HEALING SOUNDS FROM THE
MALAYSIAN RAINFOREST

COMPARATIVE STUDIES OF
HEALTH SYSTEMS AND MEDICAL CARE

For a complete list of titles in this series, please contact the

Sales Department
University of California Press
2120 Berkeley Way
Berkeley, CA, 94720

HEALING SOUNDS FROM THE MALAYSIAN RAINFOREST

TEMIAR MUSIC AND MEDICINE

Marina Roseman

University of California Press

Berkeley · Los Angeles · London

University of California Press
Berkeley and Los Angeles, California

University of California Press
London, England

First Paperback Printing 1993

Library of Congress Cataloging-in-Publication Data

Roseman, Marina. 1952–
  Healing sounds from the Malaysian rainforest : Temiar
music and medicine / Marina Roseman.
    p.   cm. — (Comparative studies of health systems
and medical care)
  Discography: p.
  Includes bibliographical references and index.
  ISBN 978-0-520-08281-6
  1. Senoi (Malaysian people)—Rites and ceremonies.
2. Senoi (Malaysian people)—Medicine.   3. Senoi
(Malaysian people)—Music.   4. Folk medicine—
Malaysia.   5. Folk music—Malaysia.   I. Title.   II. Series.
DS595.2.S3R67   1991
615.8'82'09595—dc20
                                               90-11253
                                                   CIP

15   14   13   12   11   10   09
10   9   8   7   6   5   4

*To the rainforest and the people who dwell in it,
celebrating its dangers and its beauty.*

Contents

Figures

Tables

Plates

Acknowledgments

My thanks are due to the many Temiars who gave of their time and knowledge to explain the intricacies of their culture. If this manuscript can help them to be received by the other peoples of Malaysia with respect for their unique cultural accomplishments, then I will have begun to return to them all that they have given to me.

I also thank the government of Malaysia for welcoming me into the country and enabling me to pursue my research. The staff of the Jabatan Hal Ehwal Orang Asli (Department of Orang Asli Affairs)—from past Director Dr. Baharon Azhar bin Raffie'i to officers posted in various Temiar settlements—continually provided advice, logistical support, and transportation. The Jabatan Perdana Menteri (Socio Economic Research Unit) and the Director of the Regional Police, Gua Musang, Encik Mohd. Yusoff bin Hj. Ismail, allowed me to enter deep into rainforest areas to conduct my research. Dato' Shahrum bin Yub, Director of the National Museum in Kuala Lumpur, took a kind and generous interest in this project. I would particularly like to thank Encik Syed Jamaluddin bin Syed Sulong and the staff of the Herbarium at the National Museum who assisted me in innumerable ways as a part of their project on traditional medicine. Their assistance in the collection and identification of botanical specimens is gratefully acknowledged. The members of the Orang Asli Broadcast Unit at Radio TV Malaysia, including Encik Itam Habri, Encik Angai Pedik, and Encik Uda Hassan bin Itam, kindly offered the use of archival recordings in their collection.

Numerous Malaysian and Singaporean families welcomed me into their homes as I emerged periodically from the jungle. The family of Encik Ahmad Sahlan helped me get my feet on the ground upon arrival in Kuala Lumpur; their hospitality whenever I returned to the capital city made every task seem easier. In Kota Bharu, Dr. Mat Hussin bin Hassan Gul, President of the Traditional

Malay Healers Association (Persatuan Pengobatan Tradisional Melayu), extended his support and guidance, placing me under the care of a network of students and clients that extended throughout Kelantan to the edge of the jungle. He and his family provided a place in Kota Bharu to periodically refresh myself and review my material. In Gua Musang, the frontier town where a railroad stop connected with red dirt roads into the rainforest, the District Officer Encik Ismail bin Hj. Hassan and his family offered me a warm and friendly place to rest and replenish my supplies. The families of Pamela Sodhy and Sharifah Zaleha bin Syed Hassan, colleagues from Cornell now at the Universiti Kebangsaan Malaysia, were precious old friends in a land of new acquaintances. During trips to Singapore for equipment renewal and repair, the family of Kamaldin and Bibijan Ibrahim similarly hosted me.

I am indebted to Dr. Hood Mohd. Salleh of the Department of Anthropology and Sociology at Universiti Kebangsaan Malaysia, my sponsoring institution, for encouraging and facilitating this project from its inception to its realization. His interest and involvement with the Orang Asli have been a continual source of inspiration. Dr. Abdullah bin Hassan, Coordinator of the Language Studies Unit at Universiti Sains Malaysia, was also instrumental in the initial stages of this project; his sponsorship guided me through the visa process. For aid with ornithological identifications, I am grateful to Dr. David Wells, University of Malaya.

My thanks are especially due to Dr. Geoffrey Benjamin and his wife, Vivianne Lee, both at the National University of Singapore. Geoffrey Benjamin preceded me in fieldwork with the Temiar and left a legacy of friendship and respect among Temiars that smoothed the way for those who followed. He has shared his knowledge of Temiar language and culture without reserve. Sections of this manuscript have benefited from his perusal; where inaccuracies or differences of opinion occur, I alone am responsible. Various scholars in Orang Asli studies have been uniformly supportive and cooperative; in particular, I would like to acknowledge the assistance of Kirk and Karen Endicott, Robert Knox Dentan, Peter Laird, Barbara Nowak, Gérard Diffloth, Signe Howell, Anthony Walker, and Tan Chee Beng.

Field research was funded by the Social Science Research Council, the National Science Foundation (BNS81–02784), and the Wenner-Gren Foundation for Anthropological Research (Grant No.

4064), with supplementary assistance from the Danforth Foundation, Cornell University Graduate School, and the Cornell University Southeast Asia Program. The assistance of these institutions is gratefully acknowledged. The Cornell University Southeast Program additionally provided funds for a write-up period and afforded a particularly fertile environment to study, think, and write about Southeast Asia. Tufts University sponsored travel to several conferences where feedback and exposure refined my ideas. I was fortunate in my final stages of writing to join the tradition of authors in Concord, Massachusetts, where the indirect light filtering through the pine forest canopy was sufficiently familiar to enable me to write about life in the rainforest.

James A. Boon has guided and encouraged my study, research, and writing with wisdom and humor, helping me connect minute ethnographic details with larger questions in anthropology. Everyone should have a colleague like A. Thomas Kirsch, who was willing to listen to ideas in their formative stages. William A. Austin provided invaluable musicological advice; his support for ethnomusicological research at Cornell has enabled many projects such as this one to reach fruition. The work of Carol Robertson has been an inspiration since the days that I pursued my Master's studies at Columbia University. Her exemplary scholarship in ethnomusicology showed me that music could indeed be studied as culture, engaging the fields of both anthropology and music. Fellow rainforest workers Steve Feld and Anthony Seeger have enriched my life and thought through our exchanges over the years. This manuscript has also benefited, directly and indirectly, from the comments and insights of Ben Anderson, Joe de Rivera, Byron Good, Will Haye, Billie-Jean Isbell, Charlie Keil, Arthur Kleinman, Carol Laderman, Hal Rees, Jim Siegel, Barbara Tedlock, Mary Watson, and Oliver Wolters.

James L. Gulledge, Gregory Budney, and David Wickstrom at the Library of Natural Sounds, Laboratory of Ornithology, Cornell University, provided top-notch technical advice and transcription facilities for audio recordings. In a true act of trust, Roland Tan, representative of Electrovoice in Singapore, lent microphones to take into the jungle when my own needed repairs. Lynn and Helen Meek monitored long-distance photographic development and advised me on technical adjustments.

For my father, the Southeast Asian rainforest brought memories of World War II and the Philippines; he welcomed me home like a returning soldier, showing photo albums, swapping malaria experiences, and sharing painful stories he'd never told before. My voluntary travel to the rainforest was somewhat incomprehensible to him; nonetheless, he and my mother, who wrote in letters that the rainforest seemed as far away as Siberia, always taught me to follow the path wherever it leads. I thank my parents, friends, and family, nuclear and extended, for their unflagging support and encouragement throughout this endeavor.

Orthography

Temiar orthography follows Benjamin (1976) with slight changes:

Vowel length is indicated by doubling: /aa/
Vowel nasalization is indicated with a cedilla: /ąą/
Vowels (in their short, non-nasalized forms):

- /a/ as in English "father"
- /ɛ/ as in English "bet"
- /ə/ as in English "the"
- /e/ as in English "bait"
- /ɔ/ as in English "or"
- /o/ as in English "boat"
- /ʉ/ high central half-rounded vocoid [ʉ], approximately English "tune"
- /u/ as in English "boot"

Consonant nasalization:

/ɲ/ = /ny/
/ŋ/ = /ng/ as in English "sing"

/'/ = glottal stop

Throughout this text I have used single quotes following the Temiar word for linguistic glosses that identify the word with a rough English equivalent. Where I have focused on a more detailed discussion of the semantics or when I supply the English gloss without the Temiar word, I use double quotes.

1

Introduction

JUNGLE PATHS AND SPIRIT SONGS

Traveling through the Malaysian rainforest, one first senses the presence of a Temiar settlement through a change in the density of jungle foliage: primary forest gives way in patches to secondary forest. These once-tended fields, now overgrown with brush and young trees, might indicate that one has only reached a former settlement site. Such plots are left behind to be reclaimed by jungle growth when the semisedentary Temiar move on after fertile garden sites surrounding a village have been used up, every three to five years. But when the shaded path the traveler has been following through the jungle opens out onto currently tended plots of tapioca plants, their leaves shoulder-height and open to the sun, or onto a field of hill rice farmed in the slash-and-burn, nonirrigated manner of the rainforest peoples, the presence of a current settlement is firmly announced.

Even before one sees the sun upon the tapioca leaves, the sounds of birds unique to lower brush and thickets at the fields' edge hint of an approaching settlement. The path becomes more clearly worn; dogs sensing the traveler's scent begin to bark. Voices of people calling from one house to another, or children playing outside, can now be heard. This mixture of human voices, dogs barking, and birds of the settlement edge replaces the calls of forest canopy birds and mammals which had earlier accompanied the traveler's journey through tall, dense trees. The path ceases to be a narrow trail for single-file travelers, and joins the firmly packed earth of the village, where brush around dwellings has been cleared.

If approached instead by boat or bamboo raft along the river, a footpath winding down to the riverbank announces a village's presence. In the absence of sandy beach or flat river stones, a floating bamboo platform might be attached to the shore here.

Women washing clothing and fetching water, or men preparing to set off on river travel, call to people further up along the path, who in turn announce the travelers' arrival to inhabitants inside their dwellings: "Stoke the fire, put some water on to boil, your child's father has returned."

About 12,000 Temiar live in small settlements of 25 to 150 inhabitants along five major rivers and their tributaries flowing down from the mountainous divide that runs through the center of the Malay peninsula. The watersheds spread east into the state of Kelantan and west into Perak. Temiar settlements, from ten minutes to several days' journey apart, range across 2,500 acres of rainforest. Temiar horticulturalists grow tapioca, hill rice, maize, millet, and other crops. They also hunt, fish, and gather jungle products for their own use and for exchange. Speakers of an Austroasiatic, Mon-Khmer language of Central Aslian stock (see Wurm and Hattori 1983), Temiars belong to the Senoi ethnic division of the Aboriginal peoples (Orang Asli) of peninsular Malaysia.

Highland Temiar villages near the rivers' sources reach altitudes of 4,000 feet above sea level; lowland villages downstream are about 1,000 feet above sea level. These small-scale segmentary villages comprise cognatic descent groups or "ramages" in which membership is traced through both parents. Temiar villages are agamous; inhabitants may marry within or outside the village group, with marriages contracted according to the preference of both bride and groom (see Firth 1966; Benjamin 1967b). Villages consist of extended families linked by kinship or marriage to a core sibling group.

Temiars are relatively egalitarian, with village leaders and headmen who use influence and persuasion rather than coercion to coordinate community tasks. Village leaders are usually elder males of the core sibling group, some of whom received additional sanction as headman from traditional Malay authorities, a process continued today by the Department of Orang Asli Affairs. Relationships between the sexes, discussed in greater detail in chapter 4, reveal a complementarity in everyday tasks that tends toward incipient stratification. While most mediums are male, potential gender inequities are counterbalanced by the structure of ceremonial participation and theories of dream-song composition.

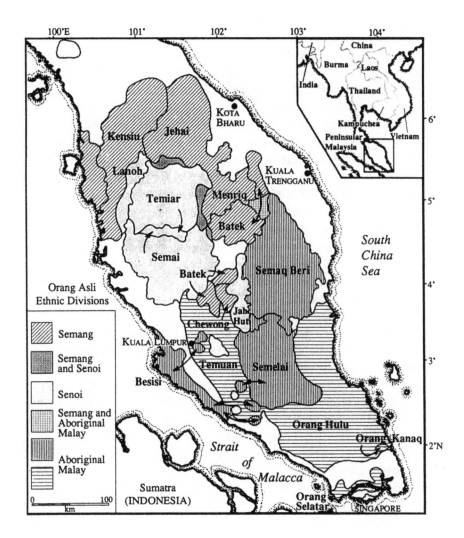

Figure 1.

Temiars practice an economic system of generalized reciprocity (see Sahlins 1965: 145–149), in which food, manufactured implements, and labor are given to others without any direct form of immediate repayment, but with the expectation that other members will be equally generous in the future. This form of economic interaction is mirrored in concepts and actions surrounding self and other, illness and health, voice and performance to be examined in subsequent chapters.

Following a jungle path or a path from the riverbank as it opens out into a Temiar settlement, one realizes that the "settlement" (*deek*) is distinguished from, and yet intimately connected with the "jungle" (*bɛɛk*). Temiar house construction further emphasizes the interpenetrability of jungle and settlement. Thatched houses, raised about 8 feet off the ground, have walls made from bamboo tubes laid horizontally one above the other, similar to the horizontal wooden logs of a North American log cabin. But in Temiar walls, about an inch of space is left between each tube. Similarly, floors are constructed of bamboo slats lashed together with about an inch of space between each slat. Clearly these spaces between wall tubes and between floor slats have utilitarian value: smoke from hearth fires escapes through the space between the tubes; excess bits of food fall through the space between the slats to the chickens below, while young children's feces fall through to the dogs. But when the cold night wind whistles through the spaces between the tubes, and uncomfortable sleepers awaken to huddle for a while around hearth fires, one realizes that this mode of construction has not survived merely for its pragmatic value. Rather, Temiar speak of the need to see out into the jungle, the desire to be sheltered but not enclosed. Neighboring nomadic Semang groups build shelters on the ground completely open on one side to uncleared forest; downriver, the Malays split the bamboo tubes and weave opaque walls. Seminomadic Temiar hunter-horticulturalists, midway between these groups in their relationship to the rainforest, build permeable houses in clearings that mark limits, yet express the intimate interpenetrability of settlement and forest.

The entities that form and inhabit these interpenetrable domains are conceived of as having similar structures and modes of action. Temiars posit a homologous division of potentially detachable souls among humans (who have head and heart souls), plants

Plate 1. The Temiar settlement of Kelaik (*Kelyet*), surrounded by rainforest. This house in the foreground is built according to the traditional building method, leaving space between poles, but the poles are aligned vertically according to a vision the builder received in a dream. Houses in the background follow lowland Malay style, weaving split bamboo into a more opaque wall. In the unwalled shelter in the center, women pound rice.

(which have leaf and root souls), animals (which have upper and lower souls), and landforms (such as summit and underground souls of mountains). Bounded souls can be liberated as unbounded spirit during dreams, trance, and illness (see Benjamin 1979). The shared properties of upper:lower and bound:unbound souls make interaction and the flow of information possible between human and nonhuman entities. In Temiar ideology, this relationship of resemblance enables dream and trance encounters, promoting song composition and precipitating illness. When unbound as spirit, entities of both jungle and settlement are capable of engaging humans in benevolent interactions as spiritguides, or malevolent ones as illness agents. Jungle is not opposed to settlement as the realm of danger versus the realm of safety, as is sometimes found among Malays; rather, both domains exhibit positive and negative dimensions.

During dreams, the detachable, unbound head soul of the dreamer meets with detached upper- or lower-portion souls of entities (such as trees, river rapids, tigers, houses) who express their desire to become the dreamer's spiritguide. The relationship is confirmed through bestowal of a song from spiritguide to the dreamer. Later, singing that song during ceremonial performance, the person becomes imbued with the voice, vision, and knowledge of the spiritguide. Singing the song links person and spiritguide; thus transformed into a medium for the spirits, a person can diagnose and treat illness.

When I first heard mediums sing during ceremonial performances, I was told what they were singing: *"nɔŋ."* *Nɔŋ*, I wrote in my notebook, must mean "song." When I asked what the female chorus, vocally responding to each line sung by the medium, was doing, they responded with the word: *"wɛdwad."* That must be "choral response," I thought. One day, as I was walking with Temiars through the forest on the way to the rice fields, someone pointed out a path between the trees and commanded: *"Wɛdwad nɔŋ-na'."* What are these people doing talking about songs and choral responses out here, I wondered in surprise. What I had been told, they explained, was to "follow that path." I realized, then, that songs were paths, and choruses were following the path. The spiritguide shows a path, a way, a route; the medium sings of the route traversed by the spiritguide, describing the visions and vistas seen by the spiritguide during its travels. The path links spiritguide, medium, and other ceremonial participants.

Plate 2.   River and footpath provide a "way" or *noŋ* through the dense jungle foliage.

My experience on the path points toward a fundamental method in the study of ritual performance: if you want to understand the building blocks of ritual, the movements, the music, the colors, the shapes, you cannot spend all your time taping rituals and playing them back for transcription and analysis. Even moving from documentation to performance and singing with the chorus or dancing with dancers gives but a partial picture. You must live the life of a people, follow their paths, dig in the dirt, gut a fish, ford a stream, and always be alert for the links between daily life and ritual activity. These links, which Gregory Bateson called "the pattern that connects," are the threads that give coherency to culture.

The patterns may connect in a straightforward pattern of iconic resemblance, as the Javanese calendar's intersecting cycles are reiterated in the coincidental cycles of the various instruments forming their *gamelan* orchestra (Becker 1979; Becker and Becker 1981). Or the patterns may connect through twists, turns, and symbolic inversions, as the street masquerades and celebrations of Brazilian *carnaval* invert the roles and playfully transgress the prohibitions of everyday life (Parker 1987, DaMatta 1984). In order to understand the medical or musical dimensions of culture, the anthropologist or ethnomusicologist must investigate the whole with all its nicks and undersides, much as a filmmaker moves from close-up view to wide-angle lens or from negative to positive image and back again.

For Temiars, the symbolic power of the image of the path arises from their daily travel along land and river routes running through the jungle and settlement. The pervasive sensate experience of the path is given symbolic expression in the root metaphor *nɔŋ*. Negotiating the path, knowing the way through the jungle, constitutes essential knowledge in Temiar life. Getting lost, losing the path, can be fatal in the jungle. Consequently, in Temiar etiology, illness often results when a person's detached head soul gets lost or waylaid; treatment then involves singing a "way," finding the head soul, and leading it back home. If the chorus fumbles when repeating the medium's initial phrase, their mistake is also spoken of as "losing the path." The foot path or *nɔŋ* links jungle and settlement; the path of the river links one settlement and another. As a song describing the path of the spirits, this gift from the dream-time sung during ceremonial performance conjoins human and nonhuman realms; as a metaphor, it links domains of traveling, knowledge, singing, and healing.

THE ARTICULATION BETWEEN MUSICAL
AND MEDICAL DOMAINS

Temiar mediums sing when they cure. A major technique of healing involves singing/trance-dancing ceremonies in which mediums sing tunes and texts given to them during dreams by spiritguides. Songs are paths that link mediums, female chorus members, trance-dancers, and patients with spirits of the jungle and settlement. Even treatment of less serious cases, which occurs outside the ceremonial context, involves singing by the medium.

How is it that singing is considered able to intercept the course of illness? What are mediums doing when they "sing"? To answer these questions, I explored the articulation between Temiar concepts of illness etiology and their strategies of diagnosis and treatment, on the one hand, and indigenous ideas about musical composition, speech, performance, and affect, on the other. I used healing performances as a point of entry into the domain of Temiar illness and well-being, letting performance acts and native exegesis lead me into issues regarding relations between humans and their rainforest environment, as well as relations among self, society, and cosmos.

During twenty months of field research among the Temiar of Ulu Kelantan (1981–1982), I observed, recorded, and participated in numerous singing and trance-dancing ceremonies, some of which were held for curative purposes. Others were held to mark the agricultural cycle, to herald the advent of the fruit season, to end a period of mourning, to strengthen or publicly celebrate connections with spiritguides, to entertain guests or inaugurate travels. Often, a ceremony held for other purposes became the stage for curative ministrations, when an attendant sufferer took advantage of a singing medium empowered with the vision of his spiritguide. These ceremonial performances were analyzed in terms of their (1) symbolic structure: an aggregation of multivocal metaphors in visual, auditory, kinetic, proxemic, and olfactory modes; (2) value structure: these symbolic codes convey meaning in terms of the values of a believing community; (3) role structure: rituals are social facts,

reiterating, inverting, and realigning Temiar social relations; and
(4) emergent structure: Temiar ceremonies are socially constructed
and reconstructed, continually transformed as extemporaneous improvisation takes place within conventionalized boundaries, and
capable of effecting transformations from illness to health through
the process of performance (Durkheim 1915/1947; Turner 1968;
Schieffelin 1985).

These ritual singing and trance-dancing performances are embedded in a network of social life that extends far beyond the
parameters of the ceremonies themselves. Commenting on the dif-
ficulties of delimiting the range of inquiry, Margaret Mead jokingly
bemoaned how anthropological residence involves attending to a
village full of "people whose every word, grunt, scratch, stomach-
ache, change of wearing apparel, snatch of song sung on the road
or jest flung over someone else's wall is *relevant*" (1977:200). Never
content to limit the range of my inquiry before I knew how far I
must trace the network of associations, I observed and documented
the range of Temiar daily and seasonal life—from hunting among
the men to gathering tubers with the women, from clearing swidden fields to collecting fruits. During my stay among the Temiar,
minute details of social interaction among women walking to the
river, chance observations out amidst the jungle foliage, and labo-
rious translations of song texts would suddenly combine to reveal
the meaning of a ritual gesture recorded months earlier. To understand the ritual form of bending, swaying dance movements precipitating trance, for example, I traced an aesthetic value that led
from the supple swaying of a woman's walk, to rainforest foliage
waving in the breeze.

The way Temiars pattern their daily actions in relation both to
one another and to the rainforest reveals as much about the ordering of their cosmos as time- and house-bound ceremonies do.[1]
When the order of daily life is disrupted by a promise broken, for
example, or when a food is incorrectly prepared, consumed, or
named, then illness might occur. To study that moment of articulation between medical and musical domains exemplified by healing ceremonies, I traced the fabric of meanings leading through
settlement and jungle, person and cosmos, dreams and performance, ritual and everyday life.

THEORETICAL CONSIDERATIONS

Accompanied by an interactive female chorus playing bamboo-tube stampers, Temiar mediums sing to heal. To approach this extension of musical performance into the domain of illness and healing, I have integrated theories from interpretive anthropology and performance theory with ethnomedicine and ethnomusicology. Although the domains of music and medicine are usually separated in Western cosmopolitan practice, their confluence in other cultures invites us to reexamine the pragmatics of aesthetics, to investigate how appropriate forms of sound, movement, color, and odor become repositories of cosmological and social power.

Western cultures have not always proclaimed a radical disjuncture between medical and musical, or human and nonhuman realms; at certain times, in certain places, trees were considered to have spirits in a manner not wholly unlike that of the Temiar. In Europe, however, the collapse of the medieval cosmos resulted in the separation of humans from nature and laid the foundation for two enterprises: the empirical investigation of nature, on the one hand, and hermeneutic interpretations of God's revelation, the Bible, on the other. While empirical science and interpretive understanding coexisted during the early Renaissance, the Enlightenment saw empirical science, joined by pragmatic utilitarianism, begin to claim supremacy (Dallmayr and McCarthy 1977:1–9). Utilitarianism aligned with positivism, a doctrine proposing that "knowledge" consists only of the empirical and scientifically useful and is only approachable through the "scientific method" (1977:9). In response to the growing predominance of positivism in the late nineteenth century, Max Weber, building on the work of Dilthey and others, began to develop an alternative approach in which social phenomena were examined in terms of cultural meaning, while natural phenomena (at least, in his early works) were relegated to the realm of empirical laws. "Empirical reality," he wrote:

> becomes "culture" to us because and insofar as we relate it to value ideas. It includes those segments and only those segments of reality which have become significant to us because of this value-relevance. Only a small portion of existing concrete reality is colored by our value-conditioned interest and it alone is significant to us. . . .

> "Culture" is a finite segment of the meaningless infinity of the world process, a segment on which *human beings* confer meaning and significance. (Weber 1905/1977:27,31)

This concern with meaning and significance, with a value orientation that plucks particular experiences from the infinite realms of possibility and makes them culturally relevant, guided the phenomenological philosophy of Alfred Schutz, and later the interpretive anthropology of Clifford Geertz. Durkheim and Mauss's focus upon symbolic classification, their study of how categories are formed and systemically related, similarly reflects a concern with the way social groups place differential values on the experiential world (1903/1963:7–8). Lévi-Strauss proposed chromaticism as a prime example of differential valuation. Each half-step of the diatonic scale in Western music renders the continuous natural realm of sounds into a discontinuous cultural reality (1964/1969:16).

A concern with meaning and value informs my own research. How do human beings, as historical and individual entities interacting in cultural groups, make sense of their experience, order it, and share it with one another?

The study of illness and health thrusts us into the midst of these concerns. An illness, with its seemingly blatant symptoms and sensations, seems at first glance so empirically *real* that it appears to be on a plane above or prior to illusive cultural relevancies. But when a Sahkalin Ainu hunter distinguishes between a headache that sounds like the light gallop of a musk deer, and a headache with chills that feels like a lamprey eel boring into a rock; or differentiates between a dry boil whose pain simulates the cry of a bat, and a boil with fluid that feels like a lamprey digging into the flesh, something else is going on. The Ainu are classifying illness in terms of the acoustic and sensory range of hunters; and their distinction between illnesses associated with land versus aquatic animals replicates the Ainu spatial classification of the universe into land and water (Ohnuki-Tierney 1981:49–59). And when Ainu consider most scratches to be merely *scratches* treatable with herbal preparations, but the scratch of a *bear* to be a metaphysical illness necessitating shamanistic rites, we realize that illness definition and concomitant treatment is not in the scratch itself, but is located rather in the source of the scratch, the bear, and its position as a deity (Ohnuki-Tierney 1981:36–37).

To deal with the dilemma posed by empirical realities and cultural interpretations, Fabrega proposes the distinction between "disease," a "biomedical thing" defined in terms of biological system malfunction, and "illness," defined by social and psychological criteria (1972:168,213; 1974; 1975:969). However, the biomedical categories of Western cosmopolitan medicine themselves express cultural influences and cannot necessarily stand as "etic" categories representing an empirical reality.

My research draws upon the ethnomedical approach in medical anthropology. Ethnomedicine studies how particular groups of people conceive of and deal with health and illness. Illness experiences, practitioner-patient transactions, and the healing process are sociocultural phenomena, constituting what Kleinman (1980) terms the "health care system," a cultural system integrally interrelated with local patterns of meaning, power, and social interaction.

A health care system is composed of many sectors. In Kleinman's study of the Chinese health care system in Taiwan, he identifies three overlapping sectors: popular, folk, and professional (1980:49–60). The popular sector is "the lay, non-professional, non-specialist, popular culture arena in which illness is first defined and health care activities initiated" (1980:50). The popular sector includes family, social network, and community beliefs and activities; it involves activities such as self-treatment by the individual or the family. The professional sector includes both the Western professional (e.g., Western cosmopolitan medical doctors) and the indigenous professional (e.g., Chinese acupuncturists). The folk sector includes nonprofessional, nonbureaucratic specialists, who may be closely related to the professional or the popular sector. In the Taiwan study, this includes folk healers such as shamans (*tâng ki*).

Temiars similarly operate within a multisectored health care system that includes self- or family elder's application of herbal remedies from the jungle, in addition to the more specialized herbal knowledge of mediums and midwives. More complicated cases require the services of mediums, who may perform ministrations outside of the ceremonial context or may call for a spirit seance. During nighttime, house-bound, singing and trance-dancing ceremonies, the medium performs diagnosis and treatment. Temiars also have access to Western cosmopolitan medicine through government-trained Orang Asli paramedics posted at various jungle sites, "flying doctors" and dentists who travel from settlement to settlement by helicopter, and an Orang Asli Hospital in Gombak, located in a forested site ten miles outside of the national capital, Kuala Lumpur. The Gombak Hospital, staffed by Orang Asli, Malays, Tamils, and Chinese, is administered by the Department of Orang Asli Affairs. Orang Asli are also beginning to visit clinics and hospitals located near the jungle's edge. Temiars move among these sectors, trying Panadol or vitamin C from a jungle paramedic, visiting a medium, trying another medium or spending time at Gombak if the mediums have been unsuccessful, returning to the mediums if Gombak has been unsuccessful—drawing upon their repertoire of options and seeing what works.

Since illness concepts and categories are closely linked with therapeutic strategies and thus are systems of knowledge *and* action (Kleinman 1980:34; Friedson 1970), it was vital to investigate how Temiars think about, talk about, act out, and act upon illness—and how they contrive to avoid meeting with illness in the first place. In this study, I focus upon daily activities of rainforest life and the ceremonial treatments performed by mediums, dealing tangentially with other sectors of the health care system as these intersect with ceremonial treatment.

Symbols and meanings come alive in the intersubjective world of ritual action and social interaction, whether that be diagnostic discourse between patient and physician in the West or the singing of a Temiar medium empowered to heal through the voice and vision of his spiritguide. Meanings take public form in the animated symbols of ritual and social action (Geertz 1973:17,18). George Herbert Mead's hermeneutic studies of meaning in social interaction (1934) informed subsequent research into the social construction of reality in everyday life (Berger and Luckmann 1966) and religion (Berger 1967) and influenced the development of social interactionism (Blumer 1969). With "frame analysis," Goffman provided a framework for examining speech and gesture in the interaction rituals of everyday life (1974, 1967). In a related trend within sociolinguistics, a focus on the communicative event as the arena in which symbols are formulated and negotiated gave rise to the ethnography of communication (Hymes 1964, 1971). Folklore studies of verbal arts bolstered the ethnography of speaking by expanding the research frame of performative folklore to include not only text, but context (Bauman 1977; Bauman and Sherzer 1974).

Turner advocated "performance-analysis and event-analysis" of ritual symbols in action in his "processual symbology" (1975:149–50). Tambiah (1977), Kleinman (1980:311ff), Csordas (1983), and Errington (1983:554ff) suggest fruitful ways of incorporating the analysis of performance into medical anthropology. The performance-oriented approaches of Kapferer (1979*a*, 1979*b*), Schechner (1983), and Schieffelin (1985) push these considerations even further, urging us to attend not merely to the semantic content of ritual symbols, but to the dramaturgical and rhetorical aspects of performance. Performance theory focuses on the ways symbols are put across through manipulation of ritual frames; aesthetic distance; performance roles; audience participation and commitment to the performance reality. Developments in the ethnography of communication and performance theory were incorporated into ethnomusicology under the rubric "the ethnography of performance" (McLeod and Herndon 1980; Béhague 1984).

Cosmological theories take sensate form in Temiar dreams and ceremonial performances: bounded souls of entities emerge in imaginal human forms, sing through the voices of mediums, and move with entranced dancers. The way Temiars order their universe and position themselves within it informs the texture of performance—the particular configurations of sounds, movements, odors, colors, shapes, and shadows. Meaningfully patterned sounds and movements set the cosmos in motion, releasing spirits from their bounded forms so they can interact with humans.

In order to entice the spirits to attend ceremonial performances and to prepare humans to meet with them, the sentiment of longing is intensified through symbol-laden sounds and body movements. Temiars say that pulsating sounds of the Malaysian rainforest, such as calls of particular birds and insects, move with the beat of the heart, and thus move the listener to feel longing. The pulsing of the bamboo-tube percussion that accompanies Temiar singing ceremonies is similarly structured, alternating high and low pitches in continuous duple rhythm. These socially structured sounds, sonic icons of the heartbeat, move the heart to longing.

This linkage of beating tubes, pulsing hearts, and moving spirits is culturally mediated: the evocative power of Temiar music is situated in a web of local meanings. These include a concept of being that locates memory and feeling in the heart. The web of meanings further includes a theory that posits detachable souls in both human and nonhuman entities, encourages both to meet when disengaged from their physical manifestations, and saturates the relationship between them with overtones of longing, attraction, and enticement.

Sounds that move with the heart set the cosmos in motion and effect the transformation of Temiar trance. The patterned sounds of Temiar ceremonies are socially constructed, performed, and interpreted; they constitute, to use John Blacking's phrase, "humanly organized sound" (1973). Studies in ethnomusicology demonstrate how musical performances embody cultural values and express aspects of social structure (Merriam 1964; Nettl 1983; Robertson 1976, 1979). Indeed, performed musical sounds often reflexively comment upon and actively reinforce, invert, negate, or diffuse social relations of power (Seeger 1979, 1988; Feld 1984; Roseman 1984; Koskoff 1989). Sounds are ordered and rendered intelligible within particular aesthetic, evaluative, and social codes. High-pitched Brazilian Suya *akia*, sung with individualized tonal and rhythmic organization, reach across the physical and social distance separating a man living in his wife's home from the sisters of his natal household (Seeger 1979); Javanese *gamelan* music incorporates indigenous concepts of coincidental cycles and powerful moments (Becker 1979; Becker and Becker 1981); bird sounds and waterfalls become musical metaphors with underlying meanings that move Kaluli to tears (Feld 1981, 1982, 1988).[2]

Musical sounds are differentially defined and manipulated in the healing contexts reported for various societies. Musical form highlights textual meanings in Piman curing songs (Bahr and Haefer 1978). Rhythm, melody, and sectional form are manipulated to direct the patient's attention to semantic oppositions in the song's text. When the opposition thus highlighted is then resolved, the patient is affectively calmed. The highlighted portions of text also convey messages cognitively: the patient learns about the "way" of a dangerous object as part of his or her cure.

In Malay spirit seances, musical and kinetic metaphors encoding maleness provide a symbolic repertoire that can be momentarily appropriated by female patients (Kessler 1977). During the spirit seance, a female patient temporarily transcends her everyday domestic subordination to her husband. She employs the sonic and kinetic language of the male role as part of her cure by dancing the warrior's ritual dance (*bersilat*) to the warrior tune (*lagu ulubalang*). This symbolic inversion, the affectation of a prototypically masculine form of behavior, allows the female patient a temporary symbolic ascendancy. The participatory texture of the seance supplies Malay women with a ritual arena in which to mobilize the support of kin and friends, who align themselves with the female member of the marital couple through clapping, cheering, spatial placement, and mere attendance.

Among the Ndembu of Zambia in Central Africa, when the illness of a particular individual is traced to the breakdown of social cohesion, collective musical participation in curative rites is used to help mend social and political factionalism (Turner 1967). Here, the cure of an afflicted individual involves remedying the ills of a corporate group. The ritual specialist skillfully orchestrates collective participation in the curative rites, exhorting participants to sing louder and cooperate together from within their respective ritual roles and thus "give their power" to help the patient (Turner 1967:389–390).

In each of these examples, the nature of the illness, the strategy of the cure, and the textures of performance vary according to the particular associative links operative in that culture. In this research, I trace the particular configurations of meaning and power that inform Temiar curative performances.

THE ORANG ASLI

Two-thirds of the over 66,000 Orang Asli (original people) are speakers of Austroasiatic, Mon-Khmer languages subdivided into three Aslian groups—*Northern Aslian*: Kensiu, Kentaq Bong, Jehai, Mendriq, Batek dialects, Mintil, Chewong, with an additional three-hundred Tonga' and Mos speakers found in Southern Thailand; *Central Aslian*: Semnam, Sabum, Lanoh Jengjeng, Lanoh Yir, Temiar, Semai dialects, Jah Hut; and *Southern Aslian*: Semaq Beri, Semelai, Temoq, Mah Meri (Besisi). The remaining 20,000 are Austronesian speakers of Malay dialects collectively termed *Aboriginal Malay*, including Temuan, Orang Hulu (Jakun), Orang Kanaq, and Orang Selitar (Wurm and Hattori 1983; Benjamin 1986).

This linguistic classification differs from the three categories based on ethnic and cultural criteria commonly used to describe the Orang Asli: *Semang* or *Negrito*, *Senoi*, and *Aboriginal Malay*. The 2,700 Semang comprise all Northern Aslian speakers except the Chewong, as well as the Lanoh, Semnam, and Sabum. Sometimes called Negritos due to their wooly hair, dark skin, and broad flat noses, the Semang were traditionally nomadic hunter-gatherers living in small bands in the lowland tropical rainforests of the foothills in northern Malaysia. The wavy-haired Senoi, basically Mongoloid peoples, are slightly taller and lighter-skinned than the Semang. The Chewong, linguistically North Aslian, exhibit Senoi physical characteristics. The Senoi, semisedentary hunters and horticulturalists, include the two largest Orang Asli groups, the 19,000 Semai and the 12,000 Temiar. Except for the Mah Meri and some Semaq Beri who exhibit Senoi physical characteristics, the South Aslian and Austronesian-speaking Orang Asli groups are ethnically and culturally placed in the third descriptive category: Aboriginal Malays (or Proto-Malays). The Aboriginal Malays are Mongoloid peoples dwelling from the rivers of the interior to the coast in the southern portion of Malaysia. They subsist on swidden and wet-rice farming, fishing, and trading. Currently administered by the Malaysian government's Department of Orang Asli Affairs, the Orang Asli have recently formed an indigenous pan-tribal political organization, POASM (*Persatuan Orang Asli Semenanjung Malaysia*; Orang Asli Association of Peninsular Malaysia).

In his search for the origins of the Orang Asli, the archaeologist W. G. Solheim II (1980:69–71) hypothesizes a widespread population 50,000 years ago that extended from Sri Lanka through Eastern India to South China and Sundaland (which joined in one continent Indonesia from Bali and Kalimantan west, a portion of the Southern Philippines, and Mainland Southeast Asia). The Hoabinhian population and related populations of Island Southeast Asia would have evolved from these people, with their common but variable gene pool, through parallel evolution under similar ecological conditions. The Orang Asli, he posits, are descendants of the West Malaysian Hoabinhian people. Until population pressures forced them to move, the Hoabinhian population of 10,000 years ago evolved rapidly in two ecologically similar niches: the lowland rainforest near the coast and river mouths, and the rainforest of upland karstic formations. The Semang, he suggests, descended from the former, the Senoi from the latter.

According to Solheim's theory, the Senoi developed into a neolithic culture with the addition of cultural elements brought by Austronesian-speaking peoples of Southern Mongoloid stock. Bellwood agrees that "the Negritos and their hunting and gathering traditional lifestyle must be considered as autochthonous to the Indo-Malaysian Archipelago, whereas the agricultural lifestyle of the Austronesian speakers is to a great (but not total) extent the result of an original expansion from more northerly latitudes" (1985:130). Solheim posits that these maritime-oriented trading people reached Kelantan from the east beginning about 2000 B.C., and continued to come for two thousand years. Some of these traders went upriver and merged with the Senoi, whereas some settled on the coast and on small islands south of Singapore toward Sumatra, where they mixed genetically with the Negrito and the Senoi but continued to speak Austronesian. These were the ancestors of the Orang Laut (Sea People) and the Aboriginal Malays.

Some of these migrants mixed less and can be considered the first Malays. More Malays joined them beginning in A.D. 1000, arriving from the east and south. Later, more Malays arrived from Sumatra. These peoples make up the present day Malays, who now comprise about 55 percent of Malaysia's population of nearly 17 million (1989 est.). According to the most recent census conducted in 1980, the Orang Asli comprise less than 1 percent of the nation's population, which also includes 33 percent Chinese and 10 percent Indians, primarily Tamils (Department of Statistics, Malaysia 1983). Together with the now dominant Malays, Orang Asli share the official designation *bumiputera*, 'children of the earth,' 'natives of the country.'[3] However, their status within the nation of Malaysia, like that of many indigenous minorities, lies suspended amidst Malaysia's often-conflicting goals. These include Malaysia's competition in the international economy with subsequent demands upon rainforest land, timber, and hydraulic power; the religious persuasions of the Islamic Malay majority; and Malaysia's attempts to celebrate the diversity of its pluralistic heritage.

TRANSLATING WORLDS

This text emerges from a dialogue between Temiars and myself—
from fumblings patiently corrected, moments graciously (or accidentally) shared despite their intimate nature, and events carefully
explained. Many weeks after observing a particular curing ceremony, I would return to a medium's house to question him about
a detail of the performance. The gathered group would chuckle,
noting that I pursued knowledge with my questions just as a hunter pursued his prey with an arrow. They gave me a nickname that
describes the straightness of an arrow and the directed course of its
path. Anthropology and the way anthropologists direct their attention and questions toward understanding was equivalent, in
Temiar estimation, to the trajectory of a hunter's arrow.

The hunter's arrow selects its mark through a singular confluence of training, intent, and coincidence. When anthropologists
observe, describe, and interpret cultural experience, they impose
their own values through processes of selection and organization.
To compress a multidimensional world into a linear presentation,
to encapsulate sounds and movements within prose, to gloss
Temiar concepts with English words entails a series of inevitably
incomplete translations. "It is a long way from the mouth of the
native informant to the mind of the English reader," Malinowski
reminds us (1935/1965:4).

Malinowski's corrective for the untranslatability of individual
words was to describe the cultural context in which those words
became meaningful. In his analysis of the language of Trobriand
magic and gardening, he writes:

> Thus it is only because we know the world of ideas, the various
> activities, the economic rules of Trobriand gardening that we can
> grasp the linguistic side of Trobriand agriculture. It is what we might
> call their *context of culture* which supplies us with the relevant ele-
> ments whereby we can translate these words. Translation then be-
> comes rather the placing of linguistic symbols against the cultural
> background of a society, than the rendering of words by their equiv-
> alents in another language. (1935/1965:18)

So too, Temiar musical and healing performances are rendered
intelligible within a network of ideas, feelings, values, and actions.
Among these are Temiar concepts of being, outlined in chapter 2.

The concept of multiple, detachable "souls" in humans and non-humans alike fuels the dynamics of the Temiar world. The upper-portion or "head" soul is the vital, animating principle, while the lower-portion or "heart" soul is the locus of thought, feeling, and awareness. "Odor" emanates from the lower back, creating a sense of personal space that extends behind the body. One person must be careful not to intrude upon another person's air space, or odor will pass from one body to another. Out of place, odor causes illness. Another essential component, the "shadow-form," is a separable duplicate image associated with the shape of the human body. Just as odors pass, shadows mix. Thus, in certain situations, care is taken not to let one person's shadow fall upon another's.

So many Temiar behaviors are dependent upon these concepts of self-essences—multiple, separable, and permeable. Concepts of being take public form in the value placed on guarding the social space around the person. Codes of action and interaction elaborate upon the need to protect, the need to maintain, the need to heal, to fill or empty that space. The principle of separability is operative in many explanatory systems, including those of musical composition and performance, and illness etiology and treatment. This property of detachment and reattachment is thus central to the performance of healing.

The process of becoming a healer, charted in chapter 3, is rooted in concepts of being which posit separable, multiple essences in both humans and nonhumans. During dreams, the detachable head soul of the dreamer meets with that of other entities (such as trees, flowers, rivers, or birds), who may express their desire to become the dreamer's spiritguide. A study of dream narratives in which the dreamer receives a song or "way" from a spiritguide highlights what has become mythologized as the pivotal moment in becoming a *halaa'*, a master singer of the landscape empowered to heal.

While all Temiars are theoretically capable of dreaming such encounters, men tend to receive dream songs more than women—and some men more than other men. This sets up a subtle differentiation within an otherwise fairly level social system. The consequent contradictions, introduced in chapter 3, are modulated and adjusted in the context of ceremonial performance, discussed in chapter 4. In the typical dream format, the spiritguide sings an initial phrase repeated by the dreamer. In ceremonial performance, this format is transferred to the realm of human actors. The medium now sings the initial phrase, repeated interactively by a female chorus.

I begin chapter 4 by considering the various formal musical genres and ceremonial cults that have developed from the dreams received by mediums. The genres exhibit characteristic scalar structure, melodic and rhythmic patterns, textual content and vocabulary, dance movements, trance behavior, instrumentation, leaf and flower ornaments, and extent of male and female participation. These stylistic parameters vary by historical period, regional location, and individual revelation. I continue by examining the various theoretical and performance devices whereby the potential for incipient stratification located in the virtuosity of the medium is undone. These include performance constructs such as overlapping medium/chorus vocalizations and repetition of the medium's material by the chorus. They also include indigenous theories underlying performance, such as the peculiar nature of the relationship between medium and spiritguide. Symbolic inversions of everyday male and female roles in ritual performance also serve as leveling devices.

Abstract notions of separable souls take sensate form in the imaginal world of dreams, where spirits emerge into perceptibility and interact with dreamers. In the sensate world of performance filled with sound, movement, and odor, spirits are again coaxed to emerge into perceptibility. In illness, as well, abstract theories are rendered sensate, and bodily sensations construed as categories of experience. Chapter 5 discusses the transformation of entities into illness agents, including those who intrude into the patient's body and those who coax the patient's head soul out of the body. The transformations in Temiar illness etiology are matched by the transformations wrought during healing ceremonies, where activated illness agents are countered by activated spiritguides. The medium's singing provides the appropriate form for unleashing the transformative process. In vocalized song, speech is transformed, sound humanized, and head soul disembodied.

Chapter 6 reexamines healing sounds as they modulate sentiments of longing and effect the transformations of Temiar trance. Uncontrolled longing leads to soul loss as human souls are attracted *out* to live in the jungle with spirits. However, when the emotion of longing is controlled in the contexts of dreaming, singing, and trancing, spirits are instead attracted *into* the human realm of ceremonial performance. During ceremonies, the sentiment of longing is focused, intensified, then momentarily satisfied through the use of symbolically weighted musical sounds and body movements. Chapter 6 concludes by examining how the emotional meanings and healing powers of these sensate symbolic forms are invoked through a particular network of associations that Temiars recognize and realize in the participatory texture of performance.

2

Concepts of Being

Temiars have a peculiarly intimate relationship to the land of the jungle, its flora and fauna, hills and rivers. They move through it daily, hunting, gathering, fishing and gardening, garnering cues as they travel from the sounds of various birds, insects, and animals that penetrate the dense jungle foliage. They cut each stalk of rice by hand, dig for tubers, climb up into the trees to gather fruits. This closeness to the land comes out in the way they think about it. In the Temiar worldview, all entities—humans, other animals, plants, mountains—embody bounded souls that can be liberated as unbound spirit. The world resonates with life, with potentially animated being.

Instead of alienating flowers, trees, or cicadas as inherently different from humans, Temiars stress an essential similarity. All entities exhibit two fundamental sets of distinctions: first, that between bounded soul and unbound spirit; and, second, between upper- and lower-portion souls. Bounded soul is the condition of everyday waking life, health, and safety; unbound or detached spirit is the condition of dreams, trance, illness, singing ceremonies, and danger.[1] Humans have head and heart souls; plants have leaf and root souls; mountains, summit and underground or cave souls (see Benjamin 1979:13–14). Temiar cosmic distinctions thus homologize humans and all other entities.

Dreaming, trancing, illness, and singing are linked through this homology, which makes interaction and the flow of information possible between human and nonhuman entities. The Temiar social world consists not merely of interactions with other humans, but with the upper- and lower-portion souls of all entities. By positing shared properties of bound:unbound and upper:lower souls in humans and nonhumans, Temiars conceptualize the world around them as having form and functions similar to those of their own bodies. This perceived resemblance facilitates communication

24

between human and nonhuman entities, thereby enabling dream and trance encounters, promoting song composition, and precipitating illness.

During dreams, the detachable head soul (*rəwaay*) of the dreamer meets with detached upper- or lower-portion souls of entities (such as trees, river rapids, tigers, deceased humans) who express their desire to become the dreamer's spiritguide (*gonig* < Malay *gundik* 'consort', 'concubine'). The relationship is established through a song given from spiritguide to dreamer. Later, singing that song during ceremonial performance, the singer, imbued with the vision and knowledge of the spiritguide, has become a medium. The song represents the knowledge that forms the basis for the ability to cure. The dynamics of the Temiar world thus rest upon the concept of multiple "souls" or "selves" in their bound states and unbound transformations.

HEAD SOULS

The *rəwaay* (head soul, upper-portion soul) is the vital, animating principle.[2] In humans, it is situated in the crown of the head (or fontanelle) or the top of the forehead (*wɔɔj*) and is closely associated with the roots of the hair.[3] During dreams and trance, the head soul takes shape as a tiny mannikin two to three inches high replicating an individual's body form. Proper situation of the head soul during everyday, waking life is essential to well-being and the continuance of life. The head soul is one of the focal points of illness etiology and curative treatments; consequently, during the course of treatment and at other times when a person is vulnerable and the head soul is endangered (such as following a death in the community), haircutting and haircombing are curtailed.

The human head soul is often metaphorically referred to as a pliant "plant shoot" (*labɔ'*). When a curer places his hands around a patient's crown and "shapes" the head soul during curative treatment, his ministrations are compared to patting and shaping the earth around a young plant. During trance, and even more intensely in illness, the head soul is said to be twisted and broken off (*na-gəyɛg* 'twist', *na-tɛgrɛg* 'break off') like a snapped twig. This image points toward the essential detachability of the head soul.

Potential detachability underlies Temiar concepts of dreaming, trancing, illness, and etiquette. Dreaming and trancing are contexts of controlled detachability; the human head soul is momentarily detached and interacts with the upper- and lower-portion souls of other entities during dreaming (*pɛ'pɔ'*) and trance-dancing ceremonies (*pɛhnɔɔh*). Care is taken not to disturb sleeping persons: if a sleeper were to be abruptly awakened, the head soul might not find its way back to the body. During dreams, the detachable head soul of the dreamer meets with the unbound souls of entities who are also detached from their concrete manifestations (e.g., trees, fruit, flowers) and anthropomorphized. In some cases, the upper-portion spirit of an entity expresses his or her desire to become the dreamer's spiritguide (*gonig*),[4] and confirms the relationship by teaching the dreamer a song. Metaphoric associations between the upper-portion soul and pliant plant shoots are again apparent: Temiar often receive songs from the upper-portion souls of matured fruit trees or flower bushes that they had formerly planted and tended, shaping the earth around the young shoot.

Prolonged absence of the head soul outside of the contexts of dreams and trance leads to the illness of soul loss (*rɛywaay* 'to lose one's head soul')[5] (see Benjamin 1967a:137–140). Marked by weariness, excessive sleeping, weeping, and eventually coma, delirium, and death if untreated or unsuccessfully treated, the illness of soul loss highlights the importance of the head soul for the continuance of life.

Abrupt occurrences such as sudden, loud noises and voices raised in anger may cause one to "be startled" (*kəjʉd* < Malay *kejut*), thereby disembodying the head soul and causing soul loss. Many Temiar rules of etiquette are predicated upon avoiding such occurrences. Objects are passed slowly and carefully between persons to avoid dropping the objects and startling the recipient's head soul. The person carefully passing the article comments: "I guard your *rəwaay*"; an accidentally dropped article is met with cries of "*Rəwaay hah!*" "Your head soul!" The article itself is a participant in the interaction, for the abruptness of the drop both startles the human participants and offends the upper-portion soul of the dropped article, which may then act to cause soul loss in the humans. Though the Temiar distinguish between bound substance and unbound spirit, the distinction is extremely subtle. The external form of the interaction and the spiritual essence underneath it are intrinsically intertwined; the spiritual effect has behavioral manifestations, and vice versa.

The Temiar concern with startling as a cause of illness shares some similarities with an Indonesian and Malay culture-bound syndrome, *latah*. In this syndrome, certain individuals prone to hyperstartling respond to abrupt occurrences with echolalia (imitation of words and movements) and obscenities. Both the Malay and Temiar focus upon startling show a concern with boundaries. When startled, a Temiar's head soul escapes the boundaries of self, becoming detached, disembodied, dislocated. The Malay *latah*, when startled, loses boundaries between self and other and repeats others' words and gestures as if they were his or her own (Yap 1952:561; Simons 1985:56; Laderman 1988). The two cultures differ dramatically, however: whereas Temiar social etiquette generally reinforces the intent *not* to startle, Malay villagers take great delight in provoking hyperstartlers into displays of *latah* responses.

Loud and sudden noises, like thunder, can startle and disembody the head souls of Temiar babies and young children, whose head souls are more labile than adults.[6] In the moments between a flash of lightning illuminating the household and the subsequent clap of thunder, older household members cover the ears of babies and young children to protect their head souls from being startled and detached. Adults can also become startled and lose their head souls. Face-to-face arguments are avoided; illness may, however, still be traced to having been startled by the relatively indirect Temiar form of critique: a harangue loudly uttered from house to house or room to room. Though walls and often darkness separate the speaker and the person criticized, this formalized discourse of anger is considered hyperdirect by the Temiar and thus capable of startling and detaching the head soul. As uttered sentiment, these disembodied words forcefully projected remain hyperdirect despite the minimal bow toward indirection contained in the performance constraints of nighttime darkness and intermediary house walls.

Angry utterances increase their potential to startle by using the autonym or "true name" (*kənɨɨh mɨn*) of the person criticized. Speaking the true name of persons, ceremonial leaves gathered for use as props in singing sessions and trance-dancing performances, or medicinal plants constitutes direct and abrupt behavior capable of startling the upper-portion soul of the item named. Abruptness and activation are thus juxtaposed to indirection or circumlocution. Names that "fly above" the "true" name are employed so as not to startle and detach the upper-portion souls of persons, ceremonial leaves, or medicinal plants. Uttering a person's true name (often connected with the person's birthplace) is avoided by a system of kinship reference terms, birth-order terms, teknonyms, and nicknames (see Benjamin 1968a). The naming of ceremonial and medicinal plants prior to a ceremony (or raucous behavior, loud-voiced harangues, and babies' cries nearby) startles the upper-portion soul of these plants into taking flight, rendering them ritually ineffective.

Ritual efficacy, however, often lies in the properly contextualized manipulation of the true names of entities. During a dream encounter, a mountain, the sunset, or a fruit might reveal its true name, then give a song text containing that name. Later, during ceremonial performance, singing this true name embedded in the song text helps to activate the upper-portion soul of that mountain or sunset. Abrupt or startling activation engenders mishap and illness, while controlled activation constitutes power.

The *rəwaay*, then, is intimately connected with the unspoken name as it embodies essence, and with the vocalized (i.e., disembodied) name as a way of unbinding and activating that essence.[7] This, in turn, is mediated by a person's knowledge of the name, claimed variously through access to the common stock of Temiar knowledge and through individual dream revelation. Controlled activation constitutes power, whereas startling activation prompts illness; this is seen in the behavior surrounding food preparation. Certain animals (and other foods) when hunted, gathered, or prepared for consumption must be referred to by names that "fly above" the true name; otherwise the upper-portion soul of the animal is startled and, when the food is eaten, it transforms into a small cat and bites the heart of the consumer, causing diarrhea, fever, and possibly death.

The act of naming certain illness agents (such as *jɔɔŋ* and *yoog*) located in the jungle startles, awakens, and attracts their attention, activating their potential to cause illness. On the other hand, the controlled uttering of names of illness agents that are located within the context of *human* interaction (or are mediated by human carriers) is used in invocations to startle and shame the illness into departing.[8]

Illnesses mediated by humans include (1) the potential for illness that adheres to violating a promise or denying a request (*pərɛnhɔ̧ɔ̧d, sərɛnlɔɔk, səlantab*); (2) *baad*, which dwells in the river, and *sɛmyaap*, which dwells in the jungle, both of which make their way into the settlement by attaching themselves to the backs of travelers; and (3) odor (*ŋɔɔy*), which passes from the back of one human into the abdomen of another. Naming these illnesses does not attract but rather startles the illness into departing. This controlled use of a name to startle an illness agent into departure is the inverse of the controlled use of a name to entice a spiritguide into attendance; both are enactments of power substantiated by the effect of the name on head souls.

The sheer movement of attention intrinsic to startling triggers the response: distraction, dislocation, and, in the Temiar scheme, relocation. This movement underlies the connection between startling, the detached *rəwaay*, and the disembodied utterance. The head soul of a speaker is said to go forth with his voice, particularly in the vocalization of singing (*gənabag*). Singers were sometimes reticent to be recorded for fear that their head souls would be captured on tape. They worried that when I took the tapes of their recorded voices away and out of the country, they would be sapped of vital force. One medium's illness of weariness, coughing, and upper respiratory infection was traced to surreptitious recording of his singing voice by a visiting Temiar from an upriver settlement. As compensation for the medium's discomfort and the offense to his spiritguides, the visitor was required to give the medium several "eggs" which, in this case, took the form of cassette radio batteries.

Adults, however, usually consider their head souls strong enough to withstand capture on tape as long as they are notified in advance of the intended recording. I was asked not to record young children of two to three years as they sang their versions of adults' songs, however, for their more labile head souls were more likely to be "captured" on tape than those of adults fortified by advance knowledge of an impending recording.

The above-ground or upper-portion souls of nonhuman entities such as plants, mountains, and river rapids appear in dreams and are reported as being visible to mediums during trance in the shape of humanoid mannikins, either male or female. During dreams, the entities reportedly indicate their "homes" (e.g., a particular plant or animal species), thereby making their origins known to the dreamer despite their generalized human form.

During curative treatments, singing, and trance-dancing ceremonies, spiritguides' head souls manifest as *kahyɛk*, a cool, spiritual liquid likened to the colorless sap of plants, the clear waters of mountain streams, and morning dew.[9] *Kahyɛk* arches in a watery thread from the jungles and mountains into the leaf ornaments adorning the interior of the house in which a ceremony is held.[10] Singers and dancers draw the cool liquid from hand-held leaf whisks and hanging leaf ornaments. Mediums draw the spiritual liquid from the leaves and from their breasts, infusing the substance into the head and heart souls of trancers and patients.

An image generated by riverine, rainforest dwellers, the cool spiritual liquid *kahyɛk* combines the essence of foliage (sap), rivers, rain, and dew—valuing water and coolness. *Kahyɛk* is the liquid form of the upper-portion souls of nonhuman entities; but when unbound and flowing in the contexts of trance, singing-sessions, and curing, this cool spiritual liquid can be transferred and infused into humans. The head soul, homologous and detachable, provides the basis for human and nonhuman interaction.

HEART SOULS

The lower-portion soul in humans is localized in the heart, *hup*. It is also associated with the blood, *lɔɔt*, and the breath, *hənum*. In most discourse, the heart soul is usually termed *hup*, although in contexts of mediumship the term *jərəək* is sometimes used.

While the head soul is the vital or animating principle, the human heart soul is the locus of thought, feeling, and awareness. One "thinks" (*na-nim* 'she/he thinks') and "becomes aware" or "recalls" (*na-bələək*) in the heart. Internal debate and rumination are functions of the heart. Memory is heartbound; songs given by spiritguides are inserted into and retained in the heart. While internalized thought is a function of the heart, language, speech, and expression are functions of the head. Temiar distinctions differ

Plate 3.   A medium blows cool liquid *kahyɛk*, drawn from his breast, into a patient's head soul.

from the traditional Western dichotomy between thought and feeling, and turn rather on the distinction between inner experience
and vocalized expression.

The Temiar words for "language" and "head" (*kuy*) are synon-
ymous. This suggests different loci for thought (the heart) and the
systemization of thought in language (the head), a differentiation
that increases in the dimension of speaking, *tɛhnuh*. Indeed, fears
that the head soul would be captured by tape-recording suggest
that the voice as "disembodied word" and the detachable head soul
are intimately connected. A comment from one of Benjamin's informants supports this distinction: "The heart soul controls our
thoughts while the head soul enables their utterance" (1967a:141).

The Temiar have a rich vocabulary of what Diffloth (1976) terms
"expressives" to describe the effect of emotions upon the heart,
especially longing, lovesickness, or homesickness. The wind sways
the leaves inside the heart; there is quickened motion in the heart,
the heart whirls and flutters. Extreme longing can lead to illness;
many of the terms describing illness are often similar to those that
describe the emotions of longing. Trance, illness, and sentiments of
longing localized in the heart are thus correlated (see chapter 6).

Young and less knowledgeable hearts are shorter than hearts of
the old and the wise. A "well" heart or "true" heart (*hup mɨn*) is
"hard" (*təgah*). In longing, trance, and illness, the heart is weak,
weary, shaky, and pliable (*bə-gɛntah* < Malay *bergentar* 'quiver-
ing'). The heart soul, like the head soul, is a focal point of illness
etiology and treatment. The heart in illness becomes shaky, hot
(*bɛdbɨd*), and narrow (*'aŋɛd*). The heart soul can be startled into
whirling and fluttering by the breaking of ceremonial restrictions or
restrictions accompanying curative treatment. Both head and heart
souls are loci for curative ministrations that involve sucking to draw
the illness to the body's surface, blowing to cool the head and heart
soul areas, and impressing the spiritual liquid *kahyɛk* into head and
heart souls, from whence it fills, cools, and strengthens the body.

Stored anger, like illness, heats and compacts the heart. A heart
narrowed by anger can be "opened" or "cleared" through invective
or harangue. During the divorce of a recently married young couple, the female relatives of the groom were angry that the bride had
run away and rejected their male kin. On the ground in the moon-
light, outside the house where male representatives of bride and

Plate 4. A medium blows *kahyek* into a patient's heart soul.

groom were negotiating a divorce, the female relatives of the groom
launched into stylized invective, graphically describing with exag-
geration the body parts of the bride, who huddled in a darkened
building several houses away. The intonation pattern of this stylized invective resembles that of the harangue: a suspended monotone leading into a plaintive downward curve. These intonation
patterns are called *jɛnhook*, a term also used to describe a song
phrase characterized by a recitation tone evolving into a downward
curve. Through this stylized verbal invective, the groom's female
kin "expanded" and "cleared" their hot, compacted, angry hearts
until finally they were seized with laughter at the absurdity and
ingenuity of their exaggerated descriptions. Yet, while the groom's
kin are cooled and cleared, the head soul of the bride is endangered, startled by bearing the brunt of this angry invective and
verbal assault.

The distinction between upper- and lower-portion souls in humans is paralleled in nonhuman entities. The lower-portion souls
(*kənoruk, kəlomaar*) of nonhuman entities are located on or below
the ground, often in an enclosure. In plants, the lower-portion soul
is in the root, trunk, or tuber. Certain animal species also exhibit
lower-portion souls. In mountains, the lower-portion soul is the
"cave" or "underground" soul (*sarak*).[11]

Just as the homology of head souls expands the Temiar social
universe by facilitating communication between human and nonhuman entities, so does the heart soul concept promote human/
nonhuman interaction. The interaction between the heart souls of
humans (*jərəək*) and nonhumans (*kənoruk*) in spirit-mediumship
and illness is analogous to the connection between human (*rəwaay*)
and nonhuman head souls (*rəwaay, kahyɛk*).

The prototypical symbol of the lower-portion soul is the tiger,
crouching on its haunches near the ground. The tiger interacts with
human mediums through a heart soul connection. During spirit
seances, the tiger sends its lower-portion soul (sometimes said to be
in the shape of miniature tiger) along a thread inserted into the
heart of the medium. The disembodied heart souls of deceased
mediums who had tigers as their spiritguides subsequently roam
the earth as were-tigers.[12] The lower-portion souls of mountains,
and *kənoruk*-possessing plant and animal species, in their unbound
manifestations, also may appear as various kinds of tigers (see also
Benjamin 1967a: 154–157).

What governs a species' possessing or manifesting *kənoruk* is not
entirely clear. Certainly, mediums tend to interact with head more
often than heart souls of species.[13] Many of the species that manifest lower-portion spirits are associated with the tiger, the prototypical representative of the lower-portion soul concept. The great
Argus pheasant[14] is mythologically connected with the tiger and is
considered to be capable of transforming into a tiger in the contexts
of dreams and spirit-mediumship. Similarly, a fish considered to be
a tiger transformation (Temiar *lɛmyɔm*[15]) possesses *kənoruk*. *Bayas*
palm-fronds,[16] which manifest lower-portion spirits, are used to
weave the walls of the hut specially built inside Temiar houses for
tiger spirit seances.

Benjamin (1967a: 154–157 and tables 2 and 6) notes that certain
birds that play a role in myth in which they carry men off to their
own domain are believed to possess *kənoruk*.[17] My data indicate
that two of these birds are intimately connected with the tiger. The
first, the bay owl[18] is said to ride on the shoulder of the tiger; the
bay owl's call announces the tiger's presence. Some say that the bay
owl itself, traveling at night, transforms into a tiger. The other,
hohuy, an owl of the *Bubu* or *Ketupa* species, can also transform into
a tiger.

Tiger associations do not account for all *kənoruk* manifestations,
however. Some lower-portion spirit associations may be experien-
tially dependent. Analysis of events preceding dream encounters
with *kənoruk* shows that mediums only made contact with them
after having slashed tree-trunks to obtain sap,[19] or pared the pith
of palms for food.[20] Here, the association with *kənoruk* involves
location: the lower- or inner-portion correlate of the human "heart"
for plants is the "trunk" or "pith."

The form taken by a lower-portion soul varies when it appears
unbound to humans during dreams and ceremonies. The tiger's
lower-portion soul inserts itself as a small tiger into the heart of the
medium during ceremonies; but during dreams, the upper-portion
soul of the tiger appears instead, taking the form of an old man or
woman. The lower-portion components of other species take the
shape of male (75 percent) or female (25 percent) mannikins of all
ages.

To complicate matters, during ceremonies *kənoruk*-identified
spiritguides may also set *kahyɛk* flowing. This simultaneous manifestation of lower-portion *kənoruk* and the upper-portion spiritual

liquid *kahyɛk* during spirit seances suggests that the upper/lower distinction is not always steadfast when souls are unbound and set in motion. Perhaps we are seeing the proportional representation of a complex whole: certain species are predominantly heart soul manifestations, but their presence also involves their vital animating principle, the head soul, which takes the form of cool liquid.

Communication between unbound head souls of humans and nonhumans is positively valued in spirit-mediumship, but has its negative side in the illness of soul loss. Similarly, *kənoruk*-possessing species, when offended, mistreated, or attracted in contexts outside of spirit-mediumship, may cause illness. In one such illness, *pacɔg*, rotting logs of *kənoruk*-possessing tree species are said to suck the blood of the afflicted. The illness *pacɔg* recalls the association between blood and heart soul, analogous to associations between hair and head soul. By establishing homologous structures and functions in human and nonhuman head and heart souls, Temiars set the stage for both beneficial interactions with their animated world in the context of spirit-mediumship, and detrimental interactions expressed as "illness."

ODOR

Another aspect of being contained within but detachable from human and nonhuman entities is odor, *ŋɔɔy*. Like the various "souls" discussed above, odor is noncorporeal yet can be traced to the entity (human body, animal, or plant) that exudes it. Hunter-gatherers moving through the rainforest experience odor's active properties daily: odor provides information to the hunter tracking an animal, whereas traces of his own smell left behind might turn the hunter into the hunted.

A person's odor is a composite of his or her labors in obtaining and transporting food. For a man, this is typified in products of blowpipe hunting: the game he has blowpiped in the jungle and carried on his back into the settlement. Women, in turn, exude the odor of items they gather and carry, such as fish caught by dredging rivers with baskets or tubers dug from the earth. As items from the jungle, game animals, fish, and tubers link people with the posited ultimate source of odor, a potent tree species (Temiar *cəhɔɔŋ*, unidentified) located at the major river's source.[21]

Human odor is exuded in sweat, but also emanates from the lower back. When activated, one person's odor can have a negative effect upon another. The primary speech event surrounding the odor complex is the utterance "ɲɔɔy, ɲɔɔy, ɲɔɔy" "odor, odor, odor"[22] spoken by a person as he passes by the lower back of another seated person. If one were to walk past another's lower back area silently without reciting, the odor becomes startled, confused, and angry, and proceeds to "eat" the silent passerby, causing illness. When one remembers to recite "odor, odor, odor" while passing by another's lower back, the odor is "ashamed" at having been openly named and remembered, and remains passive.

What is at issue here is a sense of personal space that extends behind the person, an "invisible bubble" that expands beyond the perimeter of the skin. This sense of personal space is expressed and validated through the concept of odor emanating from the lower back. As in the case of the head soul, where startling might lead to its detachment, a code of etiquette is elaborated to guard against sudden, abrupt, unannounced behavior that will unbind the odor contained within an individual and pass it on to another person. To pass someone else's back unseen and unannounced creates a potentially startling event; one learns instead to announce one's presence by reciting "odor, odor, odor" in passing.

The Temiar emphasis on avoiding startling and disruptive behavior, found in relation to head souls as well as odor, recalls Phillips's (1965) discussion of etiquette or "politeness" as a "social cosmetic" among Thai peasants:

> The cosmetic indicates that regardless of his basic intentions, the person will conduct himself properly and agreeably; it defines the presence of and prompts conformity to certain behavior rituals which simplify for the participants the kinds of behavior they may express. In a sense, the cosmetic of politeness represents one of the most "civilized" modes of social interaction: it is based on a fundamental concern with structuring one's behavior (again, irrespective of intentions) so as least to disturb others and thus permit them to act in socially easy, uncomplicated ways. (66)

Locating odor in an emanation from the lower back encourages people to give verbal indication of their presence when passing through the otherwise unguarded or "unattended" space behind the back. Concepts of being are thus translated into etiquette, a cosmetic structuring of social interaction to avoid disruption. This is ritualized social behavior coded to insure nonintrusion. Reciting "odor, odor, odor" as one passes behind another person allows verbal recognition of the other through the intermediary of odor, avoiding direct use of the other's name. The recitation at once promotes contact or social interaction *and erects a barrier*, halting the potential permeability of the other's odor into the self. Speaking obviates merging; naming the "odor" separates self from other.

Both head soul and odor involve social etiquette to minimize their potential detachability; however, there are significant differences between them. The head soul replicates the human form; it is in the image of the person to which it is attached. It is, indeed, the vital essence of that person. Odor, however, is a composite of things consumed, carried, and worn by an individual. The person is the vessel through which odor is collected, contained, and dispersed; odor is the issue of consumption and contact. Furthermore, a detached head soul can cause illness in the person who lost it, whereas activated odor causes illness not in the person who exuded it, but in the person who absorbs the exudation.[23] Finally, activated odor that afflicts another person is not returned to the emanating individual, as a lost head soul might be returned to the top of that individual's head; it is returned to the game, fish, and potent trees from whence it came prior to its residence in the human body.

Odor marks two other areas of social interaction in addition to the basic interaction ritual of one person passing behind another's back: initial contact and separation. Strangers and new arrivals to a settlement are initially kept at a distance, partly due to fear of their odor.[24] When departing, visitors (and even long-term residents) leave traces of their odor behind in the places on the floor where they have sat, or in the mats upon which they have slept. Another person subsequently sitting in that spot or stepping over the mat might get "eaten" by the departed visitor's or resident's odor. Therefore, upon departure, a person is often given a scrap of cloth to rub on his chest and back.[25] This repository of his odor will be saved for use in treatment in case someone should later manifest the symptoms of having been "eaten" by the departed's odor: a hard, swollen stomach; farting; vomiting and belching; and diarrhea.

Should someone manifest these symptoms, he rethinks the places he has sat, the mats or other personal objects stepped over, and the people's backs behind which he has passed. If he remembers passing silently behind someone's back, he approaches that person: "Oh, father's older brother, your back, I passed through your odor." The first response of the person thus approached is to joke: "Yah, you're just being ornery. It's not as if I'd been carrying game! What have I been carrying that you would be talking about my smell!" The afflicted persists: "Here, take this cloth, tear it, rub it upon yourself." His father's older brother then rolls (*lal*) the cloth on his chest and back and returns it to the afflicted. The afflicted takes the cloth, lies down, and either he himself or someone else rolls it on his stomach, reciting:

> Emerge, emerge, emerge, emerge, emerge
> You odor, you *cəhɔɔŋ* tree, you *səranut* roots,
>   you *kəraɲcęçh* tree
> You who would eat of my abdomen
> Return to the deer, to the wild boar,
>   to the barking deer, to the silver-leafed monkey,
>   to the tiger, to the water buffalo
> Eat of the dusky leaf monkey, the silver-leafed monkey,
>   the pigtailed macaque, the long-tailed macaque[26]
> Emerge, emerge, emerge, emerge, emerge
> You who would eat of the lower back
> You who would cause vomiting
> You who would cause the stomach to swell
> You who would be angry
> You who would curse
> You who would make the stomach swell
> Emerge, emerge, the tobacco leaf
> Return to the headwaters, to the river's source
> Emerge, emerge, the tobacco leaf.

The text is recited extemporaneously with variations. The basic form of the recitation involves ordering the odor to emerge from the stomach of the afflicted and return both to the *cəhɔɔŋ* tree at the river's source and to the enumerated game animals (here, the products of hunting, since the odor came from a man). If the odor was passed to the afflicted through a female, it would be ordered to return to fish and tubers. The person, male or female, from whose back the odor passed into the afflicted is not the ultimate source of the odor, but is merely a "carrier." The odor of the carrier, embodied in the cloth used in curative treatment, provides the means for prompting the odor to emerge from the swollen abdomen of the afflicted and return to the game, fish, and potent tree sources.

The human carrier is thus the mediator through which odor emerges from the jungle into the human realm. When odor has subsequently been passed from one individual to another, the odor of the prior human carrier (now transferred to the cloth used in treatment) once again mediates, prompting the odor to emerge from its new abode in the stomach of the afflicted and return to the trees and animals of the jungle.

Following the first recitation and rolling on the abdomen, the cloth is plunged into a fire. Smoking and sparking, it is then waved over the abdomen while a similar text is recited, urging the odor to emerge and return to its source. The scorching of smoke and ash startles the odor into departure. Finally, the burnt cloth is dipped in water and lines are drawn on the abdomen with the blackened ash. Some say that this cools the stomach, which was heated by the presence of the odor. The sick person then falls asleep. When he awakens, he "begins to eat tapioca and goes back to work"—the signs of health.

Children learn about odor from three speech events: the preventive "odor, odor, odor" uttered when passing someone's lower back; the gossiping around the hearth as people try to figure out whose back the afflicted passed; and the recitations of curative treatment. The speech event that forms the cure, in fact, contains the exegesis of the odor complex. For within the recitation, the origin of odor and its effects upon the afflicted are enumerated. The recitation provides a commentary on the detachability of odor from its places of origin and its ability to be returned from whence it came.

SHADOW

The shadow or "shadow-form" (*wɔɔg*)[27] is another separable component of human and nonhuman entities. The shadow-form replicates both the exterior and interior form of the body. Mediums sing about the "semblance of the body" (*badan rupəəh*) or "shadow-form" (*bayaŋ rupəəh*). This shadow component or "body soul" (*səmangat rupəəh*) is a semblance of the body similar to a person's shadow cast on the ground. The shadow on the ground is the most common, everyday, visible manifestation of the shadow-form.

Images that duplicate the outlined shape of the body are shadow-forms; Temiars refer to photographs of themselves as *wɔɔg yeh* 'my shadow'.[28]

The shadow-form as "semblance" or "image" of the body replicates not only the exterior form (as in shadows cast or photographic images), but also fills the body. Like a shadow on the ground, the outline is filled in. During curative treatment, *kahyɛk* flows from spiritguides through mediums and into their patients; the *kahyɛk* is said to fill the patient's body like a shadow-form.[29] In this, it is similar to the Batek notion of a person's "shadow-soul" (*bayang*), a "soft, transparent entity which inhabits the entire body" which visibly manifests as the shadow cast (Kirk Endicott 1979:93).[30]

Temiars say that the shadow-form is separable and can travel around by itself. The contexts in which it detaches, however, are not clear. Detachability seems to occur predominantly in the context of spirit-mediumship. Spiritguides sing through mediums about their visions of shadow-forms. For example, the female spirit of the *pəŋasɛh* flower sings through Ading Kerah of Reloy:

'ɛɛh, 'amɛɛ'
mɛɛ' mɛɛ' səlih badan
dɛh 'ɔɔy 'ɔɔy
bayaŋ rupəəh

Mother[31]
Mothers,[32] the body cool and refreshed [as the song passes through][33]
The shadow-form [separates from the body and travels around]

In another example, the *Taɲjok* Flower Spirit sings through Penghulu Dalam of Limaw, enjoying the beauty of the women[34] playing bamboo-tube percussion to accompany the ceremony: *"badan rupəəh, 'awaa' balɛy,"* "the shadow-forms of the women inside the house." The vision of the spiritguide (and thus, the medium in trance) operates on the level of otherwise invisible head souls, heart souls, and shadow-forms.

In another verse, the Tiger Spirit sings through a medium:

'iih wɔɔg wɔɔg wɔɔg
pɛnra' wɔɔg

lawɔɔg-lanɛɛl
ma-yə' yeh

Shadow, shadow, shadow
Shadow in the midday sun
The redness of the *taɲjok* flower
Behind me.

In this verse, the medium explains, the Tiger Spirit describes seeing the shadow-form of a person in the clear sun of the midday; it follows and devours the person. Whether the shadow-form was traveling separately from the body, and if so, under what circumstances, is unclear. However, the scenario recalls the concerns of another Orang Asli group, the Batek, about tigers and the shadow-souls of dreamers:

> It is thought that tigers have such good night vision that they can see a wandering shadow-soul and follow it back to its owner's sleeping place and kill him. Thus when the Batek are camping in a small group and they think there are tigers around, they sometimes make a low fence of palm-fronds around their sleeping places to prevent their shadow-souls from wandering off. (Kirk Endicott 1979: 95)

The Temiar song text similarly describes a tiger that spies a person's shadow-form and follows it to devour the person; however, in the Temiar worldview, a person's head soul is what wanders during dreams. Furthermore, the Temiar scene occurs under the clear sun of the day, not during the sleeping, dreaming time of night. The circumstances under which the Temiar shadow-form separates from the body and travels around remain uncertain.

When a patient undergoes curative treatment, he or she must observe certain restrictions to preserve the cool spiritual liquid of the spiritguide which is like "a shadow inside the patient guarding her." Some of these restrictions concern shadows. Benjamin (1967:143) observed that "sick people are often partitioned off from all but their closest relatives—parents or spouse—by a curtain to prevent the shadows of any other people from falling upon them." While under curative treatment myself, I was not allowed to read. The printed page, in addition to falling under a restriction on the use of white, glossy things (*tɛnlaa' bəregyɛɛg*), was also said to have a shadow-form in the trace of the letters against the white page. A special ceremony was performed to lift this restriction and enable me to take notes during my treatment, since handwriting on white paper also had a shadow-form. These restrictions may be intended to avoid a conflict between the liquid upper-portion soul of the curer's spiritguide, which fills the patient like a shadow-form, and the shadows of other people or things. Breach of these restrictions causes the cool spiritual liquid within the patient to be radically withdrawn by the startled spiritguide, which might worsen the patient's condition and possibly cause death.

The shadow-form is also associated with death. At death, a person's head soul leaves the body but remains around the grave indefinitely. There is no notion of a composite "afterworld" to which all head souls go. Instead, in typical Temiar fashion, the disembodied head soul continues to be associated with concrete manifestations of the visible landscape or animal species, especially the gravesite. The disembodied head soul of a dead person may also take the form of a bird, *cɛp cɛryɛj* (the dark-necked tailorbird). Encountering the voice of this "bird of dead persons," especially near a gravesite, usually harbingers illness or death.[35] This bird is sometimes referred to as the "shadow of the grave" (*bayaŋ kubur*).[36] Temiars now often possess photographs from visiting anthropologists, Malay administrators, or Orang Asli government employees. When someone dies, these photographs or "shadow-forms" of the deceased are hidden or destroyed. Some say this keeps the shadow-form from calling back the spirit of the dead person; others say it keeps the living from feeling sad.

Nonhuman entities can also have shadow-forms. This is most highly articulated in payments (Temiar *mayaŋ* < Malay *bayang* 'shadow') made to mediums and their spiritguides for curative services rendered. *Mayaŋ* payments are also made as retribution to spiritguides or the spirits of species who have been offended or disturbed, provoking their potential for causing illness. These beings usually make their requests for compensation known to the offender by appearing and speaking in the dreams of a medium, who then becomes responsible for accepting the payment. The *mayaŋ* is something given in this world (commonly about M$10 in paper and/or coins, or cloth, a ring, a woven mat) the shadow-form of which is sent off to the spiritguide or the offended being.[37] The concrete manifestation of the article can be kept by the medium himself. An example clarifies *mayaŋ* as payment:

BACKGROUND: A teenage boy, Aweng, carried white logs past Penghulu Dalam's house to use in the construction of Baleh Asɔɔd's new house. Spirit seances are habitually held in Penghulu Dalam's house; indeed, leaves had been gathered for a ceremony to be held there later that night. There is a restriction on carrying white and glossy things such as logs of certain trees, rattan, and some species of bamboo past a house where ceremonies habitually are, have recently been, or are about to be held. Consequently, Penghulu Dalam was startled and his spiritguides offended by Aweng's breach of the restriction. The ceremony scheduled for that night was held elsewhere with different mediums; Penghulu Dalam refused to participate.

CEREMONY: Three nights later, Penghulu Dalam held a spirit seance in his house to "sweep away the problem of the white logs." The spirit seance began in darkness, in preparation for the entrance of the tiger spirit, who will not attend if the lights are lit. During the ceremony, three other men in addition to Penghulu Dalam also sang the "ways" of their spiritguides, accompanied by female choral response and bamboo-tube percussion. Several hours later toward the end of the ceremony, when Penghulu Dalam's tiger spiritguide had gone and been replaced by another spiritguide, the kerosene oil lamps were lit. The flame of the lamp made visible a bowl of coins placed directly under the central leaf ornament (*tənamuu'*) suspended from the rafters. Versing in song, Penghulu Dalam called the group of male singers to end their trancing and bade the spiritguides to return safely to their original homes. The four men stood in a circle, facing the center where the leaf ornament hung, shaking leaf whisks in their right hands held opposite the open palm of their left hands. Penghulu Dalam, singing, kneeled by the bowl of coins, one hand outstretched toward the *tenamuu'*, the ceiling, and the sky beyond. Periodically his outstretched hand descended, waving back and forth over the bowl, then ascended again stretching, flinging upward and outward. He stood, gave a shudder, dropped his whisk—and the group had returned.

Baleh Asɔɔd divided the coins into four parts, M$3.50 per person, given to the four male singers. As the men received the coins, they forcefully exhaled and inhaled through open fists placed over the coins, holding the inhaled spiritual liquid *kahyɛk* in their now-closed right fists. One man gave the substance to his ailing wife; the other three blew it through their fists into the heart soul of the teenage boy Aweng.

The coins were a payment from Balɛh Asɔɔd, the person whose house was being built from the logs mistakenly carried past Penghulu Dalam's house by the young Aweng. The shadow-form of the coins was taken up by Penghulu Dalam and released to his spiritguide, the offended female spirit of a mountain. Placed in a bowl underneath the central hanging leaf ornament, the coins collected cool liquid *kahyɛk* from spiritguides who had been drawn to the ceremony. The men took that liquid and put it into Aweng's heart soul; because it was he who had shouldered the logs, he needed to be strengthened and cleared. The exchange of the shadow-form of the coins sent from the human offenders to the spiritguide and the spiritguides' upper-soul substance (*kahyɛk*) sent through the coins into the heart soul of the human offender "swept away" the dangerous situation, restoring the balance between the humans and their spiritguides. The interplay of shadow-form (*mayaŋ*), upper-portion soul (*kahyɛk* from the spiritguide), and heart soul of the teenage boy Aweng in this ceremony indicates that although these concepts of being are discrete, they intertwine during interactions between human and nonhuman entities within the context of spirit-mediumship.

SPIRITS, SOUNDS, GOODS, AND SELVES

The concept of multiple, detachable components of self in humans and nonhumans alike fuels the dynamics of the Temiar world. Form is easily translated into activated energy or detached "spirit" in the Temiar universe. This energy is exudable, permeable, and manipulable. Changes within these energy fields are spoken of, in Temiar terms, as situated souls transformed into activated spirits. People and things are constantly losing or gaining, interrupting or intruding upon energy or "spirit." This is what must be tended to during healing ceremonies.

Both humans and nonhumans are composed of a multiplicity of substantive yet permeable, detachable components: head soul, heart soul, odor, and shadow. Together, these multiple selves constitute the Temiar person (*sɛn'ɔɔy*), a social being at once separable from and connected to other human and cosmic beings, who are all capable of "having personhood" (*bə-sɛn'ɔɔy*).[38] This is a very different world than that of the individuated self of the West, generally conceived of as an isolable unit fundamentally different from anything not human (Johnson 1985). Scheper-Hughes and Lock (1987) refer to this kind of self, an interactive self that doesn't quite end at the boundaries of the individual, as a sociocentric self.

For members of societies with sociocentric selves, the beauty of interconnectedness with community and nature is offset by concern for the integrity of self. Temiar concepts of permeable, multiple, detachable selves enable a special sense of comraderie with the humans and nonhumans of their social universe, but this supportive network is also fraught with danger: spirits are there to be met and joined, but if that interaction continues beyond momentary dreams and trances, if boundaries are crossed in excess, if the integrity of self is not reestablished by waking up from a dream or returning from the trance state, then a spirit can become an illness agent.

The potential for separability and merging engenders a code of ritualized behavior to discourage components of the self from detaching or transforming in inappropriate or uncontrolled contexts. Care is taken not to abruptly startle people or things, so as not to unnecessarily activate and unbind their essential components. The space behind a person, where odor emanates, must be carefully traversed to keep one person from absorbing the other's odor. Sustained or uncontrolled activation of these components can be detrimental: a person's head soul, startled by an abrupt sound or angry invective, detaches from the body, resulting in the illness of soul loss. However, temporary and controlled activation of these components fosters benevolent interactions between entities, as spiritguides are temporarily enticed into the human realm during dreams and trance.

Temiar interactions with one another and the cosmos are driven by a dynamic tension that, on one hand, celebrates the potential detachability of self, and on the other, guards the integrity of self.

The cultural subscript of sociocentric interdependence, then, is the continual reinstatement of an independent, bounded self. It is all too easy to typify the sociocentric self as a static state, to envision an idyllic scene of interconnected entities where separation and alienation are not an issue. But I contend that societies that posit sociocentric selves are exhibiting their very concern for the relationship between self and other when they formulate and continually reinstate the sociocentric self.

Similarly, in societies commonly characterized as egocentric, such as contemporary mainstream United States, the emphasized cultural value on the independent, individuated self exists in tension with a cultural subscript that values interdependence in the family, in the community, in nationalism, in employer–employee relations or within unions.[39] And the seemingly indivisible self is variously divided into a multiplicity of selves or social roles (wife, mother, teacher, daughter, citizen) constituting the person in sociological theory, or is analyzed psychologically in multiple terms such as Freud's ego, id, and superego or Jung's anima and animus. Building on a study of these and other sources such as the imaginal beings of child's play, actor's dramatic personae, and religious visitations, Watkins (1986) proposes a contemporary Western psychotherapeutic technique that entertains a multiplicity of selves or "invisible guests."

Both egocentric and sociocentric societies, then, contain cultural subscripts that implicate their opposites. Behaviors surrounding the odor component provide a window into the Temiar concept of the sociocentric self and are a prime example of how the permeability of self and other must be balanced by its inverse, separation. The tension is articulated in terms of illness and health: excess permeability leads to illness, maintenance of the integrity of self constitutes health. In another illness complex, *pərɛnhɔ̡d* (< *hɔ̡d* 'want', 'desire'), to deny someone's request causes illness or misfortune for the person denied. This complex highlights the correlations between Temiar concepts of self and their economic system of generalized reciprocity.

Generalized exchange limits the accumulation of individual surplus or wealth by ensuring that goods obtained by one member or social unit flow throughout the village, eventually to be reciprocated. Generalized reciprocity is a sociocentric system of exchange.

To deny someone's request for something is to stop the flow of goods, which, as Mauss teaches in his analysis of *The Gift*, is more than the mere passage of things, but is rather the substance of social relations:

> [T]his bond created by things is in fact a bond between persons, since the thing itself is a person or pertains to a person. Hence it follows that to give something is to give a part of oneself. . . . It follows clearly from what we have seen that in this system of ideas one gives away what is in reality a part of one's nature and substance, while to receive something is to receive a part of someone's spiritual essence. To keep this thing is dangerous, not only because it is illicit to do so, but because it comes morally, physically and spiritually from a person. Whatever it is, food, possessions, women, children or ritual, it retains a magical and religious hold over the recipient. (Mauss 1925/ 1967:10)

The thing given is not inert, it is alive, it is often personified, it embodies an obligation to make a return gift. We recall the care with which Temiars pass items from one person to another, commenting that they thereby guard one another's head souls. To halt the flow of goods is to deny sociocentric interconnectedness. Again, Temiar concern for the interrelation of self and other is phrased in terms of illness and health, for halting the flow of goods and selves puts the person whose desires remain unanswered, whose social interconnectedness has been denied, in the state of pərɛnhɔ̹ɔ̹d, an unfulfilled wanting that leaves the person vulnerable to illness or other misfortunes such as snakebites, tigers, or accidents.[40]

Pərɛnhɔ̹ɔ̹d pertains not only to things exchanged but also to words. A promise broken leaves the person left in the lurch in the state of pərɛnhɔ̹ɔ̹d. If two men make plans to go hunting, and when the designated time arrives one of them is unable to go, the other is left in a ritual state of danger. He will either cancel his trip entirely or go at a slightly different time to a different place, thereby avoiding misfortune. To further protect himself, he chants: "Pərɛnhɔ̹ɔ̹d, pərɛnhɔ̹ɔ̹d, return it to itself, that there be no accidents, no tigers, no headaches, return it to itself."

Good exchange, then, is good health. The illness propensity of pərɛnhɔ̹ɔ̹d, which affects the thwarted *receiver* in a stunted exchange, has its correlate in *gɛnhaa'*, which affects an erring *host* who

Plate 5. Game is divided for distribution throughout the village.

fails to offer food to a guest (see chapter 5). Concepts and actions surrounding the illness complexes *pərɛnhɔɔd* and *gɛnhaaʾ* ensure the reciprocal flow of goods and strengthen the social ties of the sociocentric community. To avoid *pərɛnhɔɔd* is to reinforce inter-connection; this is the inverse of illnesses which reinforce bound-aries, such as that resulting from the absorption of another person's odor.

Exploring the relations between thought, economy, and society, Godelier (1986:6) notes that " 'infrastructure' and 'superstructures' are very poor translations of *Grundlage* and *Überbau*, the terms ac-tually used by Marx. The *Überbau* is a construction, an edifice which rises up on foundations, *Grundlage*, and it is a house we live in, not the foundations. So another translation of Marx, far from reducing the superstructures to an impoverished reality, could have empha-sized their importance." In the "house" the Temiar live in, con-cepts and actions surrounding person and cosmos both inform and are informed by the material transactions of generalized reciproc-ity. Just as issues of connection and separation exist in dynamic tension in the Temiar construction of the self, so too do issues of generosity and greed dog the path of distributive exchange. Tech-niques abound for maintaining the flow of goods while reserving enough for personal use; I was taught just how small a bit of tobacco to give to fulfill social etiquette and avoid causing *pərɛnhɔɔd*, while reserving some for myself (and my teachers, my immediate household members!). Hunters bringing home a small catch that would not spread very far through networks of distri-bution used the cover of night to hide their return and to cook and consume the small prize among more immediate household mem-bers. People traveling upstream to another village to help a relative with a rice harvest (and eventually to receive some rice in return) would carefully omit the purpose of their travels when talking with people met en route. In this way, they avoid having to fulfill the request that would probably follow mention of the impending rice yield.

In a distributive economy, an overflow of generosity can be as problematic as undue greed. In the cosmological dimension as well, Temiars alternately celebrate and are horrified by the poten-tial permeability of self. During dreams and trance, they welcome the opportunity to engage in interaction with the unbound selves of trees, mountains, and rivers; during everyday contexts they are careful not to set interactive selves in motion. To overstep the balance is to enter the realm of illness, of soul loss. In the domain of ceremonial performance, the dynamic tension between differentiated and collective selves is also evident: a song received by an individual medium from a spirit during a dream is diffused throughout the social group, who sing an interactive choral response to the medium's solo lines.

Sounds and odors, themselves detached from yet traceable to their sources, set bound form into energized motion. Examples of the interrelations between voice, person, and personal space abound. One's thoughts are stored in the heart soul; one's voice sends the head soul forth into space. The unspoken name embodies the essence of the upper-portion soul; speaking or singing a person's or entity's "true" name unbinds and activates its essence. If the true name of an animal is carelessly spoken during food preparation, that animal is startled into action as an illness agent. If the true name of an entity is carefully sung during ceremonial performance, however, that entity is activated and drawn as a helper into the ritual arena. Reciting the name "odor" when passing behind another person halts the potential permeability of the other's odor into the self, thus separating self from other. When the voice of the dark-necked tailorbird, referred to as the "shadow of the grave," is heard near a gravesite, the bird song negatively invades personal soul-space and harbingers illness or death.

Sounds and odors can transcend or demarcate the boundaries between self and other. Like components of the self, they are separable and permeable, yet they give the illusion of substance and source. The odors of fragrant leaves and flowers, gathered to make ceremonial ornaments, entice spirits to attend singing and trance-dancing ceremonies. Through the manipulation of uttered sounds and blossoming fragrances, bound souls are transformed into interactive selves during dreams and ceremonial performances. In this ritual context of unbound songs, odors, and spirits, healing occurs. To comprehend musical and ceremonial performance in Temiar society, then, we must comprehend the dynamic structure of the self.

3

Becoming a Healer

The Keralad flower.
I scattered the seed, I planted it.
It sprouted, I tended it—patting
  and shaping the earth
  around the shoot.
It arose, I tended it.
It grew and bore flowers, it gave off fragrance.
I went home, I fell asleep straight off;
suddenly taking form, there emerged a male.
He said: "I, I come to you.
    It is you that I want.
    I come home here to you.
    Me, here, to you *'ə-lah.*"
After finishing speaking, immediately he began to sing.

Boot Kəralad.
'i-rɛyruy, 'i-cəd.
Na-yah, 'i-bələəh.
Na-yah, 'i-bələəh.
Na-hịịd bar-buɲaa', na-hoos.
'i-maa' 'i-sələɔg hɛrhaj,
pəlaɲ na-həwal babəəh.
Na-tuh: "Yee' ma-hɑ̣ɑ̣' 'i-ciib.
  'i-cɛn.
  'i-maa' doh ma-hɑ̣ɑ̣'.
  Yee' doh ma-hɑ̣ɑ̣' 'ə-lah."
Habis na-tuh, kɛɛw na-gabag.
(Uda Pandak, Kengkong, 30-vi-82, DN17)

Thus the medium Uda Pandak from the settlement Kengkong, near the source of the River Bərɔk, recounts a dream he had three years earlier. In his dream, the *kəralad* flower's head soul emerged and established a familiar relationship with Uda Pandak, who is better known as Taa' Acuuc, Old Man Bitter, for his biting humor during ceremonial performances. During dreams, the soul of an entity such as the *kəralad* flower detaches itself and emerges in humanized form (often a mannikin), male or female. It speaks to the roaming head soul of the Temiar dreamer: "I come to you, I desire you. I want to be your teacher, I want to call you father." Then it begins to sing. The spiritguide sings a phrase and the dreamer repeats it. Line by line the spiritguide sings, and the dreamer repeats until, upon awakening, the song is firmly embedded in the dreamer's memory.

The ability to receive songs from spiritguides during dreams, and to later manifest those spiritguides when singing the songs and trancing during ceremonial performance, renders a person *sɛn'ɔɔy bə-halaa'* 'a person with *halaa*',' 'a person with *halaa*' adeptness' (i.e., a medium). The term *halaa'* can be used to denote the spiritguide. By shortening the longer phrase "a person with *halaa*'," the term can also be used to refer to the medium. This is a good example of Temiar dialectical compression of self and other, a tendency especially pronounced in the relationship between spiritguide and medium.[1] Spiritguides are also referred to as *gonig*, a term that may derive from the Malay *gundik* 'consort' (see Benjamin 1979:13; Wilkinson 1959:381).[2] All of Temiar vocal music and most of the instrumental flute repertoire have their source in songs received from spiritguides during dreams. Dreams are thus a primary source of musical composition.[3] As dream-song composition and ceremonial song performance show, spirit-mediumship and musical competence are aligned in the Temiar concept of *halaa'*.

As Uda Pandak's dream narrative reveals, the Temiar dreamer does not request or demand either the relationship or the song; the *kəralad* flower's head soul emerges and sings of its own accord. However, events in daily life can precipitate dream encounters with familiars and promote receiving their songs. In Uda Pandak's case, the relationship followed from his actions planting and tending the young *kəralad* shoot. Temiar dreamers often receive songs from upper-portion souls of matured fruit trees or flower bushes they had formerly planted and tended, shaping the earth around the young shoot. That the Temiar also metaphorically refer to the human head soul as a pliant "plant shoot" (*labɔ'*) to be shaped and tended by a curer (or twisted off in trance and illness) points again toward the essential homology linking human and nonhuman entities in the Temiar view of society, environment, and cosmos.

Note the sentence in Uda Pandak's narrative: Suddenly taking form (*pəlaɲ*) he emerged (*na-həwal*) a male (*babəəh*). This transformation is central to the Temiar theory of dreaming: the head soul of the *kəralad* flower detaches from its concrete manifestation and is anthropomorphized in order to interact with the detached head soul of the dreamer, which also appears as a tiny human form resembling the dreamer in waking life. The two must resemble one another—sharing human form—in order to speak the same language, to communicate. The "souls" (*rəwaay*) or, in Ellen Basso's terms,[4] "interactive selves" of both dreamer and entities encountered are detached from their concrete entities (e.g., plants, mountains) and then reified in what Barbara Tedlock (1987) and Corbin (1966, 1972) call the "imaginal world" of dreams and trance, a world of images that are not imaginary, that have an existence separate from, yet incumbent upon, concrete entities. This intimate relationship between the imaginal world and that of everyday life is demonstrated by the response of a Temiar woman to a meager crop of peanuts: she blamed their shriveled contents on a local medium who dreamt and received a song from their "interactive self," thus depleting the store of peanuts in the ground.

When a spirit takes human form in a dream, it comes into visibility, into perceptibility. We are told that the *kəralad* flower "arose" and "opened" (*na-yah*). This word is also used for the rising of the sun, coming above ground into visibility and opening the day, and for the opening of the vocal apparatus into song, coming into audibility. Singers often begin a performance by mumbling "*yah-yah-yah gəroyah gəroyah,*" and proceed to verse through metaphor simultaneously of the rising of the sun and the opening of the song.

As Uda Pandak's narrative continues, the sprouting flower bush grows even larger, buds open and flowers blossom, emitting fragrance. The noncorporeal detachability of odor as a communicative code is again in evidence here. Like the odor (*ɲɔɔy*) of game and trees potentially passed into humans who then pass odors on to one another, the flower's fragrance (*ɲɔɔy*) is both sensate and permeable.[5] Like sound, odor calls into question the distinction between the substantial and the insubstantial, for it is both perceptible or existent and yet invisible. Permeable odor easily crosses the categorical boundaries between self and other, human and nonhuman. Thus, in Uda Pandak's dream narrative, the initial sensation of the flower's fragrance embodies the incipient relationship between "interactive selves" of flower and man.

Head soul (*rəwaay*) is to singing as odor (*ŋɔɔy*) is to fragrance; both phenomena are operative in the realms of dream and ritual performance. As the fragrance emitted by the *kəralad* flower foreshadows its emergence into communicable form in the dream world, so the fragrant leaves of ceremonial ornaments are used to entice spiritguides to manifest themselves during ritual performances. Incense of roots, resins, and beeswax[6] burnt as offerings to spirits during incantations and ceremonies constitute a semiotic code that is simultaneously insubstantial yet sensable, perceptible yet permeable. These ambiguous substances, material yet immaterial, stimulate communication between human and nonhuman entities.

Olfactory channels are linked with visual and kinetic channels in the Temiars' rainforest environment. Temiars seem to be elaborating a natural code. In nature, scent is a code of attraction evolved to entice bees and birds who will then act as pollinators for the fragrant flowers. The same can be said of flower shape, color, and movement in the breeze, which allow the flower to stand out from the surrounding foliage and become notable. Similarly, fragrant flowers and ceremonial leaf ornaments attract the attention of the spirits, who then come to join Temiar ceremonies.

From a seed underground, the *kəralad* flower bush emerges into sensateness, perfuming the air and delighting the eye of the man who has planted, tended, and watched it grow. Although Temiar hunter-horticulturalists are by no means obsessive cultivators, there is a sense of ownership in the produce of what one plants. Fruit trees are one of the most enduring of Temiar possessions; village genealogies can be traced through a series of fruit trees considered to have been planted by the original settler-ancestors of the area (Benjamin 1966; 1967b:20). The flowers of the *kəralad* bush will be plucked by many members of the community, but it will be remembered who planted it. Community members may even ask the "owner" for permission to pluck the flowers, though this is observed less with flower bushes than fruit trees.

Thus, although his ownership is neither exclusive nor absolute, by planting and tending the bush Uda Pandak has established an interrelationship with the seedling that progressively emerges into sensateness in the everyday world as it grows and blossoms, precipitating its further emergence into humanized form and subsequent opening into song in his dream. The verbs and adverbs of the dream narrative trace this progressive emergence: the seed opened (*na-yah*); its fragrance wafted (*na-hoos*); the mannikin emerged (*na-həwal*); then immediately (*kɛw*) he sang (*na-gabag*).

DREAMING

When a Temiar sleeps and dreams, his or her head soul temporarily leaves the body. In its travels, it meets with similarly detached head or heart souls of other entities such as trees, flowers, tigers, deceased humans, living humans. Temiar generally categorize their dreams as "true" or "untrue." "True" dreams include those containing symbolic omens that are subsequently proved correct, dreams about contemporary social relationships, and dreams involving illness agents or spirit-familiars. Dreams containing any of a series of encoded items including, for example, tobacco or bamboo poles, are interpreted as omens foretelling events related to the next day's hunt or travel. Some dreams, particularly those involving living human beings, act as a barometer of social relationships: after waking from a dream involving a person who turned away from the dreamer, the dreamer might approach that person and gently question whether there was a misunderstanding to be mended. Many dreams are interpreted inversely: a dream in which one's mother appeared ill would indicate her good health. Dreams may contain important information pertaining to illness diagnosis and treatment.

Some dreams, including many nightmares, are disregarded as "confused" (*ŋɛwŋaw*), "unimportant" (*bɛ'bɔ'*), or "untrue"; such dreams are often said to have been caused by eating meat before retiring. Other nightmares, however, bespeak meetings with illness agents or tiger spirits. One man, clearing his fields in the presence of a large rock, returned home to dream the spirit of the rock, who emerged in giant form as an illness agent. His consequent struggle with the illness agent, during which he finally freed himself from the being's stranglehold, was discussed informally the next morning as waking household members gathered around the hearth to discover why he had called out in his sleep the night before. Some applauded his victorious struggle; others remarked he should have stayed limp and silent until the illness agent spoke about its intentions.

To become a healer, the most important dreams are those that involve meetings with the unbound spirits or "interactive selves" of entities who express their desire to enter into a familiar relationship with the dreamer. The link between familiar and dreamer is established and maintained when the spiritguide gives a song to the dreamer. This quintessential moment within dream encounters marks the turning point in becoming a medium empowered to heal with song.

Events in daily life—climbing a mountain or tending a flower bush—often precede a subsequent dream encounter. However, as in Uda Pandak's dream, the familiar emerges and sings of its own accord; the Temiar dreamer does not request or demand either the relationship or the song. The initial relationship of person with dream-spirit is ideally one of receptivity. The spiritguide "gives" (*na-'og*) a song; the dreamer "gets" or "receives" it (*'i-dapad*). Similarly, a patient "gives" himself to a medium for treatment, he does not ask for or request it. Requests are delicate matters altogether in Temiar interactions; demands are nearly nonexistent. A request denied leaves the unfulfilled requestor in a state of ritual danger (*pərɛnhɔɔd, səlɛntab*) that could result in an accident or tiger attack. The person thus refused can recite certain texts to lessen his or her danger; however, the practice puts a damper on superfluous requests and underscores the Temiar value on nonsolicitation.

I emphasize this point because reports of Temiar dream theories dating from the British colonial period (Noone 1972:51–59; Stewart 1948, 1951) and popularized in American psychotherapeutic circles (Garfield 1974, Faraday 1972) transformed this gracious *receipt* of dream songs into a *demand* by the dreamer for a gift or a song. Colonial and neocolonial ideology reworked the peculiar Temiar quality of human/spirit interaction, characterized by acquiescent receipt during dreams and gentle coaxing or enticement during ceremonies, into a relationship characterized by dominance wherein dream-self demands a song from spirit-other.[7]

In my study of Temiar dreams and encounters with familiars, I never found an instance where a Temiar requested a song or any other gift. When questioned about the possibility, Temiars explicitly stated that such a request would be unacceptable. Seasoned mediums sometimes "order" (*na-'oor*) their long-term familiars, during dreams, to go in search of a patient's lost head soul; otherwise, the spiritguide sets the agenda, not the dreamer.

Whenever I recorded Temiar singing, I would subsequently elicit a narrative recounting the dream in which the song was initially received. The majority of these narratives indicate that relationships with entities who later emerged and sang in dreams began during everyday encounters. Of fifty dream narratives I collected that described events in daily life precipitating dream-receipt of a song, 30 percent (fifteen narratives) came from plants previously tended by the dreamer, like the *kəralad* flower bush planted by Uda Pandak.[8] About half of these tended plants were located in the settlement area (eight); the other half were located in swidden or secondary forest (seven).

The ideal image of dream-song receipt from familiars, however, involves prior travel through the jungle. The traveler passes by particular plants, animals, or geographic formations; gathers jungle products; or clears swiddens. Spirits of plants or formations passed in daily life then later emerge in dreams. Forty-eight percent (twenty-four narratives) of the above sample involved such travel through the jungle.[9] The remaining twenty-two percent (eleven narratives) originated from interactions with phenomena from the settlement: plants growing around the settlement where tending was not emphasized; landforms within the settlement area; bathing in the river serving the settlement; interacting with community members who later appeared in dreams; the weaving of mats; the sifting of rice; material artifacts within the house.

Temiar mediums are singers of the landscape, translating the rainforest environment—jungle, field, and settlement—into culture as inhabitant spirits emerge, identify themselves, and begin to sing in dreams and ritual performances. Wolters (1982:7) suggests that sites, such as mountains, associated with ancestors who had achieved leadership status "supplied additional identity to the settlement areas" in prehistoric Southeast Asia. Indianization subsequently involved localizing Hindu beliefs, partly through grafting Hindu legends and spatial concepts onto local Malay sacred geography (Wolters 1982:67; 1979:438–440). However, the Temiar material suggests that the natural environment (the land, its flora and fauna) is sacralized and identified in Southeast Asia not merely through projection of "ancestors" onto the land, but in the reverse direction as well, via spirits of the landscape that moved through men who, by virtue of their ability to function as mediums, became men of prowess, people with *halaa'* adeptness.

Temiars translate the rainforest environment into a social space by establishing networks of association between humans and spirits, who then become mediums and spiritguides. Elsewhere in Southeast Asia, as among the Kaluli of Papua New Guinea, spirit people sing through mediums about the local hills and streams near their spirit homes (Schieffelin 1977:170).[10] Feisty local spirits dwelling in trees, streams, or landforms maintain and negotiate their jurisdiction over particular areas by speaking and singing through mediums during seances (Schieffelin 1977:172–175). The forest is also the home of *ane mama* 'gone reflections', spirits of the Kaluli dead, who appear to humans in the form of birds and fish and sing through mediums during seances (Schieffelin 1976:97; Feld 1988:88). The translation of the environment into cultural terms need not invoke spirits nor imply sacralization; the Kaluli intertwine geography and personal allusion in songs of the *gisalo* ceremony to evoke sorrow and nostalgia for the people and shared pasts associated with specific places (Schieffelin 1976:181–189; 1979; Feld 1982).[11]

A vibrant, continuous yet constantly reconstructed history of a people's relationship to their surroundings is encoded in the landscape. For the Temiars, the process of simultaneously decoding and encoding this information is begun during dreams which, in turn, are precipitated by interactions with the land, its flora and fauna during waking life. As the Temiar dream narratives show, travel through the jungle predominates as an ideal type of prior interaction. This is congruent with the Temiar concept of dreaming as travel of the dreamer's head soul. Comments from the neighboring Semai suggest that dream accounts may substitute for traveler's tales (Dentan 1983:31,36). Informal discussion of one's dreams in the morning with members of one's hearth group or household who happen to be present is, in one sense, the correlate of the standard Temiar greeting, *"Ma-lɔɔ'?"* "Where have you been to?" "Where are you going?"[12]

The following dream narrative, which I elicited the day after I recorded the medium's dream-song, involves an encounter with the "interactive self" of a land formation ensuing from travel through the jungle:[13]

---

1. Aŋah Busuu': There lah. That is the minister of the mountain that I sang. I sang the cool upper-portion liquid soul of the minister, a "way" from when I was still young. Like that, it ordered my father; he dreamt it ordered that I should sing of the minister. That was my father's [dream].

The minister of the mountain. That is mine: minister of Mount . . . uh . . . Bərintəəh [MMB] upriver. Berintəəh at the headwaters near Tambun. Bərintəəh, the Caldaaw group of mountains, the Tamaay group, those are at the headwaters. That was Bərintəəh that I sang. That is my spirit-familiar from when I was still small. I dreamt that at the beginning of my opening. . . .

We traveled together, [my father and I]. We traveled to the mountain I spoke of just now, the one I once pointed out to you. The one I pointed out to you formerly, that one. [We traveled to] the other side of it.

2. M: What was the name of the mountain you traveled to?

3. AB: Bərintəəh. That is what it calls itself, its name. Old Man Bərintəəh we spoke of earlier.

4. M: And after that?

5. AB: It told its name to someone formerly as "Bərintəəh."

6. M: You said earlier that you hunted game, you spent the night . . .

7. AB: We spent the night. Alone, we two. Not many. Alone, we two, we spent the night. He blowpiped game, and we ate it all up. The evening fell, he slept, he dreamt.

8. M: Your father?

9. AB: Yes, my father, he dreamt. My father [FaAB] dreamt, I his child [AB] dreamt; together we two were dreaming.

10. M: Together.

11. AB: Yes, we two together we dreamt that night. The Malays say, *"mimpi."* We dreamt, we two together. So we two dreamt, we two together, probably because he [MMB] ordered that.
   "Həə',"
he said [MMB],
   "No, I don't want you, you the father,
   I reject the father, I want your child here. I would call your child here 'father.' To you, I will call my grandfather. Like that, 'grand-father' I will call you; to the child here I will call 'father.' Like that."
[FaAB answers:]
   "All right, you can, whatever, no problem."

So I dreamt
the minister of the mountain himself said to my father, he ordered:
   "That one [AB], I want that one.
   I don't want that one there [FaAB], I want you," he said to me,
I dreamt that.
He ordered lah, immediately he began to sing. He ordered me:
   "Sing, you may do it."
[AB responds:]
   "You want me to sing?"
[MMB answers:]
   "Yes, that is what I want, I desire."
He sang this singing [you have recorded] here lah. He sang about two "mouths"[14] he sang, I followed, I repeated. I followed, I repeated. I followed completely—after two steps, three steps I would follow; that was it lah, I knew it. I returned home, I sang . . . I had a spirit-familiar lah, I treated people lah, pregnant women, babies with headaches I treated, I recited:
   "jɛg-jɛg-jɛg-jɛg."
Right up to the present: just recently you saw me take out illness. Here I'm already an old man, I've met with other familiars: the flower group I sang earlier, new ones . . .

12. M: That one was your first?

13. AB: That one was the first, the very beginning.

14. Girl from chorus: That was the firstborn.

15. AB: Yes, the firstborn, that one.
(Aŋah Busuu', Kɛlyɛt (Kelaik), 22-ii-82, DN45)[15]

The transformation of the mountain on which Aŋah Busuu' and his father slept into the Mountain Minister that they dreamt is based on the fundamental belief in a homologous division of detachable souls among humans (head and heart souls), plants (leaf and root souls), animals (upper and lower souls), and landforms (summit and underground souls of mountains) that makes communication possible between humans and other rainforest entities, who emerge as spiritguides vocalizing in song during dreams and ceremonies. Natural forms thus socialized produce an "iconography of nature" that encodes popular historiography (Taussig 1980:158, 164; see also Keith Basso 1984). Landforms traversed or cultivated become landmarks that are further anthropomorphized when their souls are dreamt and sung. Environmental resources are symbolically and materially transformed into dreams; language and linguistic classifications; ritual songs, dances, and ornaments; myth; food marked by dietary restrictions and speech taboos; and material artifacts with proscriptions on use and symbolic dimensions of form.

Temiar "adaptation" to the rainforest is best viewed as a series of choices from and responses to the natural (and social) environment. Human adaptation is inherently a dynamic historical process implicating a people's philosophy, religion, social and political organization, and performance traditions as they generate cultures appropriate to their surroundings. This is particularly evident among the Temiars, who integrate domains of kinship, leadership, spirit-mediumship, and art in their cosmology.[16] Their attempt to create order in the world, however, is neither completely homogeneous, conceptual, or static; indeed, their segmentary social organization precludes the emergence of strict uniformity in religious matters. Temiar cosmology is an imperfect cultural consensus grounded in social action and performance and is continually reconstructed through individuals' varied experiences, dream and trance revelations, and innovations. Temiar adaptation is creative composition with the rainforest as both palette and orchestra.

SINGERS OF THE LANDSCAPE

Aŋah Busuu' 's dream-meeting with the Minister of Mount Bərintəəh, occurring when he was about 12 to 14 years old, was his first encounter with a familiar, an encounter that transformed him into a singer of the landscape, a person with *halaa'*. Receipt of only one song coupled with his youthful age rendered him slightly *halaa'*. Although he compresses time and experience in his narrative ("I returned home, I sang . . . I had a spirit-familiar lah, I treated people lah . . ."), a few years passed before he began to treat people alone, rather than assisting older and more seasoned mediums. Nonetheless, the manner in which he has compressed his narrative highlights the dream receipt of a song or way from a spiritguide. This has become mythologized as the pivotal moment in becoming a medium, a master singer of the landscape empowered to heal.

Receipt of a dream song enables the dreamer to reestablish his tie with that spirit when he subsequently sings the song during ceremonies. All "composers" are thus mediums. By singing the given song, mediums engage their familiars in the tasks of illness diagnosis and treatment.

In his dream narrative, Aŋah Busuu' tells us that "Bərintəəh" is what the mountain calls itself: "It told its name to someone formerly as 'Bərintəəh.' " Dreams are also a source of language innovation. During dreams, the mountains, fruit trees, sunsets, and other entities reportedly give their "true names" (*kənʉʉh mʉn*). True names are names in the language of the nonhuman entity itself (*kuy rii' 'ə-na* 'its own language') as distinct from the language of humans (*kuy 'εε' 'our language'). The close association between the imaginal worlds of dreaming and ceremonial trancing is illustrated by another term for these appellations, "ceremonial terms" (*dɛhneeh pɛhnɔɔh*), and by their use in the poetic language of song texts.

The hazy area where speech and song fade into one another is found in *hənelad* or "versing," the metaphorical language of both sung texts and poetic speech. Thus, the setting sun might be described as *na-yuub* 'night arrives' or *ɲaab* 'the redness of sunset' (also implying the dangers inherent in this transitional period).

However, to comment *sɛrsodɛɛr sɔy maɲrɔɔy* at sunset would be to verse on the setting of the sun, calling to mind images of black silhouette against the red sun, coolness, slight melancholy, and wistfulness. *Sɛrsodɛɛr sɔy maɲrɔɔy* is drawn from song texts of a particular musical genre[17] and includes the name for sunset (*maɲrɔɔy*) given in a dream to a medium of that genre. Rather than viewing *hənelad* solely as text abstracted from song, *hənelad* or "versing" is a type of metaphorically obtuse language that is pe-culiarly adapted to the elusive and descriptive reference of sung texts. This quality of the language results partly from the use of special terms received via dream revelation, from a preponderance of descriptive adjectives and expressives (Diffloth 1976), and from techniques of meter, rhyme, assonance, and reduplicative play.

A dream narrative recounted by Ading Kerah in the settlement of Rəlɔɔy on a tributary upriver on the River Bərɔk, details the process of language innovation through dream revelation. The young female head soul of Mt. Raŋwɛɛy (located near Kampung Rəlɔɔy) reveals her true name: *'amɛɛ' sələŋɔɔy* 'Mother Fluid Beauty'.[18] She allows Ading Kerah to give this name to his new wife. Words from the imaginal world thus act to further homolo-gize people and places. The words "Mother Fluid Beauty" are often repeated in song texts the mountain spirit teaches to Ading Kerah. The song became so popular locally that members of Ading Kerah's own community as well as nearby settlements upstream and down-stream began to identify not only his wife, but he himself with the name, referring to him offhandedly as *Taa' Sələŋɔɔy* 'Mister Fluid Beauty'. Ading Kerah recounts his dream:

The male crest-soul of Mt. Galeng took the young woman crest-soul of Mt. Raŋwɛɛy, he took her, he would sleep with her, he would bring her downriver. The name of that woman is Sələŋɔɔy, Fluid Beauty. So, he took her downstream, he kept her living there two weeks, then he returned her from downstream. He brought her back from downstream—

there were three shaded river pools downstream, homes
of illness agents (they had once made my father sick,
but they'd never harmed me).

After he returned her from downstream, only then she said to my head soul, she [the upper-soul of Mt. Raŋwɛɛy] said:

"Here is a person you can use, for you."[19]
She said,
"For you; her name is Mother, Mother Fluid Beauty." After that,
then she gave me one tune. She repeated and repeated, every
week. One week, one time. One week, one time. So she gave that
tune. After she gave that tune, I was able to sing bit by bit.
So, she also asked. She asked about that name, she asked,
"To whom will you give that name, that they will become
named?"
At that time, I had just begun to sleep with my wife here [in
Rəlɔɔy]. I answered,
"No, I don't know to whom I will give the name, there's nobody,
no children.
I don't know."
She said, she ordered,
"To your wife here you can give the name Mother Fluid
Beauty."

A half a year passed before I announced that I would hold a
singing/trance-dancing ceremony with the bamboo-tube stampers,
with beating of the bamboo tubes. So I had already become com-
petent with the versing, the names of the mountains, all kinds of
things. She herself ordered that my wife should carry the name
because there were no children. Up until now I still use that "way";
up until now, I use it.

She gives the versing [in the dream], but when I perform during
ceremonies, I can sing new verses as they come—about the flowers,
about all kinds of things. She gives where we put in extra lines of
text (*jəhook*), where we fall level, where we rise narrowly,[20] where
we phrase. (Ading Kerah, Rəlɔɔy, 10-vi-82, DN5)[21]

Emerging with the form of a young woman, the interactive self
of Mt. Raŋwǝǝy speaks, gives her name, and then begins to sing.
This narrative also tells us about the learning process: Mother Fluid
Beauty returns weekly to tutor Ading Kerah until, about six months
later, he feels sufficiently secure to order a ceremony for public
performance of the song received. The timing and frequency of this
process vary from one medium to another. Some mediums say they
learn a song after only one appearance of a familiar and are ready

to perform it publicly quite soon thereafter. They either call for a ceremony to be held, or avail themselves of a performance in progress.

Repertoire size and frequency of receipt of new songs also varies; mediums may receive a new song every few weeks for a four-month period, then one or two a year, and then again return to a more concentrated period of receipt. The operative repertoire also changes: as new songs are received, old ones fall into disuse and are partially forgotten, with one major exception: the first song a medium ever received in a dream, the initial familiar encountered, remains special to that medium and is often sung first during any ceremony in which he participates.[22] Ading Kerah's narrative also indicates that some lyrics are given by the spiritguide, but room remains for extemporaneous improvisation: "She gives the versing [in the dream], but when I perform during ceremonies, I can sing new verses as they come. . . ."

Songs of mediums who have died do not necessarily disappear from the repertoire, but may continue to be sung by others. This is a dynamic tradition, exhibiting both continuity and change. The theory of dream-song composition promotes creative additions to the general repertoire through individual revelation and composition. Comparative analysis of the styles of various Temiar river valleys and regions, as well as archival studies of historical recordings, reveals consistent geographic, temporal, and individual variation. Individual dream songs and umbrella genres vary regionally and historically, rising to popularity and spreading from one medium or one river valley to another during a certain period, later to be replaced in popularity by another medium's subsequent revelations.

Temiars do not call this sonic gift received in dreams and reenacted in ceremonies a "song" (though they do speak of "singing," *gənabag*), nor do they consider it to consist merely of "sound." Rather, the spiritguide bestows a *nɔŋ*, which could be translated as a "way" or "path" describing the visions of the traveling spiritguide. The dreamer (and later, in performance, the female chorus) follows the path. The way of a particular spiritguide refers not only to melody and song text given in the dream, but also may refer to particular dance steps, leaves used as ceremonial ornaments, or rhythms for the bamboo-tube percussion; trance behavior; extent of male and female participation; whether the spiritguide will accept light or prefers to arrive in darkness; and other performance conditions. A spiritguide's way includes far more than just the tune itself.

Dwelling toward the source of the River Bərɔk near the area inhabited by the northernmost Semai of Pahang, Uda Pandak received from a spiritguide both song and dance steps influenced by the Semai style. In his dream, a young woman, emerging from the bamboo-tube stampers played to accompany singing sessions, "returns" to him the essence of the singing that has entered the tubes. He describes the dream:

> The pair of bamboo-tube stampers. The pair of bamboo tubes that we beat. It has an upper-portion soul. Our songs enter inside the tubes. I dreamt those songs were returned to me. At night I trance-danced, we put away the bamboo tubes, I returned home, I slept, she emerged, a young woman. She dances [Semai style], she invites me to dance, together, her and my head soul. Her hair falling long like rain, she comes out. She invited me—the sound of her voice doesn't reach far—she invited me to dance together with her in the settlement here. She gave the singing and that particular way of dancing together. (Uda Pandak, Kengkong, 30-vi-82, DN21)[23]

Ways are not only received from the interactive selves of upper-portion souls, but may also come from the lower- or inner-portion "heart" or "pith" soul.[24] Aluj Hitam of the settlement Kengkong was known as Old Man Rəgəəl Tree (*Taa' Rəgəəl*), for the song received from the "trunk soul" of the fallen Rəgəəl tree[25] trunk near which he built his house. Old Man Rəgəəl Tree received more songs from heart souls than any other medium I recorded. Another of his ways came from the sap of the Ipoh tree. He received this way in a dream after returning home from gashing the tree trunk to procure the sap used for blowpipe dart poison. He also received a way from the female heart soul of a *bayas* palm after having cut it, taken out the white unripe pulp from the inside, and steam-fried it. Similarly, he received a "way of the jungle" (as opposed to ways received from items identified with Malays) from the pith of the *jɛŋjɛɛg* vine[26] after having cut and gathered its products:

> A way of the jungle. The vine *jɛŋjɛɛg*. I got the song from its heart soul. The heart soul . . . one's own heart is elsewhere [when the heart soul of the spiritguide sings through one].

She was a very beautiful woman. Her hair was two arm-widths long, and she had a curving, graceful body. I cut the *jɛŋjɛɛg* vine, and it fell. I returned home, I carried on my back the cotton used for blowpiping and the vine. I slept in the late afternoon, and I got it. I got it in the late afternoon. She herself emerged. A woman. From inside the pith, she emerges, she sings, she loses her balance and shivers as she dances, she falls, she causes me to go into a dangerously powerful trance. The heart soul, she emerges, she pulls on my heart, "*Kəlib!*" Suddenly, the body is cool, filled with cool liquid. (Aluj Hitam, Kengkong, 30-vi-82, DN27)[27]

In addition to providing a format for expressing mutuality with the rainforest environment, the theory of dream revelation provides a space for Temiars to incorporate new experiences with technological devices of the developing Malaysian world. The ever-changing environment of the Temiar has increasingly included airplanes, parachute drops, perfume oils, wristwatches, Malays, Chinese, the British, Japanese (during World War II), and anthropologists, all of which have emerged in dreams and given songs to Temiar mediums. The theory of dream revelation also offered strategies for adjusting to changes in social organization as the Temiars interacted historically with traditional Malay headmen and courts, and as they interact with the contemporary Malaysian government bureaucracy.

The titles given to the mountain in Aŋah Busuu' 's dream narrative indicate this adjustment process. The shift from Mt. Bərintəəh's Temiar title "Old Man" (*Taa'*) to the Malay title "Minister" (*Mentərii'*, itself from the Sanskrit *mantri*) represents the incorporation of hierarchical bureaucratic terminology into a previously egalitarian framework. This is not to say that the Temiars did not recognize status differentiation, but traditionally prestige adhered to age, kinship, and expertise, rather than office. The mountains of Southeast Asia have long endured such shifting metaphors reflecting changes in the social and cosmological order: mountain summits locally marked by indigenous lowland peoples were re-identified by them as "natural *Sivalingas*" during the spread of Hindu influence (Wolters 1979:438–440).[28]

As spiritguides appear in Temiar dreams, they are identified as "people of the jungle" (e.g., Temiars) or "Malays" by their material origins and by their speech, clothing, and behavior. Malayo-Sanskrit titles such as *mɛntərii'* (minister), *potərii'* (princess), and *rajaa'* (king, prince) are often invoked to refer to Temiar spirit-guides, whether they be mountains, rivers, or fruit trees. Malay spiritguides are reported to emerge variously as male or female. These days, if male, they are dressed in pants and shirt. Spiritguides identified as Malays emerge from (1) the "main rivers" (*tiw boo'*) that traditionally served as passageways between the upriver Temiar and the downriver Malays such as the River Bərɔk, whose banks up to Jeram Gajah were settled by Malays in historic times;[29] (2) entities of the ground and underground, such as the underground/underwater snake *Dangaa'* (cf. Malay, Sanskrit *naga*) associated with the welling of floodwaters; and (3) trunk-souls of potent trees such as *Bɛrbɔw*[30] and *Rəgəəl*. Malay spirits speak and sing using a greater number of Malay words, sprinkling their songs with Islamic greetings and incantations. However, despite their Malay appearance and ethnic identity, they often speak Temiar and sing ways of the jungle, as one medium commented of his Malay spiritguide: "The River Bərɔk has a Malay minister. But when she arrives, that one, to us jungle folk, we sing in jungle style." Uda Pandak recounts how he received a song from a Malay Spirit of the Rəgəəl Tree, which later became his namesake:

> A way of the jungle.
> The *rəgəəl* tree.
> The birds, they returned home to the branch;
>   it fell to the ground, in all its largeness.
> It fell to the ground, I built a house there.
> I built a house, I dreamt the tree's trunk-soul.
> He emerged, a male, I dreamt he emerged, he sang.
>
> It's already been a long time, already six years.
> A young man, wearing Malay clothes—
>   pants and shirt.
> I call him "*Dato'*," that's his name.
> He himself, he speaks to me, then I can treat people,
> I take out claws.[31]
> He verses of the birds.
> (Alʉj Hitam, Kengkong, 30-vi-82, DN26)[32]

When Temiars dream the spirits of the environs and "tag" them, so to speak, with names and songs, they consolidate and legitimate their relationship to the land.[33] In his dream of the Rəgəəl Tree Spirit, Aluj Hitam translates his surroundings into the terms of Malay hierarchy. The title with which he refers to the Rəgəəl Tree Spirit, *"Dato',"* is an old Malay term for ruler or chief, now used by Malays to refer to the head of the family, elders, ancestors, and spirits.[34] His dream encompasses historical shifts in intercultural contact. The Temiar theory of dreaming thus becomes a dynamic resource for interpreting and formulating new responses to the natural and social world.

Temiars read nature as members of a literate society might read a book. A combination of road map, bible, history of civilization, and mystery novel, the plethora of animal sounds that a Temiar hears tells him or her what ecological zone is nearby, what time of day or season is approaching, what associated plants or animals may be in the vicinity to hunt and gather. But these sounds evoke not only the image of, for example, a particular bird perched in the forest canopy. For that bird is also a personage in myth, ritual, and augury. The raucous-voiced great Argus pheasant[35] gave Penghulu Dalam a dream-song that he sings during ritual performance; the great Argus's mythical association with the tiger (they once decorated one another with stripes) further marks it as a tiger transform too dangerous to be eaten by men or women who are parents of young children. The song of the magpie robin[36] foretells the arrival of human visitors, while the nighttime vocalization of the bay owl,[37] who is said to ride on the shoulder of the tiger, signals the presence of a tiger in the vicinity. Word goes out through the settlement and people travel with care. The jungle is peopled with animals and landforms imbued with meaning by the Temiars; walking through the jungle is simultaneously walking through an ecosystem and a storyland.

Abilem Lum, now dwelling in the settlement of Bawik on the Betis River, heard the sound of frogs[38] croaking during his midday nap on Mt. Bərkaay, near the source of the Betis. This narrative, recounted after he sang for me the way of the frog species, illustrates how sounds become marked as personages through dreaming:

The way of *taŋkəb*. It calls in the mountains, upstream: *"Kə-ruuh, kə-ruuh, kə-ruuh."* Frogs. They live near trees. *"Kə-ruuh,*

kə-ruuh kəruuh.'' When I got that song, I was liming birds. I
was waiting for a barbet.[39] I stuck the resinous stick up in a
tree, then slept unawares. The sound, the sound became a
young woman. You could see how beautiful her shape. That
is what I sang just now.

[I was] liming birds. The barbet I mentioned earlier. So, I stuck
in the sticks, then I waited, I slept, in the middle of the day.
I was tired, so I slept. The sound [of the frogs] was wonderful
in my unconsciousness. Only then, I dreamt. (Abilem Lum,
Bawik, 7-ix-82, DN2)[40]

How does this connection with spirits of the landscape established during dreams and enacted in ceremonial performance em-
power a medium to heal? The medium's relationship with a spiritguide constitutes a claim to knowledge. Incorporating the
knowledge and vision of the spiritguide during dreams and trance,
the medium can "see" the source of illness in a patient and interact
with or "treat" it. A medium contrasts human immobility and the
limited perspective of a human on the ground in the jungle with the
vast perspective of spiritguides who, as essence liberated from
concrete manifestation, leap across mountain crests, soar above the
clouds, and rise above the dense tropical foliage to view the rare
vista:

We know nothing. We sit at home and eat the intestines of
game. The spiritguides, they range far and wide, they return
what they see to us in our houses. We ourselves, in our
homes, we know nothing.

Extended range and overarching perspective become the metaphors for knowledge. By becoming a medium, one taps into this
range and perspective, and thus one gains the power to interact
with illness. But this power is located within the actions of the
medium as directed by the spiritguides: a medium can't tell patients
what is wrong and what to do and then have them go out and do
it. Knowledge and its enactment are mutually interdependent in
the medium. Knowledge must be connected with its source, the
spiritguide, through the *performance* of the medium. The medium is
the embodiment of knowledge translated into power that is demonstrated in song.

HALAA' ADEPTNESS: A POTENTIAL

Halaa' is a gradient of adeptness, a universal potential that is then manifested to a certain degree within particular individuals.[41] *Halaa'* adeptness enhances one's position in the social order, but does not constitute an "office" in the Weberian sense.[42] Given the homologous distinctions operative in humans and all other entities, all Temiars theoretically have access to spiritguides through their dreams. However, only some individuals actually establish such contacts. Thus, while *halaa'* potential is equally accessible in dreams, its variable realization does set up a subtle differentiation among members of a community who are otherwise on a par.

According to a few mediums in Lambok and Reloy, the ability to become a medium is not universal. The deity often said to be the "first" medium, Alɛj (younger brother of Lightning, *'ɛŋkuu'*), points to a baby still inside its mother's womb and says, "You here, eventually you will have *halaa'*." To another pregnant mother's abdomen he points and says, "You here, you will never have *halaa'*." Alɛj singles out babies that he "feels close with in his heart" to someday become mediums. Once he has pointed to them, however, they must still dream meetings with familiars and receive songs themselves. Only the potential to have spiritguides is instilled, or perhaps recognized, by Alɛj. This story is, however, more of an "after the fact" explanation for why some people don't meet familiars and receive songs in dreams, rather than an attempt to exclude anyone from possibly developing into a medium.

Halaa' adeptness enables an individual to diagnose and treat illness. Mediums also play central roles in the ritual singing sessions held at the conclusion of a period of mourning, at key points in the agricultural cycle, or to celebrate publicly the connection with spiritguides.

While all Temiars theoretically can receive spiritguides through their dreams, in actuality, men from their late teens onward receive songs from spiritguides more often than do women. Women more rarely become adepts, though the precedent exists: for example, *'amɛɛ'* Jɛrwan Lung, a female medium active in Lambok, had several types of spiritguides and vocal genres, including spirits of dead humans (*ciɲcɛm*), thunder and lightning (*'ɛŋkuu'*), and the *poɲey* flower.[43]

Among the men of a community, particular individuals distinguish themselves by receiving more songs from spiritguides and thus exhibiting a greater *halaa'* adeptness. Whoever among these men has had more spiritguides for a longer time or has access to the particularly potent tiger spiritguide, is considered to be the "larger" medium (*halaa' mənuu'*). Such a medium, however, does not necessarily work alone. Nor do people with difficult illnesses consult only one medium. Several mediums may cooperate, combining their energies to tackle problematic cases or epidemics. A differential degree of adeptness does not provoke intravillage competition. However, intervillage competition, jealousy, and suspicion between mediums has occurred.

Access to *halaa'* potential is not hereditary, but children and close relations of an adept also tend to become mediums. This is due to a secondary avenue of adeptness: being "given" a song by another medium, often a close relation. The process of bestowal involves singing and dancing in ceremonies with that medium while receiving ministrations called *pərɛnlub*: the medium conducts the cool spiritual liquid flowing from his spiritguide into the head and heart soul of the recipient. Songs thus received rarely form a medium's entire repertoire. They are an optional first step preparing him to receive his own dream songs, or they supplement his personally received dream-song repertoire.

Singers who sing other people's dream songs without having received *pərɛnlub* are not considered mediums. Rather, they are likened to singers of Malay and Tamil popular music that Temiars hear on shortwave radio: their songs are "enjoyable" to dance to or sing with, but they are songs "without substance," *tɔ' bar-'isii'*. Competence or adeptness (*halaa'*), then, links musical abilities with spirit-mediumship: evocative songs originate from and set into motion the spirits that animate the universe. With song, the medium effects a transformation from the bound-soul condition of everyday life to the freed spirit of dream and ritual performance. From this moment of transformation, stratification emerges in the prestige adhering to the effective medium.

HALAA' AND LEADERSHIP: A ROLE

Studies of social structures—be they relatively egalitarian or highly stratified—address the cultural concepts and social enactments of power, authority, and influence. Egalitarian social systems are those in which the labor or obedience of one adult cannot be coerced by another. This does not imply the absence of manipulation and social control in egalitarian societies; rather, the style of manipulation in egalitarian societies takes a different form. Members retain the prerogative of withdrawing from untenable relationships or coercive commands (Fried 1967:83; Collier and Rosaldo 1981:289). Power, defined in hierarchical terms as the ability to exert control, refers to the potential for channeling the behavior of others by threat or use of sanctions (Weber 1922/1964:152; Fried 1967:13). Whereas social-scientific discussions of "power" approach the phenomenon as an aspect of social relations (Adams 1975), indigenous Southeast Asian concepts of "power" concern a divine energy animating the universe, the manner in which this energy is tapped by humans, and the consequences of manipulating this energy for one's position in the social order (Anderson 1972).

In the Weberian paradigm, "authority" involves the exercise and recognition of legitimate power; authority is "the socially recognized and legitimated right to make decisions concerning others" (Schlegel 1977:8). Channeling the behavior of others by noncoercive methods of persuasion constitutes "influence." Leaders in egalitarian societies, such as Temiar mediums, do not command obedience through coercion; rather, they persuade others by using influence as they comment upon actions or coordinate activities.

Access to power, prestige, and material rewards is systematically differentiated in hierarchical societies but more equitably distributed among members of egalitarian societies (Schlegel 1977:3). While typologies using power, prestige, and material rewards as indices can help to distinguish inflections of egalitarianism and stratification, the Temiar data make us reconsider the discreteness of these components. For example, a Temiar medium is both a *prestigious* spirit-medium and *nobody but* the voice of the spiritguide. These theoretical formulations are necessary but inadequate in themselves for understanding the pull toward inequity within egalitarianism.

Traditionally, Temiar leadership was village-based and decentralized. Settlement groups maintained their autonomy; higher levels of intervillage organization developed minimal definition (see

Sahlins 1968:20). However, tribal leadership and more formalized headmanship have become increasingly ranked through historical interactions with the dominant Malay population. Benjamin (1968) distinguishes two categories of political authority and influence operative among the Temiar, *leadership* and *headmanship*, referring respectively to positions that are legitimized *internally* (vis-à-vis Temiars themselves) or in relation to a locus of authority *outside* of Temiar society (vis-à-vis the Malays). Historically, multiple leadership within a community has evolved into singular headmanship, as Malays sought out powerful Temiar individuals with which to interact and conferred singularity upon them.

A medium is differentiated from the other members of his community by his ability to receive songs from spiritguides. What role does such a person play within the Temiar egalitarian community? Temiar mediums are not reclusive, eccentric hermits; they are active members of the community. A person's *halaa'* ability distinguishes him as a man of respect and influence in the Temiar sense, that is, as a coordinator and commentator, not coercer. The medium's ability to mediate between spirit and human realms correlates with his ability to mediate between the members of his community in the everyday world of social relations. The nature of the medium's relationship with spiritguides parallels his method of political persuasion in community affairs. The medium does not control spiritguides through force, he entices and coaxes them into presence. Nor does he impose his will upon the community; rather, he subtly influences the course of events through suggestion and example. Yet his suggestions carry the weight of prestige and respect which adhere to him as a person of *halaa'* adeptness.

Halaa' competence propels an individual into a particular position within the social structure. *Halaa'* adeptness is one characteristic among others that marks potential leaders and headmen. *Halaa'* adeptness confers and expresses what we might term charisma; and that attribute, combined with position in the kinship network, is a major factor in determining Temiar leaders and headmen. Temiar household-cluster and village leaders derive their influence from the kinship domain, particularly as members or spouses of members of the core sibling-group of the ramage. Kinship elements being equal, other characteristics such as hunting skill, spirit-mediumship adeptness and concomitant musical virtuosity, agricultural knowledge, and the ability to move discussions toward consensus and to coordinate activities distinguish men, primarily, as leaders (see Benjamin 1968:28–32). Malay language skills and the resultant ability to interact with outsiders distinguish village leaders to some extent but are of primary importance in determining headmen.[44]

Temiar village leaders and headmen are usually mediums. In villages where the official headmen are not mediums, both the headman and the most adept medium of the community are consulted in situations of community-wide concern. *Halaa'* adeptness thus becomes a guide to inflections of persuasion.

A medium's influence on community affairs outside of singing ceremonies can be seen during discussions (*bə-caraa'*)[45] among male household-heads. Such talks are held to coordinate activities such as swidden placement, rattan gathering, house-building and village-site location, or to mediate problematic situations such as divorce. In these discussions, men of the community "speak in turns" as various "opinions" (*nɔŋ* 'paths') are expressed and moved toward consensus. Both the opinions or "routes" expressed in discussions and the songs or "ways" received from spiritguides are referred to as *nɔŋ*. Just as his songs mediate with the spirit world, a medium's opinions are especially valued and carefully considered.

THE NONADEPT:
ALTERNATIVE STRATEGIES FOR WIVES AND WOMEN

Competence as a medium enhances one's role in the social order and colors one's participation in ritual and everyday life. What alternative modes of expression are open to the nonadept, or to those in particular kinship relations to the adept? The wife of the medium, who knows her husband's repertoire better than any of the other women, is a cornerstone of the chorus and a particularly astute foil to the medium's wit during performances. The medium's wife also plays an equally important role in conflict resolution and adjudication, but in complementary fashion. While the speech of the medium is calm and judicious during discussions, the medium's wife often engages in community critique in the form of a monologue harangue uttered at high volume.

Temiar arguments and monologue critiques are rarely face to face; when harangues are uttered, the vocalizer is either in a separate compartment or building from the person being criticized. The harangues are often in third person: the object is referred to as "he" or "she" rather than "you" to further distance the confrontation. Yet for all its indirect structuring (separate cubicles, third person pronouns, often cloaked in the obscurity of nighttime darkness), Temiars still consider this a hyperdirect form of interaction capable of shocking the souls of participants or bystanders into taking flight, resulting in the illness of soul loss.

Men and women both engage in intra- or interfamily arguments and monologue critiques in this fashion. But in matters of community-wide concern, the wife of the medium often takes the stage and harangues from within her own house, her voice spreading out into the community. I have seen a medium's wife enter directly into the house of the parents of a neglected, wailing child and proceed to criticize them for endangering both the child itself and the community at large with soul loss. During an epidemic,[46] desperate community members may still come to the medium, himself struck by illness, in search of treatment. In one such situation, the medium's wife began a loud harangue after midnight from inside her house—criticizing the community for overburdening her husband, reminding them how essential his services were, and admonishing them to respect his own need for rest and recovery. Her role as commentator and guardian of the smooth flow of community relations parallels that of the medium, but her harangue presents a counterpoint to his dispassionate demeanor. The medium himself is unable to engage in angry harangues without loss of respect for his ability to adjudicate dispassionately. In this instance of rhetoric as a cultural system (see Sapir and Crocker 1977), an almost courtly restraint and indirect imposition of will are juxtaposed with the hyperdirect harangue. The relatively indirect rhetorical mode of persuasion practiced by the medium (in contrast to his wife) appears to be linked to the displacement of self that characterizes Temiar spirit-mediumship.

The intonation pattern of the harangue, a suspended monotone leading into a plaintive downward curve, resembles the melodic contour of the song phrase called *jenhook*.[47] In the arbitrarily inserted *jenhook* phrase, the medium works in text that won't fit into the melodic pattern of other song phrases. Women, peripheral to men's "speaking-in-turns" discussions, provide a layer of commentary from the sidelines, and sometimes *jɛnhook* the tail end of comments they throw in from side cubicles or from outside.

The harangue, the complaint, the *jɛnhook*—these are all the things that ordinarily *don't fit in*, inappropriate behavior made appropriate through stylized presentation. These are the rhetorical devices developed by wives of mediums and other women as alternatives, balancing the expressive forms characteristic of the medium. During trancing ceremonies, when the medium "forgets" himself and his surroundings, participants (particularly women) will call out jokingly, "Remember! The dogs will bite!"—countering his fall toward oblivion with a joke. Differentiation emerges at the level of rhetorical modes reserved for the medium and the non-adept respectively, a distinction often based in gender.

LAND, PERSON, AND SONG

Temiar mediums are singers of the landscape, translating their rainforest environment into culture as inhabitant spirits emerge, identify themselves, and begin to sing in dreams and ritual performances. Traveling daily across the land, tending its flora, hunting its fauna, Temiars return home to sleep and dream encounters with the unbound spirits or "interactive selves" of these rainforest entities. Dream narratives trace the progressive emergence of spirits into perceptibility: from seed to shoot, from flower bush emitting fragrance to emergent human form, from speech to song. These narratives mark the pivotal moment in becoming a healer: receipt of a song from a spiritguide during dreams.

The ability to receive songs from spiritguides while dreaming renders a person *sɛn'ɔɔy bə-halaa'* 'a person with *halaa'* adeptness'. *Halaa'* serve as mediums, conduits through which spiritguides flow into the ceremonial realm. The dream song is the path or way linking mediums and other ceremonial participants (dancers, chorus members, patients) with the song's source: the spiritguide. The spirit's presence flows through the medium's voice as song and through the medium's body as a cool spiritual liquid. Imbued with the overarching vision and vast perspective of the spirits when he sings, the medium is empowered to see and counteract illness. The act of singing demonstrates the translation of the spiritguide's vision into the medium's knowledge and power. Places become persons, landforms become specific locations. Singing songs of the landscape, a healer counterbalances the dislocation of illness with locations of the spiritguides.

Through dreaming and singing, Temiars locate themselves in their surroundings according to concepts of being that encourage exchanges between humans and nonhumans. While the framework of this theory is consensually held, the details are continually modified by historical experience and individual revelation. Various formal musical genres and ceremonial cults have developed from the dreams received by mediums. These genres exhibit particular scalar structures, melodic and rhythmic patterns, texts, dance steps, trance behavior, instrumentation, leaf and flower ornaments, and the extent of male and female participation. Genres vary historically, regionally, and individually. Temiar cosmology, grounded in social action and performance, is thus an imperfect cultural consensus continually constructed and reconstructed. Temiar dreaming and singing are exquisite examples of the interpretive process as a continuously dialectical interaction between humans and the world they perceive around them.

4

The Dream Performed

In dreams, the spiritguide teaches a song to a dreamer by singing a phrase that the dreamer then repeats. In performance, this dream format—the spiritguide singing an initial phrase repeated by the dreamer—is transferred to the realm of human actors. The dream-teaching relationship is thus echoed in performance, recapitulating the creation of the song in the dream transfer: the medium now sings the initial phrase, which is repeated by a female chorus ranging from young girls to older women. The female chorus also provides the essential percussive accompaniment: pairs of bamboo-tube stampers (gɔɔh) beat against a log in duple rhythm. The performance is optionally accompanied by one or two single-headed drums (bəranɔ'; batak) and/or a small hand-held gong played by males or females.

Men dream encounters with familiars more often than women, and some men are more prolific than others at receiving dream songs. Due to their primary access to spiritguides, these men occupy central roles in ritual singing sessions. They initiate the singing; the female chorus repeats their phrases. In an ingenious display of egalitarian flair, Temiars undermine this potential stratification through the structure of performance. Leveling devices include performance constructs such as overlapping medium/chorus vocalizations; indigenous theories underlying performance; and the ritual inversion of everyday male/female roles.

Dream songs, when performed, become socially organized sounds. The people producing the sounds are positioned within the role structure of the ritual event. Sound, person, and power are intertwined in the social relations of ceremonial performance. When dream songs are performed, the relationship between mediums and spiritguides also takes public form. Before examining the social structuring of sounds in performance, I will trace several formal cult and musical genres that have developed from dreams

Plate 6. Male medium and female chorus playing bamboo-tube stampers during a trancing ceremony (*peɬmooh*).

received by mediums. While the underlying dynamics of dream receipt remain the same, these various dream-song genres take different shape in particular historical periods, river-valley regions, settlement areas, and individual repertoires. They exhibit characteristic scalar structure, melodic and rhythmic patterns, textual content and vocabulary, dance movements, and other parameters outlined by the spiritguide during dreams.

Ritual singing sessions (*gənabag* 'singing' > *gabag*, the verb 'sing') and singing/trance-dancing ceremonies (*pɛhnɔɔh* > *pɔɔh*, the verb 'trance-dance') are housebound, nighttime events. The two are not discrete types of ceremonies, but rather represent points along a performance continuum, with greater emphasis on trancing and leaf ornaments in *pɛhnɔɔh*. *Gənabag* can refer to singing as it occurs in the jungle or settlement, outdoors or indoors, in the course of work or play.[1] It also refers to nighttime ritualized singing sessions which, like trance-dancing ceremonies, involve interactive choral response and bamboo-tube percussion. These extend from after sundown until anywhere up to an hour after sunrise. To hold a singing session or trance-dancing ceremony in the daytime, or to beat the bamboo-tube percussion in the open air rather than from within a covered structure, is considered *gɛnhaa'*, a breach of ritual rules capable of engendering illness and misfortune.

When asked what formally differentiates "trance-dancing ceremonies" (*pɛhnɔɔh*) from "singing sessions" (*gənabag*), Temiar often answer: "In *pɛhnɔɔh*, there are flowers." The leaf and flower ornaments are pivotal in the movement of spiritguides from jungle into settlement that is effected through the ceremonies. Foliated ornaments and hand whisks serve as camouflage to lure the spiritguides from the jungle and make them comfortable inside the thatch and bamboo homes in which ceremonies are held. The central hanging leaf ornament (*tənamuu'* < Malay *tamu* 'guest') provides a place for the spiritguides to alight as they initially enter the ritual space.

These days, traditional longhouses have been replaced by clusters of extended and nuclear family dwellings. Singing ceremonies are usually held in the house with the largest central room in a settlement or in the home of the ministrating medium or an immobilized patient if the session is held for curative purposes. For

Plate 7. These young women use bamboo tubes as cutting boards to prepare leaf ornaments for the coming evening's ceremony.

major ceremonies such as the four- to seven-day set of sessions held to mark the end of a mourning period (*tɔrɛnpuk tɛnmɔɔh*) a special raised and thatched structure without walls may be built to house the numerous guests arriving from surrounding settlements. The flexible, raised bamboo floors of Temiar houses rebound under the dancers' feet and cushion the fall of fainting trancers. Ceremonies are held variously at the conclusion of a period of mourning, for curative purposes, at key points in the agricultural cycle, before a long journey or following the return of a community member, to welcome guests to a settlement, to conclude the construction of a new house (somewhat like a housewarming), to celebrate publicly the connection with spiritguides, or for the enjoyment of singing and trance-dancing.

How does the ceremonial performance of dream songs fit into the total scope of Temiar musical experience? The Temiar musical repertoire is primarily vocal. The entire indigenous vocal repertoire is made up of the songs taught to dreamers by spiritguides. Temiars also listen to popular Malay, Chinese, and Tamil songs and learn Malay songs by shortwave radio and cassettes. These songs, however, are not in the same category of meaningful sound as indigenous songs. During the second stage of Temiar mourning restrictions, for example, no Orang Asli music is allowed (either live, radio broadcast, or tape); but Malay, Chinese, and Tamil radio stations that are "not real singing" can be played.

Songs sung by children playing, groups walking through the forest, or a sleepless person singing solo into the night are drawn from the spiritguide repertoire. In these contexts (except perhaps the last of the three), the songs do not reach their maximum potency; that is, they do not manifest the spiritguide who originally bestowed the song. The song's potency is determined by the links between performer and the spirit-source of the song, a link forged through dreams or through the passage of *kahyɛk*. Mediumship, which involves realizing the spiritguide, adheres in singing only if (1) the singer is the one who actually dreamt the song; or (2) the singer has learned the song from the original dreamer (or in a line of succession from that dreamer) accompanied by ministrations passing along the cool spiritual liquid *kahyɛk*. Dream songs may be sung by anyone in informal contexts of work, travel, and leisure without invoking their spirit-mediumship potential; but only qualified performers singing with the intent to invoke the spirits can activate the power of their dream songs.

Formal genres of the nonvocal repertoire are defined by the instruments on which they are played. Instrument construction dictates formal parameters such as scale, range, ambitus, and timbre. Temiar musical instruments include *pensɔɔl* (noseflute), *si'ɔɔy* (mouthblown flute), *kərəb* (two-stringed tube zither), *geŋgɔɔɲ* (metal mouthharp), and *raŋgɔɲ* or *raŋgɔɔ* (mouthharp made from the mid-rib of the palm, *Eugeissona tristis*). There is no overarching Temiar term for "music"; rather, gerunds are formed from instrument names and refer to the particular act of "fluting" or "zithering" or "singing."

Flutes are played by both males and females, just as dream songs are performed by males and females. The mouthharp, however, is reserved for men and has its counterpart in the tube zither, reserved for women. These instruments are usually played singly, not in ensemble. Sometimes two noseflutes are played together, but as a single voice rather than in counterpoint or harmony.

The solo instruments are differentiated from the vocal repertoire in terms of time: ritual singing sessions are designated as nighttime activities, often extending throughout the night but concluding with the firm establishment of daytime about one hour after sunrise. Flutes, mouthharps, and tube zithers, however, are played during the day. To play these instruments at night would be *genhaa'*, a breach of appropriate ordering capable of causing death or illness.

The flutes draw their repertoire from dream-song melodies. The melodies, abstracted from the songs, are not played with intent to manifest the spiritguide or engage in mediumship. The repertoire of the mouthharps and tube zither consists primarily of imitations of sounds of the jungle and settlement: the calls of various birds and insects, the chopping of trees to clear swiddens, the bamboo floor rebounding beneath dancers' feet. Nature is thus transformed into culturally constructed sounds in two ways: by dreaming the voices of spirits of the landscape, or by iconic imitation of environmental sounds. The former technique is primarily the domain of vocal music, the latter, instrumental music.

Plate 8. A Temiar woman plays the two-stringed bamboo-tube zither (*kərəb*).

SPIRITGUIDE GENRES

Dream songs vary by spiritguide source, such as the way of the annual fruit season cycle (nɔŋ tahun), the way of the underwater dragon-snake (nɔŋ səlumbaŋ), the way of the deceased humans' souls (nɔŋ ciɲcɛm, sometimes termed 'acɛm in Kelantan). These constitute formal cult and musical genres, with characteristic scalar structure, melodic and rhythmic patterns, textual content and vocabulary, dance movements, trance behavior, instrumentation, leaf and flower ornaments, and extent of male and female participation. These genres vary historically, regionally, and individually. The overall picture of Temiar spiritguide genres is one of rich and detailed complexity, challenging our Western tendencies to present so-called "simple" societies as flat or one-dimensional. Temiar musico-religious practice has a history as multifaceted as that resulting from the interplay between Catholicism and the Protestant reformations in Europe and contains a depth of interpenetrating influences similar to that which we would expect to find in almost any period of Western music history.

Paramount among Temiar genres are Pɛnhəəy (the way of the Pərah fruit tree)[2] originating in Perak, and Tangəəy (the way of the flowers, fruits, and mountains) from Kelantan. The spiritguide genres of the Temiar are themselves situated among crisscrossing influences from surrounding Orang Asli groups. Material collected by Benjamin, including a myth regarding the distribution of types of spirit-membership, suggests that the Lanoh and Jehai in the West specialize in "off-the-ground" genres associated with the seasonal fruit trees, while the Mendrik of the East are practitioners of "things in the ground" associated with tigers. The Temiar, positioned between these two poles, are specialists of "intermediate things" (baraŋ 'ɛn-gagid), "typically the flowers and mountains that effect a sort of mediation between the Ground and Off-the-ground" (Benjamin 1967a:277–278). To illustrate the depth of variety and interplay of influences involved in the composition of Temiar spiritguide genres, the origins of four genres will be examined below.

PɛNHəəY

Anthropologists and ethnomusicologists are not the only people capable of (or interested in) reflecting upon the interplay of Temiar spiritguide genres. Temiars themselves are cognizant of the historical influences generating contemporary performances. A Temiar with whom I worked closely, Ading Kerah (Adiŋ Kərah), is particularly unique in this respect, for from 1963 to 1979 he worked with the Orang Asli Broadcast Unit of Radio-TV Malaysia. In this capacity, he traveled through Orang Asli areas recording musical performances and ceremonies for broadcast on the daily two-hour Orang Asli program. He thus has a wide comparative base from which to evaluate Temiar practices. He also was a major informant during the late 1950s for Iskandar Carey's Temiar grammar and wordlist (Carey 1961) and is thus experienced in analyzing and presenting the details of his culture. Ading Kerah's grandfather, Dato' Perawas, was born in Kampung Timah in Perak, then moved to Betis where he was designated Dato' of the Betis area by his relative, the *Mikong* (Temiar, To' *Mikoŋ*), a mixed Malay-Temiar headman or chief who served as a bridge between the Malay courts and Temiar leaders/headmen.[3] Ading Kerah himself was born around 1931 in Teruleh near Kuala Betis. Here he recounts the origins of Pɛnhəəy, the paramount genre of the Perak Temiar, also practiced among the Temiars of Kelantan:

> Pɛnhəəy branched out during the time of the Japanese [December 1941 through September 1945]. During that time, Pɛnhəəy reached Kelantan. Keranih Laloh is the person who brought Pɛnhəəy to Kelantan. He married my older sister[4] in Kampung Mawa' near Betis. Keranih Laloh is from the settlement Pos Kemar on the Təmɔgɔ̥ɔh River.
>
> Keranih Laloh holds the Grandmother Fruit Spirit (*Yaa' Bərəək*), the spirit of the Perah[5] and Giyɛs[6] fruit trees. No special event precipitated her arrival. The spirit-medium of Pɛnhəəy originally used the Perah fruit. Secondarily, fruit trees of other types were used. So the woman of the Perah fruit became Young Woman Perah (*Mənalɛh Pərah*) and gave a way to Keranih Laloh in Perak. So that medium used Pɛnhəəy, which was the name given for Perah by the spirit-guide. Pɛnhəəy, like Tangəəy, is a jungle type of singing (*gənabag bɛɛk*), not like Səlumbaŋ [which is Malay type].
>
> The origin of Pɛnhəəy also has a story. This Pɛnhəəy, the *halaa'* itself, has its origin in the fruit season. During the fruit season, we carry the fruits and bring them into the house. We

carry, bring the fruits into the house, and eat them as usual. We bring them into the house.

So, Keranih Laloh tried to make a certain creation. For example, the fruit *caɲɛh*[7] or *ləgɔs*[8] or whatever kind of fruit, such as *pərah*—the fruits current that year, Keranih Laloh ordered us to open them, to eat the seeds of those fruits. After swallowing the seeds, we would reclose the fruit skins. All the fruits, such as *ləgɔs, caɲɛh, rarɔh,*[9] *tampuy,*[10] *kabaak,*[11] *kɛlwɛɛk,*[12] *huuh,*[13] *lɛɛg,*[14] *pərah, giyɛs,* from each of these seven, seven, seven; from each species seven seeds are taken. One closes the skin; it is empty inside, since the seed has already been eaten. We take a tray and group the fruit skins, seven per species, inside that tray. This tray is covered by placing another tray over it. After covering the tray, we place it on the floor, and we ourselves sit around it on the floor. We sit, talking and chattering, to watch and witness the proof that the fruits will return [to their original, complete form]. About a half an hour passes. Then Keranih Laloh orders us to open the tray of fruits. Earlier we had eaten the seeds; now the seeds have returned, the fruits have become hard. We eat again, swallowing the seeds once again.

That, then, is the starting point of the spirit-genre (*halaa'*) Pɛnhəəy from the time of the Japanese War, the Second World War, 1942–1945. At that time, I was still small, but I could work and walk. I was somewhere between 11 and 14 years old. I have witnessed the seeds return. Keranih Laloh is my brother-in-law; he married my older sister. Keranih Laloh himself would open fruits and swallow seeds, as the rest of us would open and swallow. We would group the fruits on the tray ourselves. Then it was covered with another tray. Earlier, we would have seen the fruits with their seeds as normal. Keranih Laloh wanted to make a witness, a proof of that Fruit Spirit so that we would see and know.

Keranih Laloh has already died. He has passed on [this genre] to a new medium in Grik, in Kemar.[15] To Hitam Kɛnwɔl in Grik. Because that spirit-genre, with time more people became involved and connected with it.

Kelantan is the origin for Səlumbaŋ genre, for the Tiger genre (Mamuug) with its " 'oy-'oy" and " 'aaw-'aaw" in the song texts, and for Tangəəy [the flowers, trees, and mountains genre] as its type of jungle spirit-genre. Here in Kelantan is the end point of Pɛnhəəy. The Temiar of Kelantan have stolen and transformed it. Its starting point is in Perak. (Ading Kerah, 9-vi-82, Rəlɔɔy, OR84–3)

TALƐŊ

Ading Kerah recounts the origins of the genre Talɛŋ as it has entered Temiar history and legend:

> Talɛŋ originates from Pɛnhəəy. Pɛnhəəy broke off a long time ago, and survives until now, because the way of Pɛnhəəy is "lively" (*rəncak* < Malay *rancak* 'lively'), so all people like it. After that, around 1957, they added another spiritguide, Talɛŋ, to Pɛnhəəy. The name of the person who became the first medium of Talɛŋ is Gombɛɛ'. He himself holds the spirit Talɛŋ. He is from Perak state, the settlement of Grik. So Gombɛɛ' got the spirit of Talɛŋ.

> The beginning point was when the female child of Gombɛɛ' died. After that, the father and mother cried, they were unable to bury their child because they cared so deeply for this their only child. So Gombɛɛ', sitting cross-legged, held the child on his thighs. He held his child on his thighs from morning to night for seven days. He didn't eat, he didn't smoke. So after that, there was an event on the seventh day, the day when the corpse truly should rot.[16] But the corpse of the child had not rotted. So on that seventh day, Gombɛɛ' lost consciousness (*na-bəralii'*). It was in the middle of the night, around 1 or 2 A.M. So he flew off (*na-pəlaaw*) bringing the child with him to the mountains Pɔ' Cənolɛ̧ɛ̧s and Pɔ' Rəlaay, on the other side of Grik. There he got[17] two young women of the mountain. They helped that child, they sang and trance-danced. They trance-danced on the crest of the mountain (off there in the jungle, not in Gombɛɛ' 's house) until the child awoke. The child came back to life. So two or three days after the child had been awakened, they returned the child to the house. The young women of the mountain ordered Gombɛɛ' to hold a trance-dancing ceremony to care for[18] and sweep the child clean[19] of illness and of the restrictions followed during the course of treatment, until the child was truly cured.

Gombɛɛ' held trance-dancing ceremonies for a solid week until the child was well, as she lives to this day. The child still lives; she is grown now and has a husband.

So Gombɛɛ' is a renowned medium. I once met him when I went to Perak.

That is the point of origin, the coming into being of Talɛŋ. Whereas the origin point is actually Pɛnhəəy, to which was added the spirit of Talɛŋ. Gombɛɛ' still lives; his home is in Dalah, a new government-sponsored regroupment settlement near Grik. That then finishes the story of the spirit-medium Talɛŋ which is Gombɛɛ' himself. After that, it was passed on to many people. They wanted it because it was a spirit-genre of life (*halaa' gɛsgoos*). They dreamt, they trance-danced. They trance-danced, they thought they could replicate Gombɛɛ' himself. So it was passed on until it reached here to Kelantan, to Pos Cəbaay on the other side of Bihay. That spirit-genre reached Kelantan in 1959. So the people thought that with that spirit-genre they could rekindle life, whereas only Gombɛɛ' himself had the singular fortune that the two young women should help his one child. That, then, Talɛŋ is the name. Up until now.

There are special leaves. They make a *paley* hut, weaving together *bɛltɔp* leaves.[20] The hut is also called *bumbun jərasɛɛm*. The true name for *bɛltɔp* is *jərasɛɛm*. *Kəwar* leaves[21] can also be used; the flowers of the fields and settlement areas (*bot səlaay*) can also be used. Those are the floral ornaments. I have seen it.

If you want to record Talɛŋ, you can go to Kampung Grik. They know where Gombɛɛ' lives. When I went to Cəbaay in 1953–1955, they still knew Talɛŋ. I'm not sure if they still hold ceremonies of the Talɛŋ type in Cəbaay.

(Ading Kerah, 9-vi-82, Rəlɔɔy, OR84-3)

Nɔŋ Tahun

The Way of the Annual Fruits (*nɔŋ tahun* < Malay *tahun* 'year'), referring to the yearly cycle of the seasonal fruit trees, is also called the Way of the Seasonal Fruits (*nɔŋ bərək* or *nɔŋ kəbəh*). The fruit trees blossom annually in April and May, and their fruits begin to ripen in June and July.

I was fortunate to work closely with two major mediums of *nɔŋ tahun* 'The Annual Fruit Way': Abilem Lum (Abilɛm bin Aluŋ Lum) of Bawik, and Jelit Adon of Pulat (Temiar *Pɛrlat*). Abilem Lum has been known as Taa' Ariŋ since he first received the Annual Fruit Way about sixteen years ago while posted along the Aring River under the employ of the Department of Orang Asli Affairs. He is the originator of an important variant of the Annual Fruit Way called the Rambutan Fruit Way or Taŋgɔɔy, the name given in a dream by the Rambutan[22] Fruit King (*Rajaa' Taŋgɔɔy*), who Abilem Lum considers paramount among the various spiritguides of the fruits. Jelit Adon, twelve years younger than Abilem, is rapidly consolidating a cult variant of the Annual Fruit Way which he and the members of his community have been practicing for the past five to seven years. He is known as Balɛh Kənaseh; balɛh is the teknonym for a parent of a female child, while the term *kənaseh*, 'giving, especially love or affection',[23] is found repeatedly in his song texts.

The annually fruiting trees, particularly Perah, mark the subtle seasonal changes for rainforest-dwelling Orang Asli groups.[24] Benjamin notes:

> At the low latitude of 5 degrees North the seasonal changes are so slight that they are well known in their entirety by the forest people, who use them to order the annual cycle of subsistence activities. Chief of these trees is the perah [Elateriospermum tapos], the leaf-fall of which around January marks the arrival of the proper time for felling the millet swiddens. Rice, on the other hand, is planted once the perah have opened [July or August]. (Benjamin 1967a:55)[25]

Abilem Lum uses the term *lɛgsaaj* in his song texts to describe the reddish tips of the young Perah leaves.

The rain and flood season (December through January) is followed by a relatively dry period (February and March) which precedes the blossoming of most fruit trees (April and early May). The fruits ripen between June and September, a period marked by pleasurable fruit-gathering expeditions and an abundance of fruits. Jelit Adon distinguishes eight stages (*huru'*) of the fruiting cycle:

1. The wind blows, causing the leaves to sway.
2. The flowers appear.
3. The flower blossoms open.
4. The blossoms fall.

5. The fruit buds (*goldɛɛŋ*) appear.
6. The fruit grows larger.
7. The fruit becomes ripe.
8. We eat the fruit.

Annual Fruit Way song texts are filled with images of blossoms opening, fruit buds, and fruits hanging heavily from the trees, as this example illustrates:

> *Yee' 'i-maa' na-gɛwgəyɛw*
> *Yee' 'i-maa' gəlocɛɛw Taŋgɔɔy*
> *Səpooy maŋrɔɔy.*

> I [the Fruit Tree Spirit] return, the fruits hang heavy
> I return, the drooping weight of the rambutan fruit
> Dancing slowly,[26] the sun sets.

> (Abilem Lum, Annual Fruit Way, 14-ix-81, OR25, A15–16)

The Annual Fruit Way has been influenced from two directions. The first is Pɛnhəəy, the Way of the Perah Tree,[27] known as *podɛɛw* in the language of the spiritguides. The genre Pɛnhəəy, which originated in the west among the Perak Temiar, is itself influenced by the practices of the Lanoh, a group of about two hundred Central Aslian-speaking Senoi living on the northwest border between the Temiar and the Kensiu Semang.[28] In their ceremonies, the Lanoh celebrate the spiritguide *podɛɛw* of the Perah tree. The Jehai Semang, living to the north of the area inhabited by the Temiar, also term Perah *podɛɛw* (Benjamin 1967a:147, table 7).

The second direction from which the Annual Fruit Way has received influence is from the Semang to the east of the Temiar, particularly the Batek De'. Taŋgɔɔy, the name that the Rambutan Fruit King gives as his true name in Abilem Lum's dream, is cognate with the Semang word for rambutan, *tangoi* (Kirk Endicott, personal communication).[29] Abilem Lum received his dream of the Rambutan Fruit Way while posted in the Batek De' area of the Aring River. The Batek De' "explain the periodic appearance of fruit by its movement, in some form, between the upper world and the earth. And they all affirm the crucial importance of the superhuman beings and the thundergod in the production of fruit" (Kirk Endicott 1979:57). Similarly, in Abilem's dream recounted below, the fruits are let loose in the form of a fog (also described as an ash-like or flour-like substance) from a bag controlled by the

Rambutan Fruit King. The bees, who appear around March, are also let loose and later recalled by the Rambutan Fruit King and his cohort, the Tiger King.[30] Finally, the Batek "hold one or more singing sessions immediately following the floods each year to ensure that there will be an abundant crop of fruit" (Kirk Endicott 1979:57). In Abilem's dream, the female child-wife of the Rambutan Fruit King orders that offerings be made to her each year. Accordingly, in January, before the arrival of the fruit blossoms, a special singing ceremony is held by followers of the Rambutan Fruit Way to ensure an abundance of fruits. Later, around July when the fruits have ripened and are about to be harvested, another ceremonial offering is made to ensure that the gathering expeditions will proceed without mishap.

The two directions of influence, from Pɛnhəəy of the Perak Temiar in the west and from the fruit ceremonies of the Semang in the east, are conjoined in a myth reported by Abilem. According to this myth, the Rambutan Fruit Way comes from the "base" or "beginning" of the day (*kɛd 'ish* 'east') at Gunung Tahan, a mountain at the source of the Aring River in Kelantan; while Pɛnhəəy comes from the "tip" or "end" of the day (*sɔy 'ish* 'west') at Mt. Cɛŋkey along the Kəbɔɔ' River (Gunung Chingkai in Ulu Plus, Perak). Mt. Cɛŋkey, in this myth, is associated with the Perah tree. A long time ago, it is said, only these two mountain peaks remained above the floodwaters when the sea rose.[31] At that time, there were two brothers, an older and younger. They leaped from a large rock to the crest of Mt. Cɛŋkey. There they constructed two *paley* huts by plaiting the tops of *bɛltɔp* palm fronds inserted into the ground in the shape of a circle. They sang and tranced, and the ground fell into a depression, like a grave or a pool. Abilem says that when he was a young boy, along with his father he saw the circle of bɛltɔp fronds that took root and grew atop Mt. Cɛŋkeh. This myth conjoins the mountain peaks associated respectively with Pɛnhəəy and Taŋɔɔy, as the Annual Fruit Way itself combines influences from both directions.

Abilem Lum, the originator of the Rambutan Fruit Way, was born in Kelantan around 1926 at Taŋąąs along the Pagar River, a tributary of the Betis River. His father, mother, and maternal grandfather were from this area. Following the death of his mother, his father took him and his mother's older sister to Jalong, along the

Simpak River in Perak. He lived there until the end of the Japanese
War (which lasted from December 1941 to September 1945) when,
at the age of about 17 years, he returned to Betis. After the capit-
ulation of Japan came a period referred to as the Emergency. During this period, extending from 1948 to 1960, the previously anti-
Japanese communist forces rearmed and reorganized against the
government. Some of the Kelantan Temiar moved (both voluntarily
and involuntarily) downstream to Kuala Betis, while others fled
upstream into the jungle.[32] Orang Asli loyalties vacillated between
the government and the communists during this period, as the
aboriginal peoples of the jungle tried to survive interactions with
both parties. After the Emergency, Abilem entered the service of
the Department of Orang Asli Affairs. He was posted first to
Gunung Tahan, then to Pos Aring along the Aring River, a tributary of the Lebir. Postings in Bertam, Gemalah, Blue Valley
(Cameroon Highlands), and Blau followed. Around the time of his
posting in Aring he married a woman whose mother was from
Gemalah and father from Bawik, near Kuala Betis. Bawik became
the settlement to which he returned between postings and which
he considers his permanent residence.

From his grandfather Dato' Bawan, an important headman and
medium in Jalong, Perak, Abilem received the way of *cincɛm* (the
spirit of deceased humans).[33] As a young boy, he also followed
along in ceremonies of the Poŋeey genre (the way of the *kəralad*
flower), of which his classificatory older sister Jɛrwan Lung was to
become a renowned adept. While living in Cəbaay[34] with his father
following his mother's death, he received his first personally
dreamt way from the female spirit of the hill rice. He still sings this
song solo when curing outside of the ceremonial context, for the
spiritguide told him that she did not know how to sing with
bamboo-tube percussion or chorus.[35]

Around the age of 40, Abilem received his posting to Aring, a
tributary of the Lebir with its source at Gunung Tahan. The Aring
River is a home of the Batek De' (see Kirk Endicott 1979:3–5). The
Batek De' had deserted the post, however, leaving Abilem alone
there. At that time, he dreamt an encounter with the Rambutan
Fruit King (*Rajaa' Taŋgɔɔy*), his subject the Tiger King (*Rajaa' Ma-
muug*), and the Fruit King's child-wife from whom he received the
Annual Fruit Way:

At the Lebir River; Kuala Krai is its headwaters. From Kuala Krai it becomes the River Bərɔk, or the Lebir River on the other branch. I worked there in the beginning; it was already three, four years I had lived there. From here [the Betis and Bərɔk regions] I went over there; at that time I still didn't know much about things, about dreaming.

I went over there, the people of that land had run off into the jungle. I lived alone in the post, for a week I lived all alone. Nobody.

I lived there, and I slept that night. Then I dreamt. Here I got nothing. There I first dreamt of the Rambutan fruit.

I was about 40 years old when I dreamt that. So, I dreamt I saw a *halaa'*. This person, I could see this person was a *halaa'*. Taŋɔɔy stood before the entrance of a rock face.

I dreamt in total unawareness, no people around. I dreamt I met that fruit. He entered and shut the door. A rock like cement, a rock of cement. He shut the door. There was no path. One fruit here, one fruit here, one fruit there, circling all the way around. All kinds of fruit: *bətaar, laŋsad,* all kinds. Then he asked:

"What are you coming to get here?"

"Nothing,"
I said,
"Just walking. I would meet with you. I'm having a hard time, all alone here."

"What is your work?"
he said.

"No, there's no work, no task,
I have only come to meet with you," I said.
He said:
"What path will you take to return home later?"

I said:
"I don't know.
I don't even know where the door is to go home."
They had shut it completely!

He said:
"You will meet later, down below, a Tiger King.

You'll see later a beehive (*kusul kilad*) at the end of it, down
below."
He spoke the whole thing. A man.
He said:
"This here is the very beginning of the fruits."
He said:
"The bottom, the start.
From the beginning of the day [the east], right here, until it
arrives at the other side."
He opened his bag.
"I open this bag;
when I intend to give [fruits] in great quantity, I open it wide.
When I'm going to give just a little, I open it a little.
You'll see later."
He opened it: Pang! It came out like fog. He shut it.
He said:
"Go, meet with the Tiger King."
I went down.
Here [at the bottom of the rock face] sat the tiger,
there [hanging down from above] the beehive (*padaaw*).[36]

The Tiger King said:
"This is the origin.
That [who you've just met] is the Rambutan Fruit King. I let all
the bees loose from down below here."
The bees had become tigers.
One by one they went flying here and there, becoming tigers.[37]

After a long time, I went back home. Only then, I met with the
Rambutan Fruit Woman as well. The woman was the wife of the
Rambutan Fruit King I'd met earlier, his child. Positively beautiful.
A female child. I went back home, I slept. That day, no, I didn't
walk anywhere. That night I slept and met them. Then he said to
his child:
"You may marry.
Because you [Abilem], your character (*budi'*) is good. You may
marry my child.
This child can give you anything, can help you in many ways."
So he spoke and spoke, and I married that child just like one
usually marries.

Taŋgɔɔy was a man, his child a female. A beautiful girl. He said:
  "The Bɘtaar Fruit Spirit is small.
  I, the Rambutan Fruit Spirit, am the largest, the most powerful."
So it was the child who finally sang.
She said:
  "Wherever you go,
  even among the ministers of the mountains, you will not get lost
  because I will guide you. I will let loose, if you cannot see your
  house I will point out the way. If you have problems, I will mark
  the trees so you will see and follow them home."

That is what the child said. You see, she was already my wife.
She said:
  "Wherever you go, you will not have any problems.
  Even in Perak, you can travel safely. If you travel in cars, just ask;
  I can help wherever you are. Even guards, or people who shoot,
  you can pass through safely."

That is what the child taught to me.
She said:
  "Whatever mountain you're on, it is all ours."

  "But,"
she said,
  "every year you must make offerings."
She said:
  "Souls, the souls of children or anyone else, I can return them."

That is what she said the first time.
(Abilem Lum, 3-iii-82, Bɘlau, OC6otr2)

Abilem's dream conflates receipt of a song genre (*nɔŋ* 'path',
'way') with the Rambutan Fruit child-wife's promise to help Abilem
find his way through the jungle as well as her offer to help return
his patients' lost head souls. Metaphorically linking the three types
of travel, this transaction highlights the importance of knowing the
route (and the dire consequences of getting lost) for a people who
must daily make their way through dense jungle. In subsequent
dreams, Abilem reports that the female spirit[38] of the rambutan
fruit sometimes emerges as a young woman, and sometimes as a
child, a tiny female, and even an old woman. Her hair is beautiful,

like the hair of the rambutan fruit itself, long and wavy. In another version of this dream, Abilem mentions that she stipulated the leaves and dance style to accompany her song. The leaves were to be those of her own group, the seasonal fruits, including *bɔtaar*, *pɔrah*, *lɔhaw*, and rambutan itself mixed on the central hanging ornament "so that the smell should be good." The dancing (*kɔrɛnjɛɛr*) was to be as usual: graceful, supple, and swaying.

After returning home to Bawik from Aring, Abilem ordered that a ceremony be held. He has since received additional Taŋgɔɔy tunes from other seasonal fruits,[39] insects (e.g., Old Woman Kɔwaraay Cicada and Old Woman Hɛrɲɔɔd Cicada, whose call pervades the late afternoons during the fruit blossom season), and one mammal.[40] The Rambutan Fruit genre has spread far beyond the confines of Bawik. This has occurred in several ways: through performances Abilem holds at his various governmental postings, through tunes subsequently received in dreams by members of communities he has visited, and through continual Temiar inter-village travel.

PɛHNɔɔh Gɔb: Sɔlumbaŋ

Malay-type trance-dancing ceremonies (*pɛhnɔɔh gɔb*) synthesize elements of Temiar and Malay styles of spirit-mediumship. At certain times and places, Temiars have lived (or in some cases continue to live) close to Malay settlements. Temiars have watched Malay ceremonies and in some cases have studied with Malay mediums and curers (*bomoh*). Temiars of Betis, Perolak, and Bɔrɔk still remember observing and receiving instruction from a powerful Malay medium, Raning, who lived at Kuala Betis until the Japanese war (see Benjamin 1967a: 284). Penghulu Hitam, originally from Terabas above the rapids of Jeram Gajah on the Bɔrɔk River, studied with a Malay medium who lived below the rapids near the Temiar settlements of Blau and Sintang. The Malays have since moved farther downstream, and Penghulu Hitam now resides near the place the Malay medium once lived. Malay mediums, as well, have shown interest in Temiar healing practices and often asked me to bring them medicinal plants when I came out from the jungle.

Many umbrella spirit-genres are received by Temiars in times of personal or societal crises. Talɛŋ, described above, was received by a medium during a time of personal crisis, when his child was deathly ill. Səlumbaŋ was received during a time of societal crisis, a period of heavy flooding. However, the Temiar usually think about a person's transformation into a medium as a natural process unaccompanied by stress, merely involving dream encounters with spiritguides. In contrast, becoming a medium capable of practicing Malay-style ceremonies is often reported to involve a stressful illness. Entrance into a familiar relationship with a Malay spiritguide and performance of *pehnɔɔh gɔb* serve as a means of conquering that illness.

In the case of Penghulu Hitam, it is said that during the time of peace before the arrival of the Japanese in 1941, when Penghulu Hitam was living in Kawad upriver from Blau, he was digging by the side of a small river when he came upon what looked like an animal's cove. But it was not the home of an animal; instead, it was the home of a spirit. Penghulu Hitam subsequently went crazy, tearing up the split-bamboo walls of the Temiar houses. Temiar mediums tried to cure him but failed and finally took him to a Malay medium downriver near the present Temiar settlement of Blau. The Malay *bomoh* treated him, then taught him the ways of a Malay *bomoh* as part of the cure.[41]

Penghulu Hitam was thus initiated into being a Malay *bomoh* as a cure for his mental illness, in order to placate and control the spirit that had overtaken him. Penghulu Hitam is now said to be a specialist in curing "Malay illnesses" which include (1) illnesses from small stones that become lodged in the body of the subject as a result of eating products such as salt, sugar, or curry brought from the Malay towns; (2) illnesses that come from "downstream," traditionally the abode of Malays in relation to the upriver aboriginal groups; and (3) illnesses from small bits of wood that wash up onto the riverbanks. These "Malay" illnesses are distinguished from the typically "Temiar" illnesses said to originate from the mountains, the flowers, and the jungle.

I observed Penghulu Hitam perform Pɛhnɔɔh Gɔb during a series of ceremonies in October 1981 in Sintang. At that time, he was opening a five-year self-imposed ban on performing such ceremonies. Five years earlier, his wife[42] had died. Prior to her death, she had always accompanied him as his counterpart or assistant (*to' mindok*, from the Malay *Tok Minduk*). In this role, she played the *bəranɔ'* drum, answered the questions he posed when inhabited by his spiritguides, and sang during interludes between the spirits' visits. Filled with nostalgia after her death, he had been unable to perform without her. The period of abstinence was compounded by an intestinal illness that twice sent him to the Orang Asli Hospital in Gombak, near Kuala Lumpur, for operations. In 1981, having remarried and recovered, and with a suitable period of time separating him from his earlier wife's death, he felt ready to begin performing Malay-style ceremonies again.

The ceremonies were held in Sintang, a satellite settlement about ten minutes journey from Blau. A medium from Sintang, Pak Achak, filled the role of drum-playing assistant and Penghulu Hitam's current wife helped him dress and assemble the many props required in Malay-style ceremonies. These included a red sash worn across the right shoulder; a red cloth head-covering; *calʉn* leaf whisks; offerings of uncooked rice, store-bought cigarettes, tobacco and nippah leaves for rolling cigarettes, and lime with sireh leaves; a halved coconut shell filled with embers in which the resin *kɛmɲan* (Malay *kemenyan*) would be placed as incense; a large stone wrapped in red cloth (*taŋkal* < Malay *tangkal* 'talisman'); and popped rice (*boɲaa' bərteh*) used in divination. The Malay props were balanced, so to speak, by props used in alternating "jungle-style" sections of the ceremony, which included bandoliers, wristlets, anklets, and headwreaths made from *kəwar* and, in some cases, *bərag* leaves.

The Temiar performance of Malay-style ceremonies is distinguished as a genre by the absence of female choral response; instead, the drum-playing assistant or *to' mindok* acts as the medium's counterpart. The assistant plays two different rhythms on the *bəranɔ'*. The first is played during periods when the medium is making contact with each of the successive spirits that will enter through him:

RHYTHM I

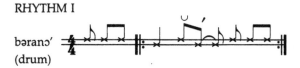

bəranɔ'
(drum)

While playing the above rhythmic pattern, the assistant optionally sings, paralleling the rhythms of the drum beat by singing six syllables per phrase. Meanwhile, the medium is seated holding the

caluun leaf whisk, which he shakes increasingly faster until suddenly
he slaps the ground with his whisk, claps the whisk with his hand,
emits the cry "Wak!" and begins to sing:

medium

Wak! 'e   ye   e _____   sa - lam ha __ lé-kum...

At this juncture, the assistant switches to rhythm II and the female
"chorus" begin to play the bamboo-tube percussion:

RHYTHM II

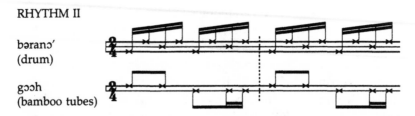

bəranɔ'
(drum)

gɔɔh
(bamboo tubes)

Sometimes each woman holds one high-pitched tube and one low-
pitched tube, which she plays in alternation. I have also observed
sequences in which one woman held two high-pitched tubes while
another woman held two low-pitched tubes, which they played in
alternation to produce the complete interlocking rhythmic pattern.
Rhythmic patterns I and II were repeated each time one spirit left
the medium and was replaced by another. Interestingly, the fluc-
tuating, syncopated rhythm I accompanies the medium's liminal
period "betwixt and between" spirits. In contrast, when the steady
duple meter of rhythm II is established, the medium has already
been entered by the spirit; he then stands and begins to dance with
his arms outstretched at shoulder height in a manner the Temiars
term *silat*.[43]

Alternatively, the medium might indicate to his wife that he
wishes to wear the *kəwar*-leaf ornaments. This signals to the participants that the medium wishes to interject a period of Temiar-
style trancing into the ceremony. During these periods, the bamboo tubes and drum are played in simple duple rhythm, and the
female chorus sings responsorially in standard fashion.

Pɛhnɔɔh Gɔb synthesizes two traditions: the Malay and the
Temiar. Penghulu Hitam's balancing of Malay-style sequences with
Temiar "jungle"-style sequences (*pɛhnɔɔh bɛɛk*) is not merely a

personal predilection, but rather is common among those Temiar who perform in the Malay style. I have repeatedly observed Abilem Lum of Bawik, who performs another variant of Malay-style ceremonies, order that two central hanging leaf ornaments (*tənamuu'*) be suspended from the rafters, a jungle *tənamuu'* and a Malay one: the Temiar ornament is hung with leaves from his jungle spirit-guides of the annually fruiting trees; the other with Malay-style beads made from the dyed inner pulp of the tapioca stem, shredded *kewar* leaves, and small wooden boards decorated with drawings of flowers, leaves, and performing mediums. (See plate 15.) If he should perform a ceremony straight through in the Malay-style without the balancing Temiar accoutrements, he says, the dangerous Malay spirits will overpower him and pull him into the ground, while the Temiar spirits would be jealous.

Malay spirits entering into Temiar cosmology are incorporated as ground-dwelling figures, and often have ominous aspects. Penghulu Dalam holds a way from the *jin bohmin*,[44] an earth spirit who can cause disease in the uncovered breasts of women; Abilem Lum holds a way from the Stumped-Legged Snake King (Rajaa' Naga' Kudoŋ), and the Bərbaaw Tree King (< Merbau tree[45] associated with Malays); whereas Penghulu Hitam's Malay spirit-guides are underwater/earth-snakes. Other Temiar report holding Malay spiritguides identified as *bahyaa'* (or *boyaa'*, the crocodile; *buaya* in Malay). But by far the most well-known spiritguide associated with the Malays is the underwater dragon-snake *daŋah*, the widespread *naga* snake of South and Southeast Asia.[46]

A catastrophic flood in 1926 caused the death of many Malays (Winstedt 1927:306) and severe damage for both the Malays living at the headwaters of the larger rivers and the Temiars upriver. The flood was personified by a Temiar medium from Perias around Kuala Wias as the spirit *daŋah*, an underwater dragon-snake welling forth from the floodwaters. The crisis generated not merely one more tune attributed to a spiritguide, but an entire genre or cult termed Səlumbaŋ. Benjamin (personal communication, 1985) suggests that the term Səlumbaŋ derives from the Hakka *selum-von* 'underwater dragon-snake.'[47] The associated term *limbaŋ* is used to designate the primordial flood reported in a version of the creation myth collected by Benjamin (1967a:38). Benjamin's informants, who sang songs of the Səlumbaŋ genre secondhand but had not dreamt the spiritguide themselves, described Selumbaŋ variously as a "great snake-like dragon" and a "dead Malay buried under-water." My informants described the spirit of Selumbaŋ as the underwater dragon-snake *daŋah*. The medium Tərohɛŋ Təlagəh, who has the *daŋah* of Səlumbaŋ as one of his spiritguides, says that this "minister" or "princess" of the river emerges during his dreams as a beautiful woman with hair ten arm-widths long that is smooth and straight like the flower of the *bayas* palm. Now known as Old Man Wind (*Taa' Pɛnhiid*) after a spiritguide he received much later, Tərohɛŋ Təlagəh is originally from Halah on the Perias River (the original birthplace of the Səlumbaŋ genre) and currently lives in Pulat (Temiar *Pɛrlat*) on the Nenggiri River near Bertam. Səlumbaŋ was the first way that he received, when he was still a young unmarried man.

Ading Kerah recounts the mythologized origins of Səlumbaŋ:

The origins of Səlumbaŋ are very old, not recent. The originator was my distant father.[48] A person from downriver, from Perias. His name is Tataa' Səliloh, from Perias. He is the originator of Səlumbaŋ. The second person responsible is Sədin, who just died recently. Sedin was an assistant. Sədin was the younger brother of Səliloh. So, in the beginning, there arrived the floodwaters, muddy waters, overflowing the banks, eroding the mountains, devouring the earth, from this river up here all the way downstream, carrying everything away. So Səliloh got that spirit *daŋah* from within the waters downstream. The Malays call it *naga*. So that animal [*daŋah*] flowed downriver from yonder, from way over on the other side, shooting the rapids, downriver, downriver, whoosh . . . until it reached the ocean. As it traveled downstream, Səliloh got it directly [from the spiritguide]. That was where he got it in the very begin-ning, Səlumbaŋ. So he sang Səlumbaŋ, and that is the origin.

So the way of executing Səlumbaŋ, I don't really know it. What I know, for the trancing ceremonies, the things that are used are like what the Malays use: the drum *bəranɔ'*, *calʉn* leaves, rotating the head to go into trance (*sənaleh*), popped rice (*boŋaa' bərteh*), kerosene lamplight. Various things. They also use props such as bandoliers made from plaited *kəwar* leaves; they make headwreaths and sashes of plaited *kəwar*. They tear the accessories into little pieces: here a bit of *kəwar* leaf is stuck, there a piece of *kəwar* stuck, like the Malays do.[49] They use the *bəranɔ* drum.[50] There is a guard, a knowledgeable person who plays the drum.[51] When the medium helps a sick person, he asks questions of the *mindok; mindok* is the name of this assistant. The medium asks questions of the *mindok* and the *mindok* answers. Other people attending the ceremony help by listening, or by responding chorally; but for answering verbally, no, only the *mindok* knows how.[52] When there are sick people that are being helped, the *mindok* knows how to answer. That is the origin of Səlumbaŋ.

MARINA: When was the flood in Perias?

ADING KERAH: It was before I was born. May 1920 . . . 1928–1929. I was born in 1931; I think it was in 1928; around that time, Səliloh got that spiritguide. A large flood; this house here was completely carried away. Even in Mering here it caused trouble. Here lah, Səlumbaŋ passed by.

(Ading Kerah, 9-vi-82, Rəlɔɔy, OR84–3)

THE SOCIAL STRUCTURING OF SOUND

Although marked formal differences exist among various genres such as Pɛnhəəy, Talɛŋ, Nɔŋ Tahun, and Səlumbaŋ, certain underlying dynamics remain relatively constant. These are contained in the relationships between the spiritguide and the medium, and between the medium and chorus.

The dramatized social groupings of Temiar ritual singing sessions and trance-dancing ceremonies are shaped by (and give shape to) cultural conceptions through which actors create, substantiate, and recreate their social world. In musical form and performance, Temiar singing/trance-dancing ceremonies integrate social groupings through devices such as overlapping alternation between initial singer and choral respondents (momentarily intermingling divided groups) and alternated repetition of the same phrase by initial singer and respondents (an equation of identity between groups) in a manner consistent with principles of egalitarian social organization and generalized exchange.[53]

The structure of Temiar ceremonial performance unravels potential inequity even as it recognizes the push toward stratification inherent in virtuosity. Yet, despite a mode of performance that simultaneously undermines distinctions while stating them, Temiar singing ceremonies do dramatize distinctions between social groups in terms of gender. In most performances, individual male singers are the nodes through which the songs of spiritguides enter into the realm of the community. Male mediums, taking turns one by one, initiate and energize the presence of spiritguides by singing songs they have received from spirits during dreams. Men sit, stand, dance, and move as they or others sing. In most contexts, an undifferentiated female chorus, seated and stationary, playing bamboo-tube stampers, repeats and responds. Women dance and trance in some regions and certain genres and can (though rarely) become mediums; but female mediumship and performance mobility seem to be the exception, male mediumship and mobility the rule.

Why are Temiar men more visible in the political and ritual spheres? Why do men predominate as mediums and headmen? To answer these questions, we must examine concepts about and actions of men and women embedded in ritual performance, cultural values, and everyday life. The Temiars organize sound and social actors in musical events in ways that both stem from and maintain their conception of relations adhering between the sexes. By examining the roles of men and women in ritual performances and in everyday life, we can come to understand both gender relations and musical expressions among the Temiar. This is because sounds, when socially performed and interpreted by human actors occupying particular roles, express (and help formulate) how members of a society think about and act toward one another and the world around them. I will thus investigate here the strategies of sound in use: how sonic forms when performed identify, invert, and reinforce the relative positions of social actors (e.g., performers and other ceremonial participants). My sphere of investigation includes not merely formal sound structures, but also the cultural logics *informing* those structures: the symbolic classifications and metaphors whereby the terms of one domain are layered with meanings drawn from another domain, imbuing both with significance.

MALE MEDIUMS AND FEMALE CHORUS

Indigenous musical theories are often articulated through terms, concepts, and practices drawn from "extra-musical" domains (see Robertson 1976). Two or more terms are juxtaposed so that each term becomes intimately associated with the other. The resultant

simultaneous perception of the alikeness in unlike terms constitutes metaphor—what Kenneth Burke calls "the thisness of a that"
(see Sapir 1977; Zemp 1979; Feld 1981). A sound performed and
experienced embodies a series of such associations as it becomes
meaningful. Renato Rosaldo, tracing the network of associations
embodied in Philippine Ilongots' red hornbill earrings (1986), refers
to this associative network as a "circle of meanings." This theory of
meaning stands opposed to one that sees a sound or visual image
as representing a particular concept; rather, the linkages are multiple and confer meaning on all the interconnected images, concepts, and practices.

We enter the Temiar circle of meanings from its emergence in the
musical performance of singing ceremonies. The crux of the performance frame is an initial phrase sung by the medium and repeated by the female chorus. While all Temiar theoretically can
receive spiritguides through dreams and thereby become mediums, in actuality, men from their late teens onward receive songs
from spiritguides more often than do women. Though women
traditionally distinguish themselves as midwives[54] and, additionally, the precedent for female mediums does exist, men tend more
often to become mediums and thus predominate as initial solo
singers. The relationships between the initial singer's phrase and
female choral response take variable forms. The standard format
exhibits substantial alternating overlap between initial phrase and
choral response, with respondents repeating both text and melody
of the initial phrase (figure 2 and table 1). Upriver on the Sungei
Bərɔk, the chorus alternates and overlaps with the initial phrase,
with respondents repeating the text while slightly varying the melody (figure 3 and table 2). Further up on the Sungei Bərɔk, where
Temiar territory borders on Semai areas, the female chorus waits
for the duration of a longer initial phrase, then responds with a
series of phrases that vary melodically and exhibit marked textual
improvisation.

The delegation of gender roles as male initial singer and female
chorus is sometimes varied when the female chorus itself transforms into a self-contained initiator-respondent unit. One woman
sings, and the others respond chorally. In this situation, however,
the initiating female singers are not considered mediums, for they
are not singing their own dream songs. This often occurs in the-
Temiar settlement of Pulat on the Ulu Nenggiri during perfor-

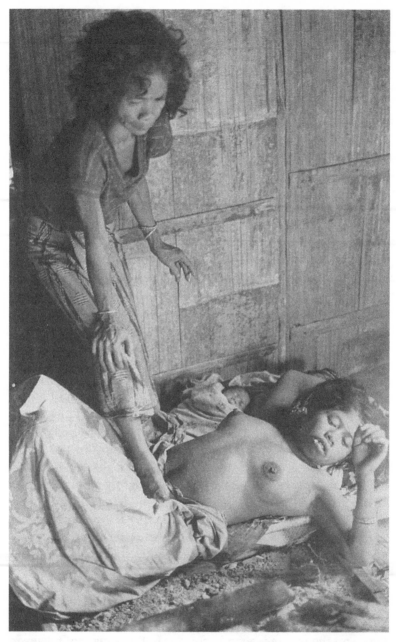

Plate 9. While men predominate as mediums, women distinguish themselves as midwives. At the end of the first week following a birth, this
midwife massages the abdomen of a new mother who warms herself
beside the hearth, in order to expel the afterbirth and tone abdominal
muscles.

Figure 2. Transcription, The Way of Old Woman Cicada Kəwaraay
Halaa': The medium, Abilem Lum, male
Chorus: Females (in this recording, approximately 8 to 10
         individuals)
Gɔɔh: Bamboo-tube stampers
Drum: Bəranɔ', a single-headed drum

Table 1 Song Text, The Way of Old Woman Cicada Kəwaraay

Song:	nɔŋ jajaa' kəwaraay		
	"The Way of Old Woman Cicada Kəwaraay"		
Singer:	Abilem Lum of Jalong, Sungai Simpak, Perak		
	now dwelling in Bawik, Sungai Betis, Ulu Kelantan		
Recorded:	14 September 1981 in Blau, Sungai Bərɔk,		
	Ulu Kelantan (Tape OR25 at 25'54")		

1 Səpooy	bəladɛɛr	lɛŋwiŋ	laaw laaw
To dance slowly, like strolling; flirtatious glance; breezy	Greenish tint at sunset	Changeable; transforming; whirling; dizzy	Onomatopoetic sound of a cicada

2 Tərolaaw	mɛŋkah	bəyɔɔl	
(Opening)	Place where sun emerges	Mountain near Bawik	

3 Sɛndɔɔl	hərabɔɔl	lɛŋwiŋ	
Dancing and percussive rhythm are strong, quick and steady	Spiritguides are pleased and enter into the hanging leaf ornament	Changeable; transforming; whirling; dizzy	

4 Mɛŋkah	na-jəna'aay		
Sun emerging in the east	Spreads its glow toward the west		

FREE TRANSLATION

1. Dancing in a slow stroll, the greenish tint of sunset and sounds of the cicada in the late afternoon mark the time of dizziness, whirling, and transition.
2. The sun emerges, illuminating Mt. Bəyɔɔl.
3. The dancing and percussion are strong, quick, and steady; the spirit-guides are pleased and enter into the central hanging leaf ornament, whirling and transforming.
4. The sun emerges in the east, casting its glow toward the west.

Figure 3. Transcription, The Way of the Female Spirit of Mt. Səwɛluu'

Figure 3 *continued*

Figure 3 *continued*

mances of the annual fruit cycle genre, a genre that generally allows greater female participation in trancing and dancing. The women of Pulat sing the Perah fruit tree genre (Pɛnhəəy), but they are not considered mediums, for the songs they sing were dreamt by others. They fill in, providing dance music for the trancers until a medium sings an initial phrase from the dance floor. Then the women switch back to their standard choral response role.

Another observed instance in which women occupied roles of both initial solo singer and chorus occurred upriver on the Sungei Bərɔk when men were detained in the jungle and unable to appear at a scheduled singing session. Fearing the cosmic imbalance that would result from disappointing spiritguides already alerted to an impending performance by the gathered leaf ornaments, the women fulfilled the promised performance by taking both lead and chorus roles. Once again, since the initiating female singers were not singing their own dream songs, they were only filling in and were not considered mediums.

The leader/chorus distinction establishes a temporal priority, but it does so in such a way that the distinction between the roles of male medium and female chorus is collapsed: first, by the overlap

Table 2 Song Text, The Way of the Female Spirit of Mt. Səwɛluu´

Song:	*nɔŋ potərii' səwɛluu´*		
	"The Way of the Female Spirit of Mt. Səwɛluu´"		
Singer:	Along Indan ('alung 'ndan bin 'agun)		
	born along Sungai Meriŋ, Ulu Kelantan, now dwelling in Blau,		
	Sungai Bərɔk, Ulu Kelantan		
Recorded:	3 May 1981 in Blau (Tape OR5-1 at 5′18″)		

1 *Ləlajəəg-ləlajɛɛg*	*potərii'*	*dan*	*ləjŋgw*
Long, wavy hair; long body; rainfall	Princess	And	The rain falls and the leaves become hard

2 *Ləjəəg-lajɛɛg*	*potərii'*	*Pahmah*	
(Same as above)	Princess	Mt. Pahmah	

3 *Pantun*	*ləmaaŋ-lɛŋləmɔɔŋ*	*rasaa'*	*gonaa'*
To verse/sing	Weary	Feeling	Use

J *'ɛm-siyab*	*gəlasəəh*	*sənɛbyab*	*liŋgan*
We prepare	Many people looking for flowers	Cause to be prepared	Central leaf ornament

kanɛɛ'	*bilɔɔ'*	*timbaŋ*	*balas*
We	Until whenever	Balance; judicious	Return; response

FREE TRANSLATION

1. The long, wavy hair and curving body of the princess of the mountain is like the slanting path of the falling rain; the rain falls and the leaves become fresh and firm.
2. The princess spirit of Mt. Pahmah has hair and body long and curving like rain falling.
3. I verse/sing of a weary feeling in the heart.

Jɛnhook: We search for leaves and flowers, then prepare the hanging ornaments now and whenever; the chorus responds graciously, accompanying the medium with voice and percussion.

between phrases, and second, through the act of repetition. The overlap at the end of the medium's initial phrase and the beginning of the choral phrase (and again at the end of the choral phrase and the beginning of the medium's subsequent phrase) conjoins the two sections in a phase of interwoven activity. The public performance of the spiritguide song thus moves the individual dream revelation into the realm of inter-sex, community participation.

Alternated repetition of the medium's phrase by the chorus conjoins the two groups in shared knowledge. The repetition of the initial phrase of the medium by the chorus establishes an identity between the two social groupings at the same time that it distinguishes them. Phrasal repetition also allows for recognition of a source. By stating something again, we realize that we have heard it before, that it *comes from somewhere*. Harkening to the source further undermines the medium-as-leader, for in Temiar conceptualization of performance, the spiritguide singing through the medium vocalizes the initial phrase.

The Temiar verb *gabag* 'sing' exhibits a Middle Voice morphology (Benjamin 1981:108–109). The Middle Voice, neither active nor passive, possesses both subject-like and object-like properties simultaneously (see Benvéniste 1971:145–151). During the public performance of mediums, singing is "conceived of as a passive experience issuing from a supposedly external agentive source, the spiritguide" (Benjamin 1981:108). Temiar mediums describe the displacement of their own self while the spiritguide sings through them as "one's heart is elsewhere" (*hup 'ɛh 'ɛn-tuuy 'əh*). The emphasis is not on self-expression, as it might be if the shape of the performance were to emphasize initial singer-as-leader; instead, the medium himself is "elsewhere" and the spiritguide is privileged.

The very structure of the spiritguide/medium relationship is ambiguous with respect to power. The spiritguide is the *child* of the medium, who is father. Yet the child spiritguide is *teacher* to the medium, who is student. The aspects of child and teacher combined in the spiritguide, and father yet student combined in the medium, counterbalance one another in a manner that undermines any potential relationship of superior to subordinate in either direction between the spiritguide and the medium.

The Temiar describe the lead vocal as occurring *nɛŋnɛŋ* 'preceding', 'initial'. The female chorus is *laŋyə'* 'occurring after', 'subsequent.' What, then, is being followed? As mentioned earlier, there is no Temiar word for "song"; the closest gloss is when the spiritguide's musical gift is referred to as the "path" or "way" (*nɔŋ*) of a particular spiritguide. In its verses, the spiritguide "causes to be returned home" (*na-tɛrmaa'*) that which it sees in its travels; the female respondents "follow the path" (*wɛdwad nɔŋ*). Thus, when viewed through Temiar conceptualizations, what might have seemed like "male leader" and "female chorus" is something else again. The choral respondents don't follow the medium, they follow the path described by the spiritguide through the medium. The focal point of power is displaced from the male medium to the spiritguide.

A similar displacement from individual to collective is expressed in performed sound structures when the solo vocal phrase is diffused by choral repetition. The Temiar image for the focus thus diffused is *kahyɛk*, the cool, spiritual liquid likened to the colorless sap of plants, the clear waters of mountain streams, and morning dew. Spiritguides manifest themselves both in song and in the flow of this liquid, which arches in a watery thread from the jungles and mountains into the leaf ornaments adorning the interior of the house in which a ceremony is held.

From a thin thread conducted into the ceremonial arena by the medium, *kahyɛk* spreads among numerous community members. Singers and dancers draw the liquid from hand-held leaf whisks and hanging leaf ornaments. Mediums draw the liquid from the leaves and from their breasts, infusing the cooling substance into the head and heart souls of trancers and patients. The medium is a conduit, his vocalization a thread that conducts *kahyɛk* from spirits to humans. The morning after a particularly long and intensive singing/trance-dancing session, the entire group of ceremonial participants (initial singers, chorus, dancers, trancers, patients) may be restricted from exposure to the heat of direct sunlight in order to avoid its conflict with the cool *kahyɛk*, the essence of the upper-portion souls of spiritguides that is now dispersed inside their bodies. *Kahyɛk* links humans and environment through the agency of spiritguides, conceptually undermining the potential thrust toward inequity inherent in the solo-choral performance format.

Some of the more recently composed ways, and ways from settlements farther downriver toward Malay communities, seem to exhibit less overlap between initial phrase and choral response. Temiars, when pointing out changes that have occurred over time in song practice, say that nowadays the women wait longer before responding; that is, there is more space between initial and responsorial phrases. Whether or not this change is statistically verifiable, what is interesting is that this is how the Temiar *perceive* their music to have changed over time. In fact, when the Temiar perform the

Malay-style ceremonies described earlier in this chapter, the chorus drops out altogether. The women lose their voice. The definitive difference between Temiar or "jungle" ceremonies (*pɛhnɔɔh bɛɛk*) and Malay-style or "foreign" ceremonies (*pɛhnɔɔh gɔb*) is the absence of female choral response in the latter. The women still play the bamboo-tube percussion, but are not allowed to respond vocally during Malay-style singing; they say that choral response during Malay-style ceremonies would result in the death of the erring respondent.

During Malay-type ceremonies, the role of respondent otherwise performed by the female chorus is taken over by a drum-playing partner who, in a mixture of Malay and Temiar languages, sings and queries the successive spirit-manifestations of the medium. These two specialists are separated from the crowd as a whole in Malay-style performances. The suppression of the chorus in Malay-style ceremonies heralds the emergence of the audience in Temiar musical events. It presents a marked contrast with the interactive choral response of Temiar-type ceremonies, which actively integrate individual medium and community on the one hand and men and women on the other. The emergent audience of Malay-type ceremonies polarizes the participant and the nonparticipant as well as male and female. This process finds its parallel in the formalization of leadership into ranked headmanship with a concomitant increase in the distance between the leaders and the led. Both trends arose through historical interactions with the more hierarchical Malay society.

If the total absence of chorus is the shape the Temiar give to performance when they contrast what is Malay to what is Temiar, an integrated male-female chorus is the shape they give to one of the most elaborate Temiar performances, the singing session that marks the end of a period of mourning. Celebrations terminating periods of mourning often constitute particularly emphatic statements of a group's concept of themselves (Goldman 1979:219–252; Huntington and Metcalf 1979). Following a mourning period of a month or more during which musical activities have been prohibited, the singing/trance-dancing ceremonies that end the Temiar mourning period are expansive performances, lasting from dusk to dawn for three to seven days. At key moments in the ceremony, especially upon reaching sunrise after the entire first night's singing, men join in singing with the female choral response.

The integration of male and female voices in the chorus during this quintessential Temiar celebration of the reopening toward life suggests that the solely female chorus of other contexts is but a contraction or an abbreviation. The expanded male-female chorus of the mourning ceremony might constitute a distinct musical genre; however, some Temiars say that this is how all singing sessions were performed in "ancient times," when men and women are said to have always sung the choral response together. Whether true or not, again it is intriguing to note how some Temiars perceive their past transforming into the present. Perhaps, then, when women alone form the chorus in ordinary singing sessions, they continue to represent the generalized community following the spiritguide's path though their chorus is formed from only the female segment.

SYMBOLIC CLASSIFICATIONS AND METAPHORS FOR SOUND

The interactive choral response of Temiar ceremonial performance integrates solo singer (male medium) and group (female chorus), simultaneously stating and undermining the distinction between individual and community, as well as the distinction between the sexes. Nonetheless, mostly men are the mediums through which spiritguides enter into the communal realm. And primarily women are responsorial members of the chorus. Why is it that men predominate as mediums and headmen? Collier and Rosaldo (1981) maintain that among hunter-gatherers and hunter-horticulturalists, an opposition between private and public spheres established in food distribution in the economic domain generates the asymmetry of the sexes in the political and ritual domain. However, my own research shows that Temiar women participate in a network of distribution that extends *beyond* the domestic sphere. Temiar women send portions of tubers and vegetables to neighboring hearth groups or houses. The extent of this distribution is comparable to the limited range of small game distribution, in contrast to the community-wide distribution of large game. But the Temiar do not differentially value small and large game distribution.[55] Secondly, distribution occurs during the act of gathering itself: women working in groups dig tubers together from each other's swidden fields, mutually sharing the products of their plots as they move from one woman's plot to the next. Thirdly, women who are ill or otherwise indisposed will receive tubers and vegetables gathered by other women, knowing that they in turn have provided and will provide for other women similarly indisposed. Finally, circulation of visitors among hearths and households (and rules that obligate visitors to partake of foods cooked or served in their presence) ensures that the products of a woman's gathering will not only be consumed by members of her immediate household but will be consumed by a network of guests that extends far beyond her own hearth group.[56]

The answer to the question, "Why do Temiar men predominate as mediums and headmen?" is not found in an economic distinction between men's "public" food distribution network versus women's "private" domestic food contribution, as Collier and Rosaldo suggest. The Temiar data indicate that both men and women participate in an extensive public network of generalized reciprocity. Neither does weighted differentiation between males and females constitute an aspect of Temiar descent or marriage practices: descent is reckoned ambilineally, and both spouses retain the right to make or break a marriage bond. Temiars live in small, semipermanent riverine settlements comprised of 15 to 150 individuals joined in face-to-face interaction: everyone knows who is related to whom, who has done what to whom, who is or was married to whom, and who might be sleeping with whom. Villages comprise cognatic descent groups or "ramage" (membership is traced through both parents) which are agamous; inhabitants may marry within or outside the village group (see Firth 1966; Benjamin 1967*b*). Temiar marriages are not arranged; they are based on mutual desires of the bride and groom. Postmarital residence is nonspecific; a period of uxorilocal residence with the bride's parents is often alternated with a period of virilocal residence near the parents of the groom.

In a manner similar to that of brideservice societies, Temiar couples work for their respective in-laws following marriage. The birth of children gradually stabilizes the initially tenuous marital bond, which may be dissolved by either partner. Polygyny is practiced; some men simultaneously have more than one wife dwelling in the same or separate villages. In general, however, Temiar marriage practices are best described as serial monogamy: initially marrying young (around the age of fifteen), individuals often work their way through a succession of two to four partners until their midthirties, by which time they have usually settled upon a permanent partner. The important thing to note here is that options are open for both the male and female partner; either or both may instigate union or separation.

Symbolic classifications exhibited in metaphors for sound help to explain Temiar distinctions between male and female domains. Symbolic classification refers to ordering, to the formation of categories and the systematic relations between categories. These culturally defined categories are often accessible through a society's terminological system (Durkheim and Mauss 1903/1963; Needham 1963; Hocart 1937).

Singing sessions are accompanied by pairs of bamboo-tube stampers (*gɔɔh*) struck against a log in duple meter by the female chorus members. Both of the Temiar instruments played primarily by females, the stamping tubes and a tube zither (*kərəb*), are fashioned from bamboo tubes. Bamboo tubes are also used as containers for cooking, water-carrying, food storage, and transport. The female counterpart of the male hunting party often consists of group forays to cut down, size, and shape bamboo stalks into tubes to prepare cooking utensils for the awaited game meat. The musical instruments identified with female players, then, are fashioned from bamboo tubes, primary utensils from the female domain of labor.

Consider the symbolic classification expressed in Temiar terminologies for sound structure as a metaphorical restatement of gender relations in terms of instrument construction, pitch, and duration. The pair of bamboo-tube stampers consists of a longer tube emitting a lower tone called "father," *bəəh*, and a shorter tube termed "mother," *boo'*.[57] A lower pitch in Temiar is referred to as "large," *rayaa'*, and a higher pitch, "small," *'amɛɛŋ* or *'amɛs*. The "father" tube is struck so as to decay naturally, resounding longer (*na-jək liiw* 'it sounds far, long'); the "mother" tube is damped to decay immediately upon striking (*'ɛ-tahan gah 'əh* 'we restrict its sound'). Similarly, two strokes are distinguished on the drum: again, the father stroke has a lower (larger, longer) pitch of extended duration and the mother stroke a higher pitch damped for short duration. The bamboo tube zither has two strings, a longer father string and shorter mother string. This symbolic classification is found in terms other than musical instruments: (1) the two-tiered fish trap has a father tier constructed from long spokes and a mother tier with shorter spokes; (2) the inner section of the blow-pipe consists of the fusion of a longer tube (the father) and a shorter tube (the mother); (3) the rainbow is said to have a short whitish section near the ground (the mother) and a long arching colored midsection (the father).

A Temiar, when questioned about this long–short dichotomy, explained in agreement with others:

> We call the longer "father" because a man is brave and travels long distances, he goes out at night, wherever, to hunt game, without a second thought. Women, they go short distances, within the community, to the swidden fields or to cut bamboo stalks. So the "mother," we make it short.

Men's domains, then, have an extended circumference; their range as hunters takes them far into the jungle. Women, constrained by fear through restricted access to weapons, have a circumscribed domain relatively limited to the settlement and the swiddens. Temiar women are prohibited from handling the poison from the sap of the Ipoh tree (*Antiaris toxicaria*) that anoints the tips of blow-pipe darts. Women may carry large knives (Malay: *parang*), but are forbidden the blowpipe. This social restriction prevents Temiar women from traveling at ease in the jungle. Women adjust to this restriction by foraging together in large and noisy groups, staying closer to the settlement, or inviting men with blowpipes along to wait for them when their tasks send them farther afield.

Sonically, the difference between men's extended range and women's circumscribed range is expressed in the contrast between larger (low-pitched), longer, resounding tones and smaller (high-pitched), shorter, damped tones. In the realm of performance practice, men's extended geographical range generates a greater number of male mediums singing the initial phrase. Unrestricted travel through the jungle increases one's contact with the rocks and mountains and river rapids that later manifest as spiritguides in dreams. Composers often mentioned that it was the spirits of particular plants or formations that they had passed in daily life that later visited them in dreams. Temiar women, relatively restricted in travel, have less occasion for the daily impressions that will lead to spiritguide manifestations in dreams. Social restrictions reciprocally affect women's perceptions of themselves and their potential: circumscribed in activity and by consensually held concepts that

Plate 10. The medium Abilem Lum plays a single-headed drum (*bəranɔ'*). His right hand plays the lower-pitched "father" stroke, and his left hand, closer to the rim, plays the higher-pitched "mother" stroke.

designate spheres of action, women have fewer expectations of making spiritguide connections.

The symbolic construction of gender correlates subsistence activities, spatial range, and communicative skill. Similarly, Michelle Rosaldo (1980) comments on the manner in which the sexes among the Ilongot of the Philippines are typified through the style and organization of their respective tasks and habitual experience. Men's hunting and traveling (and consequent acquaintance with a wider range of kin) renders their hearts "higher," with a greater capacity for knowledge and passion than women, who stay closer to home and cultivate swiddens with repetitive actions. The Semai, aboriginal neighbors of the Temiar, say: *"Lad kraal crək, lad krduur patɛi'*," "The loincloth of men is long, the loincloth of women is short." The Semai recognize ramifications of this observation in contexts of public action and influence (Robert Dentan, personal communication, 1983).

In what seems to be typical Temiar "egalitarianizing" fashion, however, there is a pattern of inversion at work once again, a leveling mechanism through which differences are concurrently stated yet undermined. This inversion works similarly to the flip-flop in which mediums are simultaneously father and student, while spiritguides are both child and teacher. Temiar mediums are predominantly male, their spiritguides are predominantly female.[58] Men, ranging extensively through the jungle during subsistence activities, are transformed into the earthbound students of female spiritguides during ritual singing sessions. Women, restricted daily to swidden and settlement, are the wandering teachers of the spirit-realm. Leaping across mountain summits, soaring above the clouds, and rising above the forest canopy to glimpse the rare vista in the imagery of song texts, female spiritguides return to the medium the knowledge gleaned from their travels. The information they bring back, passed on in dreams and during singing sessions, is essential in illness diagnosis and treatment. For example, the spiritguide, in its travels, might locate and return a patient's lost or captured headsoul. As quoted in chapter 3, a male medium comments on his position *vis-à-vis* the spiritguide:

> We know nothing. We sit at home and eat the intestines of game. The spiritguides, they range far and wide, they return what they see to us in our houses. We ourselves, in our homes, we know nothing.

Overtones of longing, flirtation, enticement, and seduction pervade the cross-sexual medium/spiritguide relationship. References from dream stories ("I sleep with her at night in my dreams, but in the morning my bed is empty"), song texts, and comments on the seductive properties of cosmetic and ornamental preparations abound. When the medium/spiritguide relationship is unisexual (male-male), the seductive nature of the relationship is subordinated to the generational dimension (father-child or older brother-younger brother). The predominant pattern of cross-sexual medium/spiritguide relationships is exhibited in the following narrative. Pandak Hibel recounts the events preceding a dream in which he received a way from the female "minister" of the River Bərɔk:

> The way of this river Bərɔk, the Mɛndrak rapids. It came around the same [time] as the ways of the *talun* banana and the *carak* flower. The banana way came one month [March], *carak* the next month.
>
> That river has a Malay minister. When she arrives, that one, to us jungle folk, we sing in jungle style. I was clearing a swidden for cassava, for rice; she watched and watched and watched, she took a liking to me. She adopted me like I would adopt and care for a chicken; like a woman would have eyes for me, she was attracted to me. She desired me, she wanted me. She was attracted to me. An adolescent girl, about 3 1/2 or 4 feet tall.
> Why would she need to speak? She just sang.
> (Pandak Hibel, Jɛlgək, 22-vi-82, DN9)[59]

The inflections of the spiritguide relationship expressed by Pandak Hibel are of interest here. They mix attraction, flirtation, desire, and adoption. Temiars use the word *bərɛcɔɔ'* ('to adopt', 'to care for' < *cɔɔ'* 'adoptee') to describe their relationship with domesticated animals they have fed and cared for, such as chickens, dogs, or the occasional abandoned infant monkey whose mother may have been blowpiped by a Temiar hunter. Temiars learned about raising chickens from Malays; however, when Temiars have raised and fed a chicken, they will not slaughter or eat it. Instead, they trade or sell it to the Malays or Chinese—or to another Temiar family who, not having fed and cared for it, is free to slaughter and consume it. "To adopt," then, is to care for, feed, and enter into a social relationship with the adoptee. The spiritguide adopts the medium, establishing a social relationship as child, teacher, lover, and adopter.

This is particularly significant given the terms of address used mutually by healers and patients. A medium who has cared and taken responsibility for a subject's health is called *tohaat* by the patient. Similarly, a midwife who has ministered to a pregnant woman is called *tohaat* by the woman, her husband, and later the grown infant. Even a modern medical doctor may be called *tohaat* by his Temiar patient. This term is also used when the Temiar speak of the creator deity *Tohaat* (< Malay *Tuhan* 'God'). *Tohaat* is said to be greater in status yet lesser in direct daily influence or power than the more immediate deities Lightning ('*ɛŋkuu'*) and his younger brother Aluj (the first medium), or the even more directly approachable spiritguides. The vagueness of the deity *Tohaat* suggests that this figure may have been appended to the Temiar cosmological scheme through historical interactions with the surrounding Muslim Malays and Christian missionaries.[60]

The complement of the term *tohaat* for "healer" or "midwife" is *cɔɔ'*, the term used by mediums to address those they have treated, and by midwives to address both parents and children whom they have helped birth. Mediums and midwives are "life-givers" (*tohaat*) to patients (*cɔɔ'*) whose lives have been sustained like adopted chickens fed with grain. Just as the medium-chorus structure of performance recapitulates the dream format wherein the spiritguide sings and the medium responds, the medium-patient (*tohaat-cɔɔ'*) relationship itself echoes the relationship between spiritguide and medium: the spiritguide adopts the medium, and the patient is symbolically "adopted" by the healer. A similar succession of transference is evident in trance performance: just as the head soul of a mountain top or flower "emerges" (*na-həwal*) in human form during dreams, the head soul of an entity is "caused to emerge" (*na-tərəlhəwal*) through the human form of the medium during trance. And while the adopter must care for the adoptee, in typical Temiar egalitarianizing fashion the direction of responsibility in the relationship is once again mutualized and upended. For the adoptee must also care for its adopter: the medium pleases the spiritguide with floral ornaments and incense, and indeed brings the spiritguide into being, causing it to emerge in ceremonial performance. As for patients, above and beyond payment for services rendered[61] given simultaneously to the medium and his spiritguides at the end of a course of treatment, or the cloth sarong given to a midwife during the eighth-day feast following childbirth, a patient is continually responsible to give service to his/her *tohaat* by cutting firewood, drawing water, working in the *tohaat*'s ricefields, or bringing the *tohaat* jungle products. *Tohaat* and *cɔɔ'* sustain one another as do medium and spiritguide.

Given the cross-sexual inflections of attraction and desire re-ported between male medium and female spiritguides, one ques-tion that arises is whether the spiritguides of female mediums are predominantly male. While I don't yet have the data from female mediums to answer this, one indication comes from the trance-dancers of Pulat, where the Annual Fruit Way (nɔŋ tahun) permits greater female participation in dancing and trancing. A Temiar woman described the singing ceremony as an intensification and culmination of longing for male fruit-tree spirits:

> It is a longing, like remembering a distant lover or looking out across a wide vista. There is a male spirit of the fruits that desires to sleep with me. Even when I dream, he's there. After a while, one doesn't feel right, one's heart is shaky, one thinks only of him, one wants to go off into the jungle, one's spirit is drawn to the jungle. I must participate in a singing cere-mony, only then can I stand it. We sing and dance, the male spirit of the fruit trees alights on the leaf ornaments, and I am transformed. (LBK, FN 1822, Pulat; July 24, 1982)

SYMBOLIC INVERSION: EVERYDAY LIFE AND RITUAL PERFORMANCE

Musical and ritual performances do not simply replicate everyday social relations. Ritual, with its intricate inversions and transfor-mations, often describes cultural fantasies rather than social reali-ties. Needham notes that the "theme of reversal" is a problem of classification, since inversions involve relations between categories (1963:xxxix). Symbolic inversions, which invert, contradict, or ne-gate categorical distinctions, perform an interpretive function, fur-nishing a framework within which to comment upon or question the accepted order of things.

In Temiar performance, categories are upended. Symbolic in-version works as a leveling mechanism. Differences are simulta-neously presented and undone in medium/spiritguide relation-ships.

Medium	*Spiritguide*
FATHER	CHILD
↕	↕
STUDENT	TEACHER

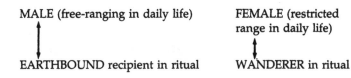

MALE (free-ranging in daily life)   FEMALE (restricted range in daily life)

↑   ↑

EARTHBOUND recipient in ritual   WANDERER in ritual

Geertz terms instances of a culture's inclusion of its own negation "counteractive patterns of culture" (1966:65). In her discussion of symbolic inversions, Babcock contends that in order to comprehend the total social fact, we must take into account "both the conventional means of articulating orders and rules *and* the counteractive patterns by which those very conventions may be profitably and recognizably transformed" (Babcock 1978:27). Bakhtin (1965/1984) calls this inverted play of culture "carnivalization."[62] Temiar symbolic inversions crisscross the categories of kinship and pedagogy: the father is student, the child is teacher. Furthermore, they reverse gender distinctions: the free-ranging male of the everyday domain becomes the earthbound male of the ritual domain, whose consort is the ritually free-ranging female component. Gender is retained, but the valences are switched.

What about the women who (though rarely) do become mediums, and the female trance-dancers who connect with male spirit-entities? Are these alternatives also leveling mechanisms, poking holes into predominant patterns? Perhaps there is something else at work here: conjuncture. The male element incorporated by females (and the female element by males) presents a dynamic conjunction of opposites which overcomes boundaries and generates the "transformation" (*leslǫǫs*) of Temiar trance. The simultaneous incorporation of male and female in the medium or trancer bridges otherwise bounded categories, setting spiritual energy into motion and sparking the transformation from bound soul to free spirit.[63]

The dynamics of Temiar ritual and social life suggest that gender is conceived of not in terms of inequity, but merely in terms of differentiation. Could the predominantly male monopoly on mediums represent a Malay or Islamic influence, paralleling both the rise of the Malay-type headman in the political domain and the emergent stratification of performer and audience as well as male and female in Malay-type Temiar ceremonies of the ritual domain? Is it possible that there were more female mediums in the past, that the scrutiny of the Malays has affected the Temiar such that there has been an increasing reticence to propel women into visible ritual and political roles?

Despite Malay and Islamic influence on Temiar gender roles, the leveling mechanisms of symbolic inversion and conjuncture suggest that Temiars continue to think of gender in terms of differentiation rather than inequity. This correlates with evidence from the economic domain: though men may range extensively through the jungle and women be confined nearer the settlement, men as hunter-horticulturalists and women as gatherers and horticulturalists participate as equally valued contributors to a common system of distribution and exchange spreading throughout the community. Through inversion, conjuncture, and the interactive singer-respondent format, Temiars play with the theme of inequity while redistributing activities and roles so that they interpenetrate. Temiar males and females both embody incipient magico-religious power: as co-creators in performance, they give substance to that power in the form of cool liquid and musical sound.

The performance event puts society on the stage; it presents an interaction among social actors cast in various roles. The dream relationship between medium and spiritguide is transferred to medium and chorus during ceremonial performance. While dream-song genres vary regionally, historically, and individually, the underlying relationships between spiritguide, medium, and chorus continue to obtain, with the significant exception of some genres patterned on Malay models. Temiar theories of composition and performance de-prioritize the medium and privilege the spiritguide. The texture of Temiar performance simultaneously distinguishes and integrates the individual and the community, as well as males and females. Temiar performances do not merely reflect an egalitarian social structure; rather, they play an integral part in diffusing social and sexual stratification.

Through interactions between medium and chorus, the social group actively co-creates the event. In this widened frame of analysis, we move from merely considering what the medium is doing to the text, to examining what participants are doing with the medium's performance. Inviting community and cosmos, men and women, humans and spirits to participate in the performance event takes on increased significance when an additional actor is added: the patient. When patients are tended during singing and trance-dancing ceremonies, the social universe composed of the community of humans and spirits participates in the cure.

5

Setting the Cosmos in Motion:
Sources of Illness and Methods of Treatment

SOURCES OF ILLNESS

To understand the articulation between domains of singing and curing in trance-dancing ceremonies held for curative purposes, three areas of questioning must be considered: (1) Where does illness come from? What are the indigenous concepts of disease etiology? (2) Where does song come from? What are indigenous concepts of song composition and performance? (3) How, then, is song able to intercept the course of illness? What are indigenous concepts of performance, affect, and treatment?

Illness (*jani'* < verb: *ji'*) is a deviation from the state of well-being (*mɛj* 'good', 'well', 'beautiful'). Several indigenous belief complexes are used by Temiars to explain illness etiology. Reputed (and disputed) sources of an individual's illness provide a familiar topic of discussion as family and community members gather from hearth to hearth. A medium usually diagnoses the cause of illness during dreams or in trance; however, information on the patient's recent travel, past history, and eating habits gleaned from hearth gossip undoubtedly inform his insights. This is not considered cheating; mediums often openly question where their patients have been walking or what they have recently been eating. This genre of discourse is similar to the diagnostic interview in Western biomedicine, but differs both in the thrust and logic behind the questions and in the manner of gathering information from patient, family, and community reports.

Indigenous concepts of illness etiology prescribe rules for behavior and outline the consequences of transgressing those rules. These, in turn, are embedded in the way Temiars continually construct and reconstruct their reality to make sense out of misfortune, deviations from health, and chaos. Like dreaming and trancing, illness takes shape within the fundamental cosmological homology joining humans and nonhumans. Head and heart souls of all entities are bound in the contexts of everyday life, the waking state, health, and the normal state of affairs. Transgressing the rules that constitute "normality" awakens these souls from their state of suspended animation, whence they emerge unbound as "illness agents," *mɛrgəəh*.

For Temiars, then, illness consists in the transformation of the essences of entities into interactive agents (souls in their unbound state) who then act upon humans in various manners. A survey of the sources of illness suggests two types of activated illness agents: (1) entities that transform into illness agents operative inside the body of the patient; and (2) illness agents that draw the head soul, the vital animating force, out of the patient. While some illness beings are intrinsically malicious (e.g., *baad*, which dwells in the river, and *sɛmyaap*, which dwells in the jungle), most entities are potentially either helpful *or* harmful. They can manifest as spiritguides or illness agents, depending on the nature of the interaction. Furthermore, Temiars do not juxtapose the jungle as the realm of potential harm against the settlement as comfort and safety. Rather, spiritguides and illness beings come from both jungle and settlement.

Once an entity has transformed into an illness agent, only beings of a similar type or origin have the knowledge, vision, and power necessary to interact with it. Illness agents come from the mountains, fruits, and river rapids; from these same origins come the spiritguides that can effectively engage them. A Temiar medium talks about his spiritguide, the soul of the trunk of the Ipoh tree[1] who emerged during his dream in the form of a man:

Na-lɛrkɔ' 'e-loo' 'e-loo' baraŋ pɛnyakid mɔ'.
'un-na' un-tɛŋlɛk ma-'ee' bɔ' 'ɛ-cɛɛd.

  Mɛn-gɛrbɔw, mɛn-batuu', mɛn-jɛlmɔl, mɛn-buŋaa',
'un-na' bə-'asal pɛnyakid. Jadii', mɛn-gonig
bər-'asal bar-bungaa', bar-boot, bə-jɛlmɔl, 'un-lɛk,
kiraa' ney jənis. 'ee' 'ɛn-deek, 'ɛ-kaceed.

He [the spirit of the Ipoh tree trunk] draws out whatever thing of illness there is. Those ones tell us what they know, and then we treat people.

The ridges, the stones, the mountains, the flowers—they contain the origin of illness. So too, the spiritguides have their

source in the flowering plants, the mountains . . . they are
knowledgeable, it's like they are of the same type. We, in our
houses, we know nothing.
(Aluj Hitam, Kengkong, 30-vi-82, DN18)

Both illness agents and spiritguides come from stones, mountains,
and flowers; they are both "of the same type." When a medium
embodies his spiritguide, he reaches the phenomenal plane
wherein he can interact with illness agents. He attains this phenomenal plane by singing the dream song or path that links him
with his familiar. Access to the path through song constitutes a
medium's claim to knowledge and consequent power to heal. The
relation of resemblance, this derivation from shared origins ("of the
same type"), enables interaction between spiritguides and illness
agents through the communicative mediums of healer and patient.

Treatment (*sɛ'no'* < verb *so'*) consists in establishing the presence of spiritguides, primarily by singing the way previously given
in dreams. While singing, the medium identifies the source of
illness. Healers suck to draw the illness to the patient's body surface and brush it off with a leaf whisk. They shriek to startle the
illness into "running away," or "blow" (*tɛnhɔɔl*) and "apply"
(*pərɛnlʉb*) the spiritual liquid *kahyɛk* to cool and strengthen the head
and heart soul of the patient. Illness is identified and treated during
trance ceremonies and dreams.

Temiar term the act of trancing "transforming" (*lɛslǫǫs*), from the
light, controlled trance of the seasoned medium to ecstatic trance-
dancing practiced by followers of particular spiritguide genres. Just
as the head soul of a mountain top or flower "emerges" (*na-həwal*)
in human form during dreams, the head soul of an entity is "caused
to emerge" through the human form of the medium during trance.[2]
Transformation begins when a medium sings in performance the
way initially given in dreams. At first, the medium reenacts the
dream song, but soon the voice of the spiritguide takes over, and
reenactment becomes enactment. A subtle shift in vocal quality can
sometimes be heard, and the medium may shift from his initial
crouched position with a hand covering one ear to intensify the
sound to a standing posture. Temiar mediums describe the displacement of their own self while the spiritguide sings through
them as "one's heart is elsewhere, to the side" (*hup 'ɛh 'ɛn-tuuy
'əh*).

The intermingling of dreaming and trancing in treatment is illustrated in the case of Lɛh Apəər, a married woman whose house
had burned down. This startled her head soul into running away,
resulting in soul loss, *rɛywaay*. She and her husband traveled upriver to be treated by the medium Along Indan. After hearing her
story, he slept and met with his spiritguide, the female spirit of Mt.
Səweluu', and ordered her to find Lɛh Apəər's head soul. The
spiritguide promised to return in four days, whether she had found
the woman's head soul or not. For the next three nights, healing
ceremonies were held for Lɛh Apəər at the home of a younger
medium, but Along Indan did not attend. Only on the fourth night,
the promised night, did he attend and participate. Singing and
trancing the way of the female spirit of Mt. Səweluu', he lifted his
palms upward and received the tiny mannikin-like head soul of Lɛh
Apəər which the mountain spirit had found in the bushes not far
from the house that had burned downstream. Singing with the
voice of his spiritguide, he blew the woman's head soul back into
the crown of her head where it belonged.

To understand how spiritguides are considered effective in the
treatment of illness, we will take a closer look, like Temiar mediums, at the sources of illness.

RULES RELATING THE EDIBLE AND SOCIAL UNIVERSE

Gɛnhaa'

Gɛnhaa' is the potential for disease inherent in proscribed objects
which is released when prohibitions pertaining to those objects are
not observed. *Gɛnhaa'* covers a complex set of actions pertaining to
a variety of objects. However, rules pertaining to *gɛnhaa'*-desig-
nated animals[3] typify the conceptual complex for Temiar. These
rules govern actions pertaining to these animals as they are brought
into the settlement and houses, prepared, and consumed.

Entrance of a *gɛnhaa'* animal from jungle into community is
specifically marked. Unlike most game, *gɛnhaa'* animals must be
brought into and prepared within the first house that the returning
hunting party passes. Once prepared, portions of the animal must
be served to all who have witnessed its capture and preparation;
and if the animal is large enough, it must be served to all members
of the community allowed to eat it.[4] The animal must be consumed

within the house in which it was cooked; portions cannot be distributed from house to house in the standard fashion of Temiar food distribution. The bones of *gɛnhaa'* animals must be incinerated in the fire and are not allowed to be dropped to the ground as would be the case for non-*gɛnhaa'* species. Breaking the rules associated with *gɛnhaa'* may lead to fits of ague; withering and whitening of the hair or hair loss; and even death. Benjamin (1967a:82–98) suggests that the actions pertaining to *gɛnhaa'* objects serve to distinguish the house and settlement as the realm of culture from the on-the-ground realm of nature.

The *gɛnhaa'* complex is not limited, however, to animal species. A common situation provoking the disease-causing propensity of *gɛnhaa'* objects involves the stipulation that any guest entering a home should be served some form of food or drink before they descend once again to the ground. A host who has no food or drink to offer an entering guest bemoans: "*Gɛnhaa'*, one dies." The propensity for illness strikes the guest, who has entered the social realm of the house but has not been appropriately incorporated into social relationships by sharing food before his/her return to the outer realm. In a manner consistent with a sociocentric society, good health requires good exchange.

Some instances of the *gɛnhaa'* complex, however, defy analysis in terms of the distinction between house or culture and the outer world or nature. For example, to hold a singing or trance-dancing session on the same night in the same settlement as a "storytelling performance" (*cənal*) is considered *gɛnhaa'*. Both ritual singing and storytelling are nighttime, housebound events. To tell stories or hold singing sessions in the jungle, Temiars say, would attract the attention of tigers or illness beings, who would then wish to participate in the chorus or to emit the interjectory "*hə'!*" with which audience members punctuate a storytelling session. Ritual singing sessions and storytelling are collapsed into one category in another context: neither is allowed to be performed during the period of mourning following a death in the community. While Benjamin (1967a:77) suggests that ritual singing sessions are opposed to storytelling sessions as housebound:jungle, it would seem rather that it is the very similarity of singing sessions and storytelling performances (as housebound, nighttime, nonmourning period, initiator-respondent performance events) that prohibits their simultaneous performance. As in the case of offering food, singing

and storytelling establish social interrelationships; to hold two such events simultaneously would divide the community, dissipating the cohesiveness that their performance formats (interactive solo/choral singing and storyteller/interjector) seek to generate.

The *gɛnhaa'* complex circumscribes areas and times of day appropriate for particular performance activities. Time is ordered: solo instruments (flutes, mouthharps, tube-zither) are played during the day, extending through late afternoon until before dusk. Ritual singing sessions and storytelling are performed after nightfall; all-night singing sessions conclude an hour after sunrise when daylight is firmly established. Space is also ordered: while the playing of solo instruments and singing unaccompanied by percussion may occur inside or outside the house, the bamboo-tube percussion accompanying ritual singing and trance-dancing can only be performed inside the house. To tell a story during the day, play the flute at night, or beat the bamboo-tube stampers outdoors is *gɛnhaa'*. The offender's hair might become dry and white or fall out, followed by illness and death.

In these cases, *gɛnhaa'* consists in the disease-causing propensity of the object that is released when the orderly state of affairs (e.g., flutes during the day, singing sessions at night) is disturbed. When spatial or temporal categories are disrupted, the potential for illness is unleashed. The death of two infants in Blau occurring during my stay there was traced to *gɛnhaa'* released by an extraordinary event: the sudden flaming of a store-bought cigarette while it was pointed in the direction of the infants' house. Should a homemade cigarette of tobacco rolled in dry leaves have thus flamed, there would have been no *gɛnhaa'*. Dry-leaf cigarettes are expected to flame up; wet-rolled and store-bought cigarettes are not. The disturbance of order exemplified by the sudden flaming of the store-bought cigarette awakens the disease-causing propensity of the object, resulting in *gɛnhaa'*.

Some Temiars commented that the upper-portion souls of particular objects were activated by the transgression of prohibitions; the offended upper-portion soul was responsible for the misfortunes of *gɛnhaa'*. This was mentioned particularly in relation to the leaves and flowers gathered for ceremonial ornaments. When the ceremonial foliage is brought into a house where a ceremony is later to be held and the construction of ornaments is begun, hearth-fires are lit to welcome their leaf souls. The fires also keep the leaves

company should the house be emptied of people while the ornaments hang in anticipation of the ceremony. Failing to light the fires
and suitably honor (or socially recognize) the arrival of the ceremonial leaves and flowers would offend their head souls, poten-
tiating *genhaa'*. Once the ornaments have been constructed, the
ceremony cannot be canceled; to do so would offend the upper-
portion souls of the leaves and flowers, causing *genhaa'*. I observed
several instances in which ceremonial ornaments had been constructed and hung, night had fallen, and suddenly the anticipated
medium had taken ill and was unable to perform, or the male
singers of the village had not returned from their work in the
jungle. In these cases, substitutions had to be made and the ceremony fulfilled: either another medium was called in, or, if no male
singers were in the village, the women took the parts of both initial
singer and chorus in order that the head souls of the leaves and
flowers not be offended.

Another *genhaa'* configuration surrounding the tools of ceremonial performance concerns the bamboo tubes used as percussion
stampers. When the bamboo tubes become dry or cracked and lose
their resonance, they must be thrown away outside. They cannot
be split and used for firewood, or used to construct another bamboo artifact. Having been used to accompany the voice of a medium, they become like a child of that medium. To reuse these
already socially integrated tubes for another purpose would abro-
gate the social relationship between the medium and his bamboo-
tube children, offending their head souls and causing *genhaa'*. This
in turn would result in various problems for the medium, including
a throat ailment, loss of voice and *halaa'* adeptness, and possibly
death.

An event I observed in Jɛlgək, upriver on the Sungai Bərɔk,
illustrates how the head soul of an offended *genhaa'* animal species
is awakened from its state of suspended animation and subsequently placated. Two boys from another river valley currently
dwelling in Jɛlgək had noticed that observances in Jɛlgək seemed to
differ from those of their own settlement, Bɛr. In their home settlement of Bɛr, the Monitor Lizard,[5] once prepared, is consumed by
community members who have gathered together in one house. It
is not distributed from house to house, as they had observed in
Jɛlgək. They thus assumed that the Monitor Lizard was not considered a *genhaa'* animal in Jɛlgək. When they caught a Monitor

Lizard one evening, they brought it past several houses before bringing it into their own house. Unbeknownst to the two young visitors, Jɛlgək residents did consider the Monitor Lizard a *gɛnhaa'* animal; the carcass should have been brought into the first house met upon entrance into the community. According to practices in Jɛlgək, only the act of carrying the uncooked carcass past other houses was considered *gɛnhaa'*. However, once the meat was cooked it could be distributed among the various houses of the community.

The next morning a young male adult member of the Jɛlgək community, Aŋah Pandak (Angah Pandak), went to the boys' house (where I also was staying) and related a dream he'd had the night before:

> Last night I dreamt of *gɛnhaa'*, of *pəmalii'*.[6] I dreamt the body of that game animal [the Monitor Lizard], it was weeping. It asked for payment in retribution,[7] seven dollars [US$3.50]: "Ask them to give me seven dollars."
> (Aŋah Pandak, Jɛlgək, 24-vi-82, FN1693–94)

The older of the two boys placed seven dollars in coins on a plate and presented it to Angah Pandak, who commented: "By virtue of this dream, I become the Tuan [< Malay 'Lord', 'Sir', 'Boss'], the one responsible." While presenting the money to Angah, the older boy recited:

> This is the retributive payment. I did wrong, I was unknowing when I brought the game directly to this house last night. This is the payment; I give it to you. I want that all should be well, that you [the Monitor Lizard] not bother us. I am ashamed; I did not know the correct actions.

Shyly Angah Pandak received the payment, ashamed to take money from the boys. But the activated head soul of the offended Monitor Lizard was thereby placated, and the potential for disease obviated.

Misik

Misik[8] is the potential for disease or misfortune resulting from an array of proscribed actions including laughing at or imitating the cries of certain animals and insects; eating an animal that has been laughed at during its slaughter, preparation, or consumption; laughing too long or too loudly at another human being; flashing mirrors or exposing white objects outside; or perpetrating in-and-out movements (such as copulation or pushing sticks into the pulpy stems of tapioca plants to remove their pith) in clearings without overhead shelter. Indulging in these actions provokes the state of *misik*, manifest as raging thunderstorms, diarrhea, or tiger attacks.

The *misik* complex implicates the thunder deity ('*ɛŋkuu*') and his younger brother Aluj. Many of the species that cannot be laughed at or imitated are said to be the "children" or "adoptees" of Aluj; less often, it is said that some of them are the children of '*ɛŋkuu*'.[9] As with *gɛnhaa'*, temporal ordering is at issue. At night, Aluj is asleep and only '*ɛŋkuu*' is awake; it is thus less dangerous to laugh at or imitate these species at night. But during the day, Aluj is awake and vigilant: if someone should laugh at one of his children, he awakens the now-slumbering '*ɛŋkuu*' who sends rain, thunder, and lightning.

When I asked how Temiars came to know that various actions would precipitate *misik*, I was told that when a child would do one of the forbidden acts, a thunderstorm would follow. After that, Temiars knew that this action could not be done without incurring *misik*. This indigenous explanation suggests that for Temiars, classes of animals, insects, and actions such as those that constitute the *misik* complex are not formed merely on the basis of shared attributes (e.g., morphological or behavioral resemblances). Rather, these classes are developed by noting the results from interactions with these species. When such experiences were followed by thunderstorms, the species in question were added to the class *misik*. Howell (1984:214), noting a similar propensity among the Chewong, suggests that these classes constitute "nomenclature." Such classes are defined by the inclusion of members named within them, rather than by resemblance. A similar process may be involved in the classification *tɛnruu'*.

Tɛnruu'

Tɛnruu', a nominalization of the verb *tǝruu'* (also referred to as *sabat*)[10] is manifest by symptoms including a wasting away of the body, convulsions or shivers, crankiness or irritability, loss of appetite, labored breathing, nausea, and imitation of animal behaviors. *Tɛnruu'* results from consumption of or contact with the meat or blood of an animal or plant species forbidden to an individual by virtue of that individual's age, sex, or parental status.

The birds, mammals, amphibians, fish, insects, and plants considered edible by Temiars are not unilaterally edible by all members of society. The Temiar community is divisible into sectors extending from those enjoying the widest range of edible foods, old men, to those with the most restricted diets, menstruating women and women who have just given birth. Table 3 presents sectors ranging from those with the least restricted diets (on the left) to those with the most restricted diets (on the right). Divisions are primarily by age, sex, and status with reference to children or childbearing potential. A person may move among categories as a woman goes in and out of menstruation, for example, or if a couple's child dies, as a child ages, or as a previously childless person becomes pregnant.

People join designated groups through reference to their children. This is because consuming a dangerous food endangers not only the parent or prospective parent, for it is passed through the parent to the child or fetus. This is another example of the permeability of self and other, the sociocentric self: the parent extends beyond the "self" to include the child. A restricted food, then, is simultaneously "consumed" by both the parent (especially the mother, sometimes the father, depending on the food and the age of the child) *and* the child or fetus. Old men, who are furthest from the childbearing state and whose children are already adults, are freer to consume the most dangerous foods. Not only consumption but also contact with the blood of a restricted animal (e.g., a baby crawling across a spot where the blood of meat may have fallen during preparation; or a mother carrying the meat of a restricted animal packed in bamboo tubes slung across her back) or the use of cooking utensils contaminated by foods outside of one's acceptable categories can cause *tɛnruu'*.

The species of animals, birds, amphibians, fish, insects, and plants that constitute the edible universe are categorized as respectively edible or nonedible in relation to population sectors outlined in table 3. The various species, then, are "socially edible," that is, categorized as edible in relation to various sectors of the society.

Table 3 Dietary Restrictions by Social Sector

LEAST RESTRICTED DIET → MOST RESTRICTED DIET

Old men	Old women	Childless women (excluding midwives)	Men with young children	Women with young children	Midwives	Menstruating women
	Childless men		Adolescents	Pregnant women		Midwives who've just assisted in birth
	Men with older children			Babies, young children		Women who've just given birth
				Women who've just completed menstruating		

A search for an underlying set of resemblances shared by a class of *tenruu'* species renders a bemusing array of responses. Many of the species with various levels of *tenruu'*-producing qualities are considered to be transformations of the tiger. When consumed by someone who, according to their social category vis-à-vis table 3, should not have consumed that food, the species "transforms" (*na-lǫǫs*) into a small cat or tiger inside the stomach and bites or sucks on the heart of the consumer (or his/her children), causing the illness symptoms described above. Drawing on detailed research into dietary classifications among the Chewong, another Orang Asli group, Howell proposes that through progressive experiences with particular species, Chewong construct and reconstruct classifications of the type termed nomenclature. By observing what an animal eats, where it lives, and what happens to the people who eat it, the Chewong gradually add members to a particular class. The basis for the classification system may have as much to do with experiences following consumption of a species as it does with species' attributes. Nomenclature "consists simply in assigning a common name to all the members of a class. It is based neither on hierarchical principles nor on shared attributes, but may nevertheless be regarded as a type of classification because, by virtue of the consistency of its application, it does locate a thing in a conceptual frame. However, the search for common attributes underlying such a system would reveal that members of a class have nothing more in common than their being named as such" (Howell 1984:214).

A Temiar comment on the origin of knowledge about actions precluding *misik* has bearing here: a child was said to have done one of the forbidden acts, then it rained. After that, Temiars knew that this action could not be done without incurring *misik*. Furthermore, the variability from river valley to river valley of species considered to precipitate the illnesses discussed above (*genhaa'*, *misik*, and *tenruu'*) supports the proposition that these classifications constitute nomenclatures constructed locally over time through contingent experiences with the species in question. Pragmatic bases for these symbolic classifications arising out of observation and experience should also be considered. In her study of Malay dietary restrictions, Laderman (1981) found that certain fish species denied to Malay women in the postpartum period under the system of food restrictions surrounding the puerperium were indeed chemically toxic.

The illness symptoms associated with *tɛnruu'* are often said to represent a transformation of the afflicted into the forbidden species consumed; the afflicted then imitates the animal's behavior. "Myths" (*cənal*) offered as explanations for the origin of *tɛnruu'*-causing propensities of various species invariably harken back to the experiences of a sibling pair. The younger brother is incorrectly advised by his older brother to eat a species previously designated as *tɛnruu'* by their parents. Protesting, then submitting to the advice of his older brother, the younger brother eats the forbidden food and begins to shiver, then transforms into the forbidden species. The experience of the younger sibling, who transforms into the forbidden species after consuming it, then stands as the mythological "origin" of that species' propensity to cause *tɛnruu'*. That the parents already knew in advance, and how they knew, is relatively inconsequential.

The medium Alung Indan bin Agun (Along Indan) of Bəlau discusses the etiology of the recurrent asthmatic-like attacks suffered by the old man Bubung, whose chronic illness and treatment I repeatedly observed:

> When Bubung was young, he came into contact with *kənɔg*, a large land tortoise of the jungle.[11] He may have gotten ahold of the meat, old bones or shell, or even passed a spot where there was an old blood stain. That tortoise is *sabat*; only the very old and the childless can eat it. It must be eaten in the home of whoever caught and cooked it. Portions cannot be carried to other homes. All bones and shell must be disposed of in one place.
>
> Bubung came into contact with the tortoise and became *sabat*. There is a liquid in his abdomen. When the sickness hits, the water rises to his heart and fills his heart to swelling.[12] He begins to wheeze like the voice of a tortoise, his body heaves and humps like a tortoise, his hands claw at his sides like a tortoise.
>
> I've checked. If I treat Bubung, sometimes it helps and sometimes it doesn't. If I treat him, in about three days the condition clears. If I don't treat him, it clears of itself in three

days. I have checked when I treat him and when I don't;
sometimes it helps, sometimes it clears on its own. It's without order, no clear "path" (*nɔŋ*). (Alung Indan bin Agun,
Bəlau, 30-x-81, FN907–908)

Illnesses traced to the activated *tɛnruu'* or *sabat*-potential of an incorrectly consumed species are often chronic illnesses, treatable to
an extent by mediums, but periodically reemerging and requiring
retreatment. Mediums often comment, like a Western cosmopolitan doctor speaking of a cancerous tumor, that the activated animal
transformation has been inside the patient for so long and become
so large that removing it entirely would cause the death of the
patient. The illness etiology thus provides a rationalization for the
failure of treatment and the tenacity of illness.

Na-cəkah: 'It gets angry'

Foods are also classified into categories that must not be cooked or
stored in the same utensils or consumed at the same sitting. Mixing
these categories gets the food's head soul angry (*na-cəkah*), causing
diarrhea (*na-cɛɛd*). The two categories are:

1. fish (*kf'*); frogs (*sɛgnug*)
2. game (*ɲam*); birds (*cɛp*); rodents (*kadeeg*).

Game, birds, and rodents have fur (*sɛntɔɔl*) that should not be
mixed with fish and frogs. One should not eat members of both
categories at the same sitting. A few hours, another activity perhaps, should separate the consumption of frogs from that of game.
When eating fish or frogs, it is likewise dangerous to touch the fur
of cats and dogs roaming about hoping for bones. The exclamation
"It's fur!" commonly accompanies the whack of a stick rather than
use of the hand to keep a cat or dog at bay while consuming fish or
frogs. The odor of fur is also given as an explanation for the pro-
hibition on eating game, birds, or rodents while under treatment
for illness by some mediums.

'ɛ-deeh: 'We utter (the name)'

Naming across categories also causes diarrhea. To utter the word
"game" (*ɲam*) while eating vegetables, fruit, rice, or tapioca will
startle the head soul of the entity being consumed. The head soul

then bites onto the consumer's heart, causing diarrhea, fever, and possibly death.

Uttering the species or "true" name of game, rodents, frogs, birds, or fish also startles the head soul of the being in question, which then bites or sucks on the heart of the consumer, causing diarrhea, fever, and possibly death. For example, while cooking or eating rodents, they can be referred to generally as "rodent" (*kadɛɛg*). But to speak the name of a particular rodent species (e.g., "large rodent," *kadɛɛg rayaa'*) would court illness. These rules are more stringent for the smaller animals such as rodents or small fish.

Temiars exhibit considerable linguistic improvisation in their development of utterable and nonutterable reference terms for edible species.[13] The unspeakable terms constitute the "true name" (*kənɨɨh mɨn*), whereas utterable terms are said to "float above" the name (*kənɨɨh puloh*). The wild boar[14] has two names that can be vocalized during its hunt, preparation, and consumption (*ta'ɔŋ, 'amboj*) and three names (*gaaw, cɑ̰ŋɑ̰', goŋgɛɛ'*) that cannot be spoken from the moment the boar is sighted to approximately one full day and night after the last bit of meat has been consumed. Ideally, the meat should work itself through the digestive system before the true name is uttered, so that the animal's head soul will not be startled into activity while its essence is still inside the consumer's body.

The one situation in which all names of the wild boar can be heard uttered in succession is when a Temiar discovers a boar has raided a tapioca patch. In anger, he or she can be head to exclaim: "That animal *ta'ɔŋ, 'amboj, gaaw, cɑ̰ŋɑ̰', goŋgɛɛ'* ate my tapioca! We'll be hungry later!" This parallels situations in which Temiars might utter the "true name" of human beings: Temiars commonly refer to one another with nicknames, birth-order terms, and teknonyms, reserving the use of a person's true name for moments when, in anger, they lash out and use it to intentionally startle that person's head soul.

NEFARIOUS BEINGS IN THE SURROUNDING ENVIRONMENT

Baad

A river-dwelling, worm-like creature whose body is approximately six inches long, dark, and very thin, *baad* attaches itself to those who travel on or in the river. It works its way inside the victim's body and sucks on the heart, causing abdominal swelling and diarrhea. The disease may attack the traveler himself or herself, or may be carried into the household and passed on to children or other household members. The illness complex is another reminder of the dangerous side of sociocentric interrelation of self, other, and cosmos, for interpenetrability of self and other in this case can aid the passage of illness. To rid themselves of *baad*, those returning from river travel smoke themselves and their baggage over the hearth. Chest and back are the two most important areas to smoke, especially for a woman who will later breastfeed her child. When mediums treat patients intruded by *baad*, they blow and suck until they extract the being, which appears in the form of a stone.

Sɛmyaap

This formless being ("like the wind") dwells in the jungle and, like *baad*, attaches itself to the backs of travelers. The afflicted show symptoms including fever, labored breathing, and a cold heaviness, prompting them to attempt unsuccessfully to warm themselves by the fire. Since Temiar travel usually involves movement through both river and jungle, *sɛmyaap* and *baad* are treated with preventive measures as a couplet. Returning travelers waft smoke from the fire onto their skin; this causes *baad* and *sɛmyaap* to run away elsewhere. Similarly, the traveler's baggage is smoked over the hearth, or placed in an isolated corner of the house. There, a person waves a torch over it and recites: "Waving the torch, waving the torch, waving the torch, *sɛmyaap*, *baad*, *baad*, *sɛmyaap!*" Waving the torch and reciting, the person gradually moves closer to the doorway and finally tosses the now smoldering stick out the door.

Reciting the names "*Baad!*" and "*Sɛmyaap!*" startles and shames these illness agents into running elsewhere. To name and thereby startle the head soul of consumed food provokes it to afflict the offender from within; in contrast, uttering the name of *baad* or *sɛmyaap* while they are still in the initial stages of being attached to the traveler's skin or belongings (rather than having entered the body where their activation might cause harm) merely startles them into running away.

Rɛywaay

The illness *rɛywaay* ('soul loss' < *rəwaay* 'upper-potion soul') results when a nonhuman entity's head soul maliciously attacks or is
sentimentally attracted to a human being. The interactive self of the
awakened entity entices the human's head soul to leave his or her
body and dwell together with it in the jungle. All nonhuman entities can be provoked into this mode of interaction with humans by
acts that either offend them or merely attract their attention. However, some entities are more inclined to cause soul loss and are
therefore treated circumspectly. These include rice, the annually
blossoming flowers, and a cicada (*hɛrɲɔɔd*) that appears during the
blossom season.

The head soul of rice is carefully approached with ritual actions,
recitations, and trance-dancing ceremonies before and at the conclusion of harvest. Children are told not to play in the rice fields
where they might attract the attention of the rice *rəwaay*. If annual
flowers worn as hair or body ornaments are disposed of in the
river, they will take the wearer's head soul along downstream.
They should be disposed of on the ground instead. The cicada
hɛrɲɔɔd should be listened to with a strong heart in order not to be
drawn to follow it into the jungle. If caught in one's hand and then
released, this cicada will carry off one's head soul with it, causing
soul loss.[15]

SETTING THE COSMOS IN MOTION

The medium Alɥj Hitam explains that people, stuck in their houses
on the ground, know nothing. It is only when people are joined by
spiritguides, who, like illness agents, have their source in the flowering plants and the mountains, the birds and the animals of the
rainforest, that they become mediums who partake in the knowledge of spirits and can heal. Temiars operate with a logic that meets
illness as they conceive of it with a tool that functions on a similar
phenomenal plane: since illness agents and spiritguides share similar origins, a medium must activate benevolent spirits to treat an
activated malevolent spirit. So too, in Western biomedicine, a bac-
terial infection, conceived of as producing cellular and antibody
responses, is treated with antibiotics, which interfere with the bac-
teria cell wall synthesis so that the invading organism loses its

integrity. Spiritguides and illness agents are also joined as one "type," to use Aluj Hitam's words, by their chance emergence "out of the blue" and "onto the horizon" of human intelligibility. Spiritguides "happen to come" to people in dreams. Though a person's everyday actions such as passing by a rock or tending a plant may precipitate a dream encounter, a person cannot ask for or demand a song. It "just happens" (*na-jadii'*) that he or she is given one. Similarly, though a person's everyday actions may include passing a grave or eating a proscribed food, it just happens that the possibility for emergence inherent in the entity does, in some cases, eventuate. If it does, he or she is "struck" (*na-kənah*) by illness.

Given this leeway of chance, Temiars do not conduct their lives rigidly rule-bound; one lives somewhat by the rules, breaks or tests them, and might (or might not) get hit by illness or misfortune. The rules of culture are more like signposts than roadblocks; they provide ways to negotiate and make sense out of experience.[16] Anyone who has seen Temiars laughing at the antics of a dog and muttering "*Misik,* thunderstorms will follow!" while trying half-heartedly to constrain their laughter, or heard a classificatory brother try to seduce a classificatory sister by saying, "No one will suspect us; they will assume we fear the thunderstorms that follow incest," knows that cultural rules are always being tested, played with, and chanced. And, too, there are the rules for when rules have been broken, the chant that puts odor back in its place, the song that lets a medium rise to the phenomenal plane of offended illness agents and set the world right again.

The patient's responsibility for misfortune is obviated by recognizing the element of chance. The concept of chance as the previously unforeseen coming into perceptibility appropriately describes the emergence of Temiar spiritguides and illness agents from the realm of possibility into the realm of human experience.[17] Temiar animism acts to locate the Unknown within the Known; the unforeseeable emerges from *within* the visible landscape. During the chance encounter of the initial contact dream, the spiritguide emerges with the upward and outward movement of a tiger pouncing—possibly a Temiar root metaphor for motion. Prototypically the worst incident is to be eaten by a tiger; on the other hand, the best, "biggest," most powerful (yet most dangerous) spiritguide is the tiger.

Spiritguides, then, arise from previously unmarked landscape formations personified through dream encounters and marked with song. Most illness agents, as well, emerge from within known foods and features of the landscape. Diagnosis involves reading the incidents of the patient's past: where did she walk, what did she eat? To diagnose is to "symptomalize contingency," to make passing incidents into clinical symptoms. The act of healing involves translating the arbitrary into the motivated, the unmarked into the marked; healing takes that which is not anticipated and serves to motivate it as if it were anticipated. The medium cures illness by turning it from something unseen and unforeseen into something perceptible and knowable.

When the medium determines the source of the illness agent during dreams or the trance of curing rituals, he marks the arbitrary misfortune of illness by identifying it. As we have seen in our survey of the sources of illness, many of the entities are startled into their animated state of "illness agent" by a human act that transgresses the rules upholding the state of order and normality. Interactive selves of entities become unbound; the cosmos is set in motion. Once unbound and transformed, they rebind themselves to the perpetrator of the original transgression by either entering inside the afflicted or enticing the afflicted into a relationship off in the jungle. When the medium "sees" the source of the illness agent with the help of his spiritguides, and marks or "knows" it, he begins to move the chaotic situation of illness back into the realm of order.

The medium treats his patient in the context of a ceremonial performance that reframes reality, reorganizing roles and codes of discourse. The performance frame presents a vehicle for propelling the cosmos into motion and moving the afflicted from illness to well-being. In the staged or "altered" situation of the curative performance, social actors are brought together in their transformed roles as medium, chorus, and patient. The unique configuration of interactive performance roles coupled with the peculiar textures of the media whereby those roles are enacted (sound, movement, touch, spatial orientation, fragrance, color, lighting) engenders an arena in which the paramount reality of everyday life has been shifted. Within this arena, activated illness agents can be countered by activated spiritguides and a reordering of the cosmos wrought.

SINGING AS TRANSFORMATION

What is it about singing that makes it a primary technique of healing particularly effective in promoting transformations and communication across domains otherwise distinct in daily life? Why do
spiritguides—transformed, detached from their concrete manifestations, and anthropomorphized—sing? Song is both speech *transformed* and patterned sound or "music" *humanized* by endowing it
with a semantically meaningful linguistic component, a text. The
transformations wrought upon speech disguise and augment, yet
never obliterate it: syllables are variously shortened or lengthened
to align them with rhythmic configurations; the intonation curves
of everyday speech are variously exaggerated or canceled to integrate them with the melody.

Temiar song texts and poetic speech are linked in the term
hənelad 'versing', describing a metaphorically obtuse language
filled with dream words and employing textual devices such as
assonance, rhyme, and reduplicative play. All these devices emphasize the sensuous sounds of words. The "versing" of sung texts
and poetic speech is opposed to ordinary language in the extent of
its creative transformation (see Ellen Basso 1984: 462) and forcefully
contributes to the transformation of reality in ritual.

Singing is also a detached, disembodied form of the emergent
head soul. Many Temiar were wary of their own or their children's
songs being recorded on tape, fearing this would deplete the vital,
animating force supplied to the individual by the head soul. The
detached head souls of spiritguides are inserted as a watery thread
into the heart of a medium. The thread flows through him as song
and liquid *kahyɛk*, which he then disperses to participants and
patients. In the enactment of performance, this infusion is effected
when the medium's initial solo phrase is repeated by a female
chorus, a sonic dispersal from individual to collective. In treatment,
infusion occurs when the medium sings through a space between
his two joined hands into the patient's head and heart soul areas.
Vocalized song is the interactive self in motion.

Knowledge constitutes the power to heal when it takes that
which is unknown and defines it. Power, institutionalized in performance, is tied to the medium's claim to knowledge, which derives in turn from his own dream encounter with chance. This

Plate 11. A singing medium ministrates to a patient during a ceremony.

chance encounter with the landscape and its inhabitant beings then ceases to be chance because the medium now knows where it comes from, he appropriates it as his "own way" (*nɔŋ rii'*). Singing enacts and demonstrates the power to take the chance out of illness.

Singing shows what the medium knows. It is an icon of soul unbound as spirit. Speech transformed, sound humanized, and head soul disembodied, singing parallels the ontological transformations of entities into interactive selves. Singing is the perceptual embodiment of the transformative process. Diagramming that which it signs, singing becomes the dynamic vehicle of transformation, linking dreams, trance, and healing as the privileged form of communication for spiritguides when they interact with humans and illness agents.

6

Remembering to Forget:
The Aesthetics of Longing

When a dream song resounds in ceremonial performance, it becomes a path linking spiritguide, medium, chorus, and patient. Singing is accompanied by bamboo-tube percussion: female chorus members each beat the high-pitched and low-pitched members of a pair of bamboo-tube stampers in alternation against a log. The duple rhythm of these beating tubes is linked in a web of local meanings that extends from pulsating sounds of the rainforest to the beating of the human heart. In order to entice the spirits to attend ceremonial performances (and to prepare their human hosts to greet them), the sentiment of longing is modulated through symbolically laden sounds of the stamping tubes and bodily movements of the dancers. The beating tubes play upon the evocative power Temiars attach to pulsating sounds; by moving the emotions, the sounds of the tubes set the spirits in motion.

The sentiment of longing pervades the relationships of spiritguides with mediums, illness agents with ill persons, and humans with humans among the Temiars. The sentiments of longing and remembrance are aesthetically coded in sound and movement within Temiar everyday life and ceremonial performance. Sounds of the tropical rainforest, such as particular bird and insect calls, are imbued by the Temiar with meaning and power to evoke longing and remembrance. Ceremonial performances make use of structurally similar sounds to intensify the longing and remembering that lead to the forgetfulness of trance. When longing is intensified beyond the proper bounds, illness occurs. The aesthetic sensibilities evoking longing and remembrance thus interweave the contexts of spirit-mediumship, courtship, trancing, and curing.

REMEMBERING TO FORGET

Toraja ritual specialists in Sulawesi act as receptacles for the collective memory or traditions of the ancestors; Coville (1984) describes these ritual specialists as "those-who-remember." In contrast, Toraja trance-dancers, whose links are with the divinities rather than the ancestors, are "those-who-forget":

> It is not surprising . . . that when [trance-dancers] return to consciousness (or rather when they are brought back by the audience and the *to minaa* [ritual specialists]), the trance-dancers have no memory about what has transpired when under the influence of the divinities. Their inability to remember makes them the inverse of the *to minaa*. So we have, on the one hand, the conscious ones who remember and, on the other, the unconscious ones who forget. Those-who-remember submit as credentials for the task their link (through birth and/or practice, and only rarely through revelation) to the beginnings of culture. Those-who-forget, on the other hand, are certified or authenticated by their direct link to the Upperworld.
>
> There is a trade-off, then, between objectified power inscribed in the knowledge of ritual and transient experience of power enacted in trance. (Coville 1984:7)

Among Temiars, a trade-off occurs within the single individual: everyday knowledge and experience is forgotten, displaced by the remembering of the dream-time and connection with the spiritguide. In his discussion of multiple realities, Schutz suggests that the various worlds "of dreams, of imageries and phantasms, especially the world of art, the world of religious experience . . ." constitute "finite provinces of meaning," each with their own peculiar cognitive style and specific "tension of consciousness" (1967:232). Participation in one province of meaning replaces participation in another province of meaning, each respectively contributing to a total frame of reference. The provinces of meaning, I would suggest, need not always be finite: participation in one province might overlay or intersect another, rendering "nonfinite" provinces of meaning.

The theme of longing and remembrance begins with the dreams in which Temiar mediums first meet spiritguides. During dreams, the soul of an entity such as a fruit tree detaches itself and emerges in humanized form, male or female. It speaks to the roaming head soul of the Temiar dreamer: "I come to you, I desire you. I want to be your teacher, I want to call you father." The acquaintance is thus begun in a melange of desire,[1] pedagogy, and kinship. Male mediums often speak of their female spiritguides as "wives" in addition to their being "children." Bemoaning the fate of transitory dream encounters, they comment: "I sleep with her at night, but in the morning, my bed is empty."

The longings initiated and momentarily fulfilled during dreams are later recapitulated and intensified during ceremonial performances. Singing at first with his own voice, crouching on the floor with eyes closed and hand cupped over his ear, listening at once deep within himself and far away, the medium "causes [the spirit] to emerge" (*na-tərɛlhəwal* < *həwal* 'to emerge'). Continuing to sing, standing, beginning to dance, the medium becomes imbued with the voice, vision, and knowledge of the spiritguide.

The singing medium is transformed; his simultaneous presence of body and absence of self is described as "one's heart being elsewhere, to the side," *hup 'ɛh 'ɛn-tuuy 'əh*. This is contrasted with the state of normal consciousness, "true heart," *hup mʉn*. The transformation is effected when the medium recalls the tune and text taught to him during dreams. Remembering the dream song, he attains the forgetfulness (*wɛlwəl*) of trance. It is both a loss and a finding, a "forgetting" of everyday knowledge and a "remembering" of the spiritguide.

This point may help us understand the seeming abandon yet stylized control of trance behavior. One dimension, the everyday dimension of bounded souls, is forgotten, while another one of dreams and spiritguides is recalled. Thus, while mediums or trancers "forget" themselves and their surroundings, nontrancing participants (particularly women) will call out jokingly: "Remember (*kɛɛk*)! The dogs will bite!"—counteracting the fall toward oblivion with a joke. Overly rowdy and haphazard movements will be met with the reminder, "Trance beautifully, remember!" The impetus to forget is thus bounded on the other side; one must remember to remain within the parameters of stylized abandon.

The medium's voice becomes the spiritguide's vocalization; his heart is elsewhere, but the potential emptiness of longing is filled by the presence of the emergent spiritguide. Uncontrolled longing leads to the illness of soul loss, in which human souls are attracted *out* to live in the jungle with the spirits. However, when the emo-

Plate 12. A medium begins to sing, initiating the emergence of the spirit-guide.

tion of longing is controlled in the contexts of dreaming, singing, and trancing, spirits are instead attracted *into* the human realm of ceremonial performance.

The spiritguide is the source of knowledge that it "returns" to the spirit-medium, who will remember upon "returning home" to consciousness that which has been revealed during trance. The general flow of knowledge in the context of trance and spirit-mediumship is from the jungle into the household. Funneled

Plate 13. As the spiritguide emerges, the medium stands.

through mediums and trance-dancers, knowledge is dispersed into
the female chorus (as they repeat each line sung by the medium),
and into the community-at-large. Both active and passive participation constitute participation; there is no audience per se. Everyone present inside the ceremonial house is a witness and therefore
a participant in the event, a recipient to some degree of the cool
spiritual liquid that flows into the household concurrently with
song. For the more active participants, a momentary displacement
of self is intensified then replaced by the emergent spiritguide.

Unrequited longing that is not fulfilled leads to the illness of
"soul loss," *rɛywaay*. Here, the direction of energy is reversed.
Instead of the movement of knowledge from jungle to household
exemplified by emergent spiritguides attracted during ceremonies,
the soul of the ill person is drawn to the jungle, seduced by a
spiritguide into residing far from that person's settlement. It is as
if there were a continuous tug-of-war in progress, with humans
attempting to draw the spirits into their realm during ceremonies,
while spirits likewise attempt to draw humans into their realm,
reportedly "twisting" and "breaking off" the head soul as if it were
a young plant shoot. But the dynamics of the interaction are rarely
phrased in terms of antagonism; rather, they are phrased in terms
of longing and attraction.

THE AESTHETICS OF LONGING

Temiar mediums are predominantly male; their spiritguides are
predominantly female.[2] Overtones of longing, flirtation, enticement, and seduction pervade the cross-sexual relationship between
humans and spiritguides.[3] The term *hɛwhəyaaw* is central to the
conceptual complex of longing and remembrance as it crosscuts
dimensions of spirit-mediumship, courtship, trancing, and curing.[4] A Temiar medium comments:

> One hears it in one's ear, like wind: "*Yaaw-waaw-waaw*." If we
> sit, dream, we hear this in our ear, it's uncomfortable. We
> must have a singing ceremony, it orders us to have a trance-
> dancing ceremony, only then are we relieved. Otherwise,
> after a while, we would go mad. [*Hɛwhəyaaw*] is like a hot, dry
> wind rustling the leaves when there is no rain; we must hold
> a ceremony. (Abilem Lum, September 1981, FN 659)

Similarly, when a man sees a beautiful woman, or a woman thinks of a man she longs for, the sentiment evoked is *hɛwhəyaaw*. It is an unfulfilled longing, the type of remembrance referred to as "pining for," pulling at one's heart.

A related term, referring both to lovesickness and the feelings intensified in trance, is *bərɛnlii' bərolaaw*.[5] A Temiar man explains:

> *Bərɛnlii'*: I lose my appetite, my heart is elsewhere, it's not right. I start walking without purpose; one eventually can become crazy. It's both good and bad, a longing, like when one remembers a boyfriend or when one looks across a beautiful vista. When we trance-dance, it becomes *bərɛnlii'* in our hearts. (Bawik, August 1982, FN 1905)

Both *hɛwhəyaaw* and *bərɛnlii' bərɔlaaw* are expressives built by reduplicative play from the roots *[hə]yaaw* and *[bə]laaw* respectively (see Diffloth 1976; Benjamin 1976:177–178). The words describing the sentiment of longing are formally linked through onomatopoeia with Temiar utterances describing sounds considered to evoke the sentiment: *yaaw-waaw-waaw* (pressure in the ears; also, the call of the cicada *hɛrɲɔɔd*), *laaw-laaw* (the call of another cicada species, *jajaa' kəwaraay*), *howaaw howaaw* (Golden-throated barbet calls).[6] This linguistic clue to the centrality and consistent patterning of sound in the complex of longing and remembrance is borne out by the structure of the sounds themselves.

The song "The Way of the Perah Tree"[7] was inspired when the medium Abilem fell asleep under a Perah tree during the fruit season, while listening to the persistently pulsating call of the cicada *hɛrɲɔɔd*. In his dream, the male Perah tree spiritguide listened to the female cicada head soul's calls and, falling in love, began to verse. The themes of attraction, longing, and courtship are expressed in Perah's verse: *"Hɛwhəyaaw rasaan hɛrɲɔɔd,"* "Pulsating, longing, the feeling of the cicada *hɛrɲɔɔd*."

In everyday life, cicada calls are said to move one's heart to longing for a loved one. The pulsating, rhythmic sounds of cicadas and certain bird species are said to pulse and whirl with one's heart. Pulsing with the heartbeat, the sounds of these birds and insects set the heart to whirling as they invoke remembrances of deceased relatives or move one to pine for a lover. Cicada calls are also very hard to localize; like longings, they are hard to find a place for.

The same expressions are used to describe the pulsating duple rhythm of the bamboo percussion as it beats with one's heartbeat, and the whirling feelings in the heart during trance. This aesthetic sensibility links longing and remembrance with the pulsating sounds of bird calls, insect sounds, and the bamboo-tube stampers of ceremonial trance-dancing sessions.

Female trance-dancers also describe their participation in singing ceremonies as an intensification and culmination of longing for male spirits. We recall a Temiar woman's comment, discussed in chapter 4:

> Bərɛnlii'. It is just like *hɛwhəyaaw*. There is a male spirit of the fruits that desires to sleep with me. Even when I dream, he's there. After a while, one doesn't feel right, one's heart is shaky, one thinks only of him, one wants to go off into the jungle, one's spirit is drawn to the jungle. I must participate in a singing ceremony, only then can I stand it. We sing and dance, the male spirit of the fruit trees alights on the leaf ornaments, and I am transformed. (LBK, Pulat, 24 July 1982, FN 1822)

The content and structure of this monologue is remarkably similar to Abilem Lum's description of *hɛwhəyaaw* quoted earlier. Both monologues describe a situation of discomfort (the pounding pressure in the ear; the longing for the male fruit-tree spirit) that can only be relieved by participating in a singing/trance-dancing ceremony.

Musical activity connects humans and spiritguides: performance of songs first given in dreams manifests the spiritguides who gave them. Singing and trance-dancing ceremonies do not, however, merely function as a "stress release" when they relieve accumulated longing and discomfort. A stress release model would not explain the aesthetic elaboration, the poetics of this particular release. The Temiar, in fact, are longing for the very activity which is the release of longing; the ceremony *intensifies* the sentiment of longing in order to effect its "release." A Temiar spirit seance gets rid of longing by *playing* on it, a modulation rather than a simple evacuation. Temiars are not escaping their longings through a quick fix; instead, they move ritually into the space of desire and let themselves live with wistful sadness. Projecting the object of desire onto the spirit-world, they create a ceremony in which they can bring the spirits back to them through song and dance, momentarily fulfilling otherwise inchoate longings.

The sentiment of longing is not only phrased in terms of cross-sexual attraction among humans and spirit-entities. The longing has to do with absence, evanescence, and the unobtainably distant. Sometimes pulsating bird calls evoke longing not for a lover, but for a deceased relative. *Hɛwhəyaaw* is also the feeling evoked by a vista—a rare and moving sight for the Temiar, who are continually submerged in the denseness of tropical vegetation. The spirit-guides commonly leap across mountains and soar above the clouds; humans only glimpse the rare vista when their trails chance to lead up hills and mountains. The evanescent moment of transition and transformation during sunset evokes *bərɛnlii' bərɔlaaw* with images of coolness, black silhouette against the red glow, and greenish tints described in song texts.

LONGING IN THE LATE AFTERNOON: INSTRUMENTAL MUSIC

Many of the rainforest species whose songs evoke longing begin to call in the late afternoon, as the sun gets lower and the time of its disappearance nears. The approaching sunset itself evokes a sense of impending loss. The solo instruments are played in the late afternoon when the day's work tapers, while sitting or lying on one's mat and thinking, perhaps, of a loved one gone away. Playing a flute, bamboo-tube zither, or mouthharp at that hour allows one to *cədʉ' hənum*, 'to clear the breath or heart of remembrances', 'to free one's feelings'.[8]

The flute, in addition to being an instrument for "clearing" or "freeing" the longings of the late afternoon, is also an instrument of courtship and seduction. During the fruit season, a Temiar man might climb the fruit trees and begin to play his flute while the women cutting fruit on the ground below listen and admire. Or a woman might play the flute to attract a man's admiration and attention. A young Temiar man comments: "The custom of the flute is the custom of [courting] women," " 'adad pɛnsool, 'adad bɛ'boo'."

Longing, sadness, and courtship are the primary motivations for playing instrumental music on flutes, zithers, and mouthharps. Like the medium's songs, these songs, too, crosscut dimensions of

Plate 14. Playing a noseflute in the late afternoon.

courtship and longing; but instrumental music remains within the realm of human desires. Playing solo instruments in the late afternoon clears one's breath and heart of longing for loved ones distant or deceased, just as singing/trance-dancing ceremonies intensify and satisfy longing focused on spiritguides.

THE AESTHETICS OF SWAY:
DANCE AND MOVEMENT

Another area crosscutting dimensions of courtship and longing, as well as everyday and ceremonial aesthetics, is movement—what I call the "aesthetics of sway." A woman's swaying stroll—soft, supple, and effortless—is prized in everyday movement *and* forms the swaying dance movements that lead to trancing.

Mediums take turns singing during ceremonies, accompanied by chorus and percussion, while other participants begin to dance. These dancers may be members of the settlement, or visitors familiar with the particular genre of spirit songs being sung. While singing, mediums voicing the spiritguides are in a state of "other-awareness" or "unconsciousness" (bəralii') with their hearts elsewhere and their "eyes changed"; but they continue to control their trance and sing without fainting. Dancers, however, commence a cycle of changing or "transforming" (lɛslǫǫs) that can lead through fainting and back to consciousness.

In one genre given by the annual fruit spirits, nɔŋ tahun, dancers begin by dancing a slow, strolling-in-place movement (səpooy), bending and swaying the torso as first one arm, then the other, swings in front of the body. The dancer continues, beginning to bend more deeply, counterbalancing the bending with slight lift and wave of the arms. The dancer begins to lose her balance, her unsteadiness and shuddery stumbling marked by the term kɛnrook. When the chorus notices a stumbling dancer, they begin to push the tempo of the bamboo tubes, subdivide the duple rhythm, sing more loudly, and if possible, push their vocal range up an octave. The medium may further intensify the sounds by pitching the song higher. At a certain point, the dancer breaks her step and begins a double-footed, low-level, rapid-paced jump. The increased tempo, rhythmic subdivision, and dynamics of the tubes (termed ba-'asiil) loosely matches the soft frenzy of the dancer's jumping.

After about a minute of jumping, the dancer falls to the floor in a faint (*na-kəbʉs* 'he/she faints'). This term, used also for "death," describes simultaneous immobility and mobility: the physical body lies immobile, while the head soul is released into movement. The raised floor made from bamboo slats loosely lashed together resounds and rebounds beneath the feet of dancers, gently cushioning their falls. Fallen dancers are laid together, often placed beneath the central hanging leaf ornament. Some dancers report a total lack of sensation while fainted; others tell of hearing the sounds of singing and percussion faintly, as if from a distance, while others describe visions of soaring above the forest canopy and circling the mountain tops.

Eventually, a medium sings over the fainted dancers, shaking his hand-held leaf whisk over them. Along with the spiritguide's voice, the cool liquid form of the spirit's upper-portion soul flows through the medium. When he applies this liquid to their head and heart souls, the fainted dancers begin to stir. Participants along the sidelines, usually members of the opposite sex who are attracted to particular dancers, now enter the dance-space. With help from others, they raise the dancers to a standing position, and, supporting them around the waist (*cɛbcaab*), begin to dance them back to consciousness. A dancer, her head rolled to the side and down, limply waves her arms as she is gently lifted up and down, reminiscent of the bending and swaying in her original movements. Slowly she comes back to consciousness and begins to dance herself, her helper retreating to the sidelines. After a few minutes of strolling in place, she too retreats to the sidelines and sits. Another spectator, perhaps her helper, again expressing attraction, rolls her a cigarette. Sitting and smoking, she comes back to her "true heart" and "true eyes," and begins to "think" again (*na-nim*).

I describe the course of movements throughout the transformation process in detail because the movements are the message, they help lead us to the meanings of Temiar trance. Temiars liken the bending, swaying motions of trance-dancing to the swaying stroll of a woman walking in everyday life. The qualities of "swaying while strolling" (*lɔŋɛ'-lɔŋa'*), "softness" and "suppleness" (*pəcii'*), and "effortlessness" (*rələmah*) are prized in women's movements generally and form the supple, swaying dance movements that lead into trancing. These motions, in turn, are associated with the

Plate 15. A Temiar woman demonstrates the bending and swaying movements of trance-dancing beneath the hanging leaf ornaments (tənamuu) from the preceding night's ceremony. The leaf ornaments for the Temiar-style "Way of the Annual Fruit Trees" on the viewer's right counterbalance the leaf ornaments for the "Malay Way" on the left.

waving of palm fronds and jungle foliage in the wind. *Lɛləŋooy* 'bending', 'swaying', an expressive found in song texts and poetic speech, refers both to the quality of swaying in human movement and in windswept foliage. This imagery is doubly exploited in the "Way of the Coconut Tree." In this song, the swaying of the coconut fronds is observed and described by the spirit of the Rambutan tree.[9] On another level, the imagery refers to the swaying of trancers while they dance:

Yee' 'i-gəəl na-lɛləŋgooy,
Səpooy mənalɛh taŋɔɔy.

I sit, [the fronds] sway gently in the breeze,
The slow, strolling dance of the Young Woman Rambutan Fruit
    Spirit.

Marcel Mauss (1935/1979) writes that the "techniques of the body" are both "effective" and "traditional," or transmitted through imitation and education. The swaying movements of walking and trance-dancing, what I have called the "aesthetics of sway," are studied and intentional. The overtones of seduction are not to be lost here: in daily life, they attract other humans; in ceremonies, they entice spirits to attend. This double intention is confirmed in the layered meanings of the term *səpooy*, the name of the slow, strolling-in-place dance step that initiates and concludes the transformation cycle. *Səpooy* also describes a seductive sideways glance from the corner of downcast eyes in everyday life. It refers as well to a gently blowing breeze and the motion it excites in the leaves. This isomorphism between seductive attributes of everyday life, trance behavior, and aesthetically valued features of the rainforest environment is also apparent in another expressive, *ləlajəg-ləlajɛɛg*, which links the long and winding leaves of ceremonial ornaments with falling rain; the cool spiritual liquid of the spiritguides; and the long, wavy hair and curving body of a woman.

Like swaying movements, the fragrant and visually pleasing facepaint, leaves, and flowers decorating people and ceremonial house interiors are said to entice the presence of spiritguides. But they also please human participants. If seduction is occurring in terms of "enticement to visitation" between human trance-dancers or chorus members and ethereal spiritguides, it is also occurring between human participants of opposite sexes. A man might flirt with a female chorus member by urging her: "Sing high, it makes me go into trance." A female on the sidelines shows her favor toward a male singer by offering him a lit cigarette. Trance-dancing, involving physical contact between the sexes in some genres, circuitously allows displays of affection that are not available in the repertoire of everyday life.

Themes of community support and interdependence are also choreographed into Temiar trance-dancing. After having fainted, when the dancer begins to stir, he or she is picked up by members of the community, who dance him/her back to consciousness by physically supporting the dancer's body. This symbolic statement of interdependence is counterbalanced when community members offering support withdraw to the sidelines as the dancer shows she can now support her own weight. Yet even as the dancer dances on her own, she is surrounded by other dancers and singers who together co-create the event. The choreography recognizes the individual within the web of connections constituting a sociocentric society.

SOUL LOSS

The sentiment of longing is transformed into a momentarily satisfying communion between trancer and spirit-entity when properly channeled within the context of trance-dancing ceremonies. Trancers speak of weightless, refreshed feelings experienced the day after trancing. But the coherence of a cultural system is incompletely grasped unless we investigate the ways that system can be disrupted. What happens when longing is not fulfilled, when the pull on one's soul is exacerbated rather than relieved? This situation, in various forms, is the basis for much of Temiar illness.

Soul loss (*rɛywaay* < *rəwaay* 'head soul') is the prolonged absence of the head soul during the waking state, as opposed to the temporary detachment of the head soul during dreaming or trancing (see Benjamin 1967a:138–140; also, chapter 5 of this text). This occurs when the head soul of a plant, a river spirit, a mountain spirit, or the like takes an interest in a person who has passed by, disturbed, or offended it. The entity's upper-portion soul entices the person's head soul to take up residence with it in the jungle, swiddens, or wherever it has its home.

Soul loss, as an illness category, can be understood within a semantic network as an idiom of distress, an "image which draws together a network of symbols, situations, motives, feelings and stresses which are rooted in the structural setting" (Good 1977:48) in which Temiars live, suspended between the often contradictory tendencies of connection and separability. The soul loss complex devolves around the detachability of human head souls and their predisposition toward entering into relationships of varying degrees with the head souls of other entities. A temporary connection maintains the level of intimacy, ensuring that it does not become overwhelming. In trance and spirit-mediumship, these relationships are temporally and spatially limited to the dream and ritual frame; in illness, the connection exceeds temporary bounds and becomes overwhelming.

ETIOLOGY: In one of many soul loss cases I followed, Angah, a young Temiar man living in his wife's village, went hunting with a rifle. He shot the rifle near some cliffs, causing the sound to reverberate. For two days he grew increasingly listless, sleeping excessively, losing his appetite, and becoming depressed. The first two days he treated himself with Panadol and vitamin C, to no avail. Through discussion among community members coupled with revelations in a medium's dream, it was determined that his head soul had gone off with the sound of the rifle and been taken by the female spirit of the mountain, who had been awakened by the sound. On the third day of his illness, he sent for the spirit-mediums.

TREATMENT: Two mediums were called to Angah's house. They treated him by sucking and blowing on the areas where the soul resides: the crown of the head and the heart. After one of the mediums, Penghulu Abeh, treated Angah, the medium slept and dreamt that his head soul met the patient's head soul in a garden of flowers replete with a house where a female crest soul of the mountain had taken the patient. Silently, the medium grabbed Angah by the hand and whisked him downriver before circling upriver toward their home settlement, choosing this circuitous route to evade subsequent forays by the female mountain spirit.

The next three nights, I observed the two mediums as together they held singing ceremonies for Angah. This allowed the medium Penghulu Abeh to return the patient's soul in the ritual realm as he had done in the dream realm. Imbued with the power of their spiritguides while in the register of singing ceremonies, the two mediums blew cool liquid *kahyɛk* into the head and heart soul of the patient, reshaping and strengthening the position of the patient's newly returned head soul.

Soul loss cases such as this one characteristically show four stages: (1) separation of the person's head soul; (2) relocation of the head soul in a new "home"; (3) a medium seeks and finds the head soul; and (4) the medium replaces the head soul into the person's crown. In Angah's case, as is typical, the relocation of his head soul in a new home involved cross-sexual attraction with the female spirit of a mountain. Here, longing has gone awry—the mutual enticement between spiritguides and humans has overstepped the bounds of dream and ritual, becoming a prolonged and unrelenting bond. This situation is even clearer in the following case of *təwiiŋ*, a variant of soul loss in which not merely the head soul but one's physical body is drawn to walk alone in the jungle.

ETIOLOGY: Biyɛh is a divorcee with seven daughters. She has trouble eating and sleeping. She often wanders off alone into the jungle.

TREATMENT: The medium Balɛh Kənaseh traces Biyɛh's illness to the attraction of a young male spirit of the fruits. If she could trance-dance, she could meet him under the proper ceremonial auspices and not need to wander off into the jungle. However, whenever she tries to trance-dance, she becomes embarrassed and is unable to go through the ritual transformation and spiritguide connection. The medium's treatment is therefore oriented toward initiating her into successful trance-dancing. During ceremonies he ministers to her, blowing *kahyɛk* from the spiritguides into her body in hopes that she will learn to trance.

In Biyɛh's case, appropriately contextualized trance-connection with a cross-sexual spiritguide is clearly juxtaposed with the inappropriate, extra-ritual connection with the male spirit of the fruit—an excess of longing drawing her to walk off into the jungle.

In another variant of the soul loss complex, *na-bərahii'* ('it draws', 'it falls passionately in love with' > Malay *raih*, 'to draw towards oneself'; *berahi* 'passionate'), fruit- and flower-spirits take a liking to people as they pass by collecting fruits and flowers. These entities both insert their "essence" into people and draw people's souls off into the jungle. Involvement with these spirit-entities during trance-dancing ceremonies which is "misunderstood" or incorrectly performed by participants also leads to this dialectical intrusion/drawing-of-the-soul by the activated spiritguides.

I witnessed treatment of four afflicted females involving extraction of the essence of the male Perah fruit tree. After releasing a sticky sap of Perah drawn from an afflicted woman toward the suspended ceremonial leaf ornament, a medium commented:

> Now I have returned the sap to Perah itself. Sometimes I give the sap to someone else to feel, because the preceding person from whom I extracted it didn't understand it. If this next person is also unknowledgeable, that person will also become ill. If I don't give the sap to someone else, I return it to Perah itself. (Balɛh Kənaseh, Pulat, 23 July 1982, FN 1821)

This contrast between the knowledgeable and the unknowledgeable illustrates again the difference between the controlled attraction and longing of trance and the excessive situation of illness. During trance-dancing ceremonies, the sentiment of longing is focused and released. The illnesses of soul loss, situations of excessive longing, are best treated in the context of singing/trance-dancing ceremonies since these are the contexts in which controlled relations with the spirit-world are possible. But how are these ceremonies capable of effecting such relations and transformations?

MUSICAL FORM, EMOTION, AND MEANING

During ceremonial performances, sentiments are modulated by sounds that have been imbued with networks of association. Sounds meaningfully situated activate emotions of longing, prompting their focus and release in the context of ceremonial performance. The call of the cicada *hɛrɲɔɔd* evokes sentiments of longing in Temiars. The formal structure of this sound exhibits a two-toned pulsation alternating between high and low frequencies (see sonogram, figure 4). The call of the golden-throated barbet, *cɛp təwaal* (*Megalaima franklini*), also considered to evoke sentiments of longing, has a similar two-toned pulsation structure alternating between lower and higher frequencies (see sonogram, figure 5).

These two-toned pulsating sounds are said to beat in rhythm with one's heart, thus moving the heart to longing for a loved one or a deceased relative. The continuous sound of the bamboo percussion in singing/trance-dancing ceremonies is socially structured as a two-toned pulsation alternating between lower and higher frequencies (see sonogram, figure 6). The sound is produced by a pair of bamboo tubes struck in alternation against a log. The pair consists of a shorter tube, producing the higher sound, and a longer tube producing the lower sound. Drumming, when it accompanies the ceremonies, follows the two-toned pulsation pattern of the bamboo tubes.

In performance, the continuous two-toned sound of the bamboo-tube percussion, structurally similar to the barbet and cicada calls, is also said to move with one's heart, focusing and intensifying longing to effect the transformation of trance and spiritguide connection. The shorter bamboo tube is termed "mother" (*boo'*), the longer, "father" (*bəəh*). When the mother and father tubes are beat in contiguous alternation, their sounds differentiate yet conjoin the male and female domain. Structurally in their two-toned pulsation, the sounds move the heart to longing; metaphorically, they replicate the momentary association of male and female which exemplifies the cross-sexual connection with spiritguides.[10]

I first became aware of the cultural value placed on pulsing sounds of the rainforest when sitting around the fire with a group of Temiar women after a morning spent working in the rice fields. One of the women mentioned a bird song she had heard, how it had moved with her heart and made her feel longing. I scribbled down the name of the bird, and asked the women if there were other sounds that made them feel similarly. They listed several, including the golden-throated barbet and the cicada *hɛrɲɔɔd*, whose songs pulsed with their hearts. I had gone to the rainforest

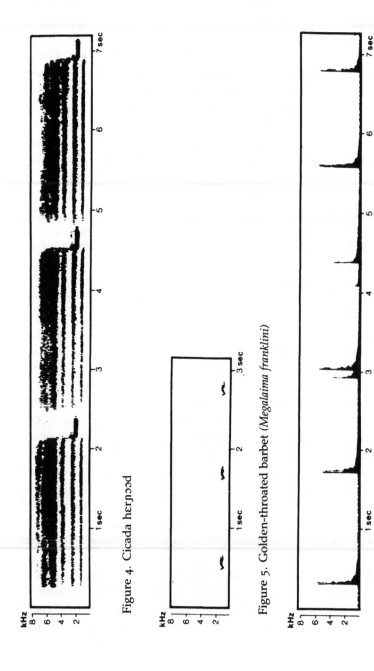

Figure 4. Cicada herpodd

Figure 5. Golden-throated barbet (*Megalaima franklini*)

Figure 6. Bamboo-tube stampers (One pair; alternation begins with higher-pitched tube)

with the necessary equipment for recording natural sounds, including parabola and shotgun mike, which Temiars jokingly termed my blowpipe. I began to notice that when I played back the recorded sounds for identification and discussion, the arioso bird songs I found so compelling, given my culture's melodic orientation, were of less interest to my Temiar listeners. They responded, rather, to the pulsating calls of several species. I also noted references in song texts to the calls of these species and the feelings they evoked. The bamboo tubes of singing ceremonies, ceremonial participants commented, similarly moved with their hearts and made them feel longing.

The pulsing beat of the bamboo tubes is an iconic sign in that it gains its meaning through the association of similar forms: the continuous two-toned beating of hearts, certain bird and insect calls, and the percussive rhythm of the tubes. As an iconic sign, it brings together sounds of the rainforest and sounds of the body and links these with a theory of selves and spirits that can be loosened and rebound. Anchoring themes of gender, boundaries, and interconnection in natural and physiological forms, the sounds of the bamboo tubes resemble Turner's dominant symbols (1967:28) which pack their affective power through the simultaneous condensation of physiological and ideological poles. The Beckers (1981) suggest that a symbol gains legitimacy and authority to the extent that it is rooted in a culture's concept of the "natural" and thus the "true"; this rootedness through similar form they term "iconicity." The beating of Temiar tubes gains affective power through its rootedness in the rainforest and the body as these are culturally transformed into signs and symbols. Daniel highlights the polychromy or multimodality of the sign, reminding us that "iconic as well as indexical aspects may be concealed within the same sign" (1984:39). To the extent that the meaning of the bamboo tubes is rooted in the body and thus contiguous with that which it signs, it also has an indexical aspect.

The iconic relation between heartbeat and bamboo-tube percussion is not merely operative on the level of biological entrainment or auditory driving as some authors have suggested when exploring the role of music in trance induction. Neher (1961, 1962), for example, suggests that drumming at certain tempi prompts auditory driving, biologically entraining brain waves and thus inducing trance. The evocative power of these sounds, however, lies in the way they are imbued with meaning and interpreted by participants. The linkage of beating tubes, pulsing hearts, and moving spirits is culturally mediated, driven by an ethnopsychology that locates emotion and memory, longing and nostalgia in the heart. Blacking (1985) argues that "the effectiveness of musical symbols depends as much on human agency and social context, as on the structure of the symbols themselves." Formal structure and social content, when interrelated, render music effective (Blacking 1985:66).

Surveying the astonishing variety of musical forms accompanying trance ceremonies around the world, Rouget (1977*a*, 1980) suggests that from within a given society's musical repertoire, certain musical genres and formal musical features are particularly categorized and valued as trance-related. These valued musical forms, then, do not so much precipitate as "socialise trance" (Rouget 1977*b*), marking contexts and moments appropriate for participating in trance behavior.

In such a manner, barbet and cicada calls—pulsing like the heart, hidden in the dense jungle foliage, persistent yet unobtainable—become culturally marked and valued. These sounds, socially reconstructed in the patterned sounds of ceremonial percussion, intensify longing focused on the spirits. When joined with a cosmological theory that posits detachable interactive selves and images songs as paths, and when joined with swaying movements that entice the spirits, the sounds set the cosmos in motion and effect the transformation of Temiar trance, a momentary intermingling of self and other.

When the pulsing bamboo tubes metaphorically "move with the heart" to evoke longing, the unsettling sentiment of longing is transformed into a momentarily satisfying communion between trancer and spirit-entity properly channeled within the ceremonial context. Singing/trance-dancing ceremonies exemplify dialectically balanced interactions with the spirits. For Temiars, the working cosmos is not a static balance, but a dynamic conjunction in alternation that is present in the continuous pulse of low "male" and high "female" tubes, the strolling sway of a dancer or the undulation of leaves in the wind. The aesthetic texture of the ceremony celebrates the momentary balancing of intimacy between spirit and human, self and other, male and female; it is thus the appropriate context in which to treat a patient whose interaction with the animated world has ceased to fluctuate and thus exceeds proper bounds. By gathering members of the community together in dance and song to periodically resituate their relationships with the spirit-world, preventive measures are taken to avoid the excess of unfulfilled desire that can lead to soul loss. And by situating a patient whose interaction with the world has become imbalanced, whose soul roams the jungle in search of a spirit-mate, in the midst of the balanced interactions of ceremonial performance, treatment is effected.

7

Songs of a Spirited World

"If I know a song of Africa . . .," Karen Blixen wrote after spending time in the Ngong Hills of Kenya, "does Africa know a song of me?"

> Would the air over the plain quiver with a colour that I had had on, or the children invent a game in which my name was, or the full moon throw a shadow over the gravel of the drive that was like me, or would the eagles of Ngong look out for me? (Dinesen 1937/1972:79)

If I know a song of the Malayan rainforest, does the rainforest or its people know a song of me? As I make sense of, record, and remember the Temiar and their world, how are they making sense of, remembering me? Certainly, history is written in many forms, and archives take many shapes.[1]

We are often so busy watching the people we are studying that we forget they, too, are watching and listening to us. Dialogic anthropology reminds us that ethnography occurs in that intersubjective space between the ethnographer and the people studied, just as culture exists in the intersubjective realm of imperfectly shared expectations and communications (Tedlock 1983; Bakhtin 1981; Mannheim and Tedlock i.p.). Ethnography, and all interaction, occurs not between a subject and an object, but arises from the meeting of two or more agents interacting in particular settings, just as the sound of a piano emerges not from one pin or the other but from the piano wire stretched between, which further resonates with the soundboard. We engage one another, turning each other into memory in our cultural engravings, inscribing each other in our respective forms of discourse: the Temiar in their historiography of song, me with my field notes, tape recorder, and publications.

Temiar songs embody the collective memory of a people, individualized by particular mediums. Individual dream connections with variegated spiritguides place a value on personal revelation; Temiar musical historiography thus encompasses individual variations and experience within a general form in a manner congruent with a diffuse, egalitarian political organization. The songs mark the natural and social landscape of the people, naming it, locating it in time and place, in history. During singing ceremonies, mediums place patients suffering from soul loss into the midst of these songs. These patients' souls are described as being dislocated, excessively detached and fragmented, the Temiar metaphorical equivalent to our "out of sorts" or "not quite myself." Such patients are surrounded by songs generated by community participation.

The community's ceremony celebrates differences as well as similarities: different mediums call on different spiritguides, whereas the dynamics of the spiritguide/medium relationship remain similar; performance roles of initial singer and choral response coordinate different genders who repeat similar song texts and melodies, their heterophonic sounds differentiating while overlapping. Such an enactment realizes what sociologist Iris Young (1986) has described as a "politics of difference," through which communities recognize their differences as an integral part of their commonality. In ethnomusicological terms, this is what Charles Keil (1987) calls a "participatory discrepancy": that space of difference that allows a jazz player to lean into the beat, a musician to add his or her sounds to a musical production, or listeners to actively participate in the event.[2] In this environment, the Temiar patient's dislocated and fragmented components of self are relocated in his body, the patient situated within the sociocentric community, the differentiated individual reintegrated within the textured fabric of the social whole.

Expressive culture records, helps makes sense of, and attempts to accommodate social and technological changes. By emphasizing individual revelation, Temiar musical historiography can incorporate new items, people, and events. The system is thus highly adaptive, enabling Temiars to call upon the spirits of old mountains and new wristwatches, rainforest birds and parachutes, connecting them with the past while moving them into the future.[3] Temiars strive to maintain a delicate balance between upriver "things of the jungle" and downriver "things of the market." When the medium Abilem performs "Malay-type" singing ceremonies, for example, he offsets "Malay" ceremonial leaf ornaments with "Temiar" leaf ornaments so his jungle fruit Rambutan Spirit "won't get jealous." (See plate 15.)

Most Temiars suggest that as long as there is enough rainforest for them to carry on their traditional subsistence forms of hunting, gathering, and horticulture so that they can continue their traditional relationship with the land, moving through it and hearing it speak and sing, then new items and innovations will not disrupt their combined economic, cosmological, philosophical, and aesthetic system. Where the balance between innovation and tradition is lost, illness occurs. For example, Temiars currently wear wristwatches, but they follow their own sense of how time should be used. To work nine-to-five daily, as they have sometimes done when employed by the government or the timber industry, rather than alternating concentrated periods of work with periods of rest as is their traditional pattern, brings illness, they say.[4] Similarly, when the land, its flora and fauna are treated disrespectfully, the spirits are offended and may cause illness. Such reasoning is becoming more familiar in Western scientific practice, in environmental toxicology and resource management, for example, as we experience how the environment "strikes back" when mistreated.

The Temiars have observed that when too many people are gathered together in a settlement on a main river, as occurs in some aboriginal resettlement projects promoted by the Malaysian government for development and security reasons, or as rainforest acreage is decreased by logging, then too much "heat" and subsequently, illness, is generated. A similar recognition of the interconnections between social life, political economy, and bodily processes is resurfacing in the Western cosmopolitan tradition in works such as Kleinman's *Illness Narratives* (1989). The Temiar phrase the impact of macro-political, economic, and social forces upon the microcosmos of bodily function (and dysfunction) in terms of interactive spirits. They also phrase macro- and microcosmic interrelations in the complementary oppositions between downriver and upriver, between the heat of the clearing and the coolness of the jungle, evidenced in the positive value placed on the cool healing liquid *kahyɛk*.[5] Could it be coincidental, one wonders, that game is more abundant and the water cleaner when the population is dispersed upriver along the tributaries (without other settlements further upstream using the water supply), rather than congregated in larger groups along the main rivers or at river mouths as recent development and security policy urges? In their traditional oppositions between hot and cool, crowded and dispersed, downriver development and upriver jungle, Temiars translate pragmatic, empirical observations into symbolic terms. Their cosmology enshrines an indigenous cultural ecology.

Temiars locate themselves in their surroundings by positioning themselves in social relations of kinship both with humans and, through dream encounters, with the interactive spirits of their environment. These positions are reiterated each time they address one another, using terms such as "sister's husband" or "mother of Asɔɔd." In their dreams, they establish kinship relations with spirits who emerge, identify themselves, and give the gift of song. Receipt of a dream song from a spiritguide marks the pivotal moment in the development of mediums and healers. The song, sung during a ceremonial performance by the medium and an interactive female chorus, links medium, chorus, trance-dancers, and patients as they "follow the path" of the spiritguide. When the ceremony concludes, spirits and humans "return home" (*mɛ'maa'*) to their respective abodes.

Dreamed encounters and the songs received therein consolidate the Temiars' relationship to their environment, situating them within a known universe. Singing charts a path, a welcome phenomenon in the dense rainforest environment. Illness, so often conceived by Temiars as the dislocation of an essential component of self such as a head soul, is treated when mediums activate their links with the land through song. Mediums are singers of the landscape who counterbalance the dislocation of illness with the "true names" of locations in their songs.

While studying with the Temiar, I quickly learned that unknown quantities must be placed within a known context to avoid the dangers of such dislocation. When I first arrived in the village of Lambok, a group of Temiars, including the headman Penghulu Dalam, asked me who I was in relation to the anthropologist who had preceded me by about fifteen years, Geoffrey Benjamin. "He is my friend, my colleague," I told them, using the Malay word *kawan* 'friend' at that early stage before I could speak and comprehend Temiar. Geoffrey and I had corresponded before I went into the field; he had been wonderfully gracious and welcoming and had told me to be sure and visit several residents from the village of Humid, now living in Lambok, whom he had found particularly welcoming and informative. I tried to explain our relationship to the Temiars, but the category of "friend" did not place me securely enough to avoid the unease felt by these members of a small-scale society where nearly everyone is referred to by kinship terms and teknonyms (see Benjamin 1968*a*).

"Who is Taa' Jamin (Old Man Benjamin) to you?" several of my Temiar hosts repeated.

"My adopted father," I finally responded in exasperation, hoping that Geoffrey would forgive my presumptuousness.

"Well, in that case, since Taa' Jamin was Penghulu Dalam's younger brother, then you are Penghulu Dalam's daughter, which would make you Awɛŋ's younger sister, and Asɔɔd's mother," and so on.

They had worked me into their system, made sense out of my presence, located me in their world of actions modulated by kinship relations by doing my geneaology, just as I would do theirs in the days and months to come.

Nearly a year later, while transcribing song texts upriver at the settlement of Bəlau, I began to find the word *Tɛtəjɔɔy* appearing. Talking with a group of men about the details of a ceremony held weeks before, the group had chuckled, comparing my line of questioning to the hunter's arrow in pursuit of its prey. *Tɛtəjɔɔy*, they had called me, using an expressive term to describe the arching yet directed, goal-oriented yet happenstance path of the ethnographer's quest and the hunter's arrow. Now I was hearing this word in song texts.

"That is the name the medium's spiritguide gave to you in a dream," some of the women explained to me. I realized they had known it for a few weeks, and I was only just catching on. Later, in a translation session with the medium who had received the dream song, the medium told me that the spirit of one of the fruiting trees had indeed seen me dancing, and given me the name *Tɛtəjɔɔy*. Had I entered Temiar historiography through the medium's song, just as Temiars' life histories were now inscribed in my notebooks? The English, Malays, Japanese, airplanes, and parachutes had found their way into Temiar songs; had I too? Would some ethnographer later record this song, translate the text, collect the dream narrative that describes the circumstances leading to the song's composition, as I had done for so many Temiar songs, and hear a story of that tall light-skinned woman with a nose like an arrow, who danced during ceremonies? That name, in the collective memories of the Temiars of Bəlau, when it resounds in their songs through the Malayan rainforest, preserves their memory of me.

THE BODY AS NEXUS

The body is a powerful locus for articulating ideas and actions pertaining to environment, society, and self, since it is the nexus where the biology meets culture, where the individual meets society. As Lock notes:

> There is, of course, a biological reality, but the moment that efforts are made to explain, order, and manipulate that reality, then a process of contextualization takes place in which the dynamic relationship of biology with cultural values and the social order has to be considered (1988:7).

The body is the medium through which self is engaged with other. It is a reference point for our isolation and for our connection. For Temiars, this dynamic is played out in the tension between bounded souls and detached spirits, between maintaining the integrity of self and extolling the interactive, sociocentric self.

In their thoughtful essay, "The Mindful Body," Scheper-Hughes and Lock (1987) distinguish three analytical constructs: the individual body, the social body, and the body politic. The *individual body* concerns the embodied self as it exists apart from and in relation to other bodies; for Temiars, this is a multiple and sociocentric self, capable of merging with other selves in dreams, ritual, and illness, yet carefully cushioned to help maintain its integrity in other interactive contexts. The *social body* develops Mary Douglas's ideas (1966, 1970) on the representative uses of the body as a natural symbol with which to think about nature, society, and culture. The relationship between pulsating sounds of rainforest birds and insects, the rhythms of bamboo tubes in healing ceremonies, human heartbeats, and the emotion of longing constitutes such a symbol, iconic in its use of formal resemblances to draw disparate domains into a meaningful relationship, indexical in its contiguous use of the body as a signifier.[6]

The *body politic* entails the regulation, surveillance and control of bodies. "Cultures," the authors argue, "are disciplines that provide codes and social scripts for the domestication of the individual body in conformity to the needs of the social and political order" (Scheper-Hughes and Lock 1987:26). Temiars, socialized to cooperate and reciprocate, are taught that illness comes from harsh words and broken contracts, from "things" withheld or mistreated, by listening to on-the-spot explanations and after-the-fact diagnostic discussions. As children, they learn that fear and flight are valued, not hostility and aggression. Historical studies of Muslim Malay enslavement of "pagan" Orang Asli, a practice that extended into the late nineteenth century, indicate that the socialization of fear and attendant strategies of flight may have been adaptive responses to encroaching Malay settlement and slave-raiding (Jones 1968:289; Roseman 1980; Kirk Endicott 1983).

Temiars partake of an elaborate code of etiquette that encourages them to avoid being startled, which may lead to detachment of self.[7] Their intimate interactions with the landscape and its flora and fauna lead them to posit a universe resonant with being. They learn to move through the landscape carefully in hopes that it might awaken in the whirling spirits of singing ceremonies rather than in the whipping winds of thunderstorms.

The body is both the work of culture and culture at work. The Temiar concept of upper and lower selves, shared by humans and all other entities of their universe, demonstrates culture at work in the body. In this homology, Temiar recognize that body, social order, and cosmological order are interwoven like a cloth, to draw on an analogy from Barthes and Kristeva.[8] For Temiars, the perception of association between body, society, and cosmos is heightened in the contexts of dreams and ritual performance, when spiritguides take human form to speak and sing with their human companions. It is no coincidence that a "paradigm of embodiment" (Csordas 1990), with an emphasis on experience and practice, is emerging as anthropological theory combines studies of symbolism and practice in processual analysis;[9] indeed, the study of performance is a study of the socially informed body (Bourdieu 1977), of culture worked and working, of symbols in action.

The musical transformation of human speech into spiritguide's song signals that the healing ritual is indeed a reconfigured realm. In singing and trance-dancing ceremonies, the body moves within an expanded social universe, a cosmos in motion. Time is restructured in the beating of the bamboo tubes, which metaphorically draw the human heartbeat into their duple rhythm as high-pitched "mother" and low-pitched "father" tube beat in alternation, conjoining male and female. The ceremonial house is filled with fragrant jungle foliage; this is a place and time where forest spirits and human selves can interact. The ritual reframing of reality and the consequent personal and cosmological transformations it facilitates are hardly limited to the Temiar case, but may indeed constitute a universal property of healing ceremonies, though the particular sets of associations that render them effective are grounded in local knowledge. In this context, where colors, odors, sounds, and movements are reconfigured, a patient can move from illness to health.

ENSOULING THE WORLD

> I imagine myself today something like the ancient Greek as Hegel describes him: he interrogated, Hegel says, passionately, uninterruptedly, the rustle of branches, of springs, of winds, in short, the shudder of Nature, in order to perceive in it the design of an intelligence. And I—it is the shudder of meaning I interrogate, listening to the rustle of language, that language which for me, modern man, is my Nature.
>
> Roland Barthes, *The Rustle of Language*

To understand the process of singing to heal, I have examined Temiar musical performance, affect, and composition processes, asking where songs come from and what they do. I have examined illness etiology, categorization, and treatment, asking where illness comes from, and how one responds to it. Using the healing performance as a point of entry, I saw how Temiar musical and medical knowledge and practice are pervaded by a value system, an ethos or sensibility that intricately interconnects Temiar concepts of self and society, human and cosmos, male and female. When Temiars sing and play bamboo tubes during healing ceremonies, the sounds and movements performed by members of the community give symbolic form to a fundamental sensibility that is experienced in many other dimensions: in everyday relations with the potentially animated environment, in the subsistence practices of hunter-horticulturalists moving through an acoustically rich rainforest environment, in a diffuse political organization that coordinates through persuasion, and an economic exchange of generalized reciprocity.

As I prepared to leave the Temiar after nearly two years of living among them, they also prepared me for my reentry into a world of jostling landrovers and car horns, a world they were convinced was as set on causing startle as they were set on trying to avoid it, a world into which they enter and interact with care. While I worked my way downriver towards the lowlands, mediums in each village performed ceremonies to strengthen my head and heart souls for the assaults to come. "There will be longing tomorrow," one sang in his song texts, "No more singing and trance-dancing tomorrow." Several Temiars cautioned me not to promise when I might return, so that they not be left in the unfulfilled state of *pərɛnhɔɔd* should I not fulfill my word.

I returned to the pigeons and sirens of the urban landscape and surrounded myself with tall pines and old oaks of the eastern United States while writing. I was alternately filled with images of the magnificently dense rainforest and of clearcuts I had seen in areas of Malaysia. What kind of landscape will enable us to resonate with it? Can we find healing sounds in the city, in the drums of Cuban and Puerto Rican *santería* ceremonies held in New York City and Miami, in our tape and record collections, in our concert and jam sessions, in the engine's roar or a nearby stream, or must we take to the country to hear the spirits sing? Are groups such as the Art Ensemble of Chicago our "Urban Bushmen," as their album title suggests, glorifying in sound the spirit of the urban community? Even if the soundscape of each type of environment can potentially resonate in its residents' musics, it is still imperative that we ensure the diversity of environments and associated cultural adaptations to those environments—of which the musical and healing arts are but a part. For diversity promotes survival; diversity is the very basis from which the processes of selection and adaptation proceed (Wilson and Peters 1988; Wilson 1989).

Art forms are shaped by, and give shape to, the cultures from which they emerge. This is what Geertz means when he writes that art forms "are meaningful because they connect with a sensibility they join in creating" (1983:101), that "such a sensibility is essentially a collective formation, and that the foundations of such a formation are as wide as social existence and as deep" (99). The term "sensibility" is particularly apt, for it simultaneously refers to the cognitive, affective, and sensate. Music is heard, thought, and felt, just as the experience of illness combines the conceptual, emotional, and sensate. When Temiars beat bamboo tubes or sing the way of a spiritguide with interactive choral overlap, they are giving form to a cultural configuration that links ritual and everyday life, a sensibility that posits a world "ensouled" (Hillman 1982) and charts strategies for bringing the potentially spirited world out of suspended animation in some contexts, while putting it back in place in others. Temiars are listening to the rustle of language in the world around them; they structure their ceremonies to participate in that rustle, to celebrate the shared terms of bird songs or insect calls, bamboo tubes, and heart beats. The music of the beating tubes mediates between the rainforest's pulsing sounds and the body's beating heart, bringing nature spirits into conjunction with the human spirit, collapsing the boundaries between nature and culture. But even in their celebration, as Temiars bring the cosmological into the performative dimension (Tambiah 1977), they confine the ritual within boundaries of time and space—in house, between sun down and sun up, in the temporal patterns of the bamboo-tube stampers—to give order to a world so resonant with being.

The healing sounds of Temiar ceremonies make sense when they are situated in the social world of ideas and actions from which they arise and in which they become an "affecting presence" (Armstrong 1971; 1981). Temiar musical and medical practices are part of the same social fabric. From Boas's early definition of culture, which redirected anthropological theory away from evolutionary extraction and comparison of isolated cultural traits toward an examination of the integrative dimensions of culture, to interpretive anthropology, which uses the language of "coherence systems" to address the way culture is experienced as meaningfully ordered, even in its disorder, anthropologists have examined the interrelations among cultural elements.[10] The power of healing performances emerges from the shared assumptions guiding Temiar musical composition, performance, and affect, on the one hand, and indigenous cosmology, dynamics of illness and health, and the composition of the person, on the other. As we move analytically between Temiar cultural constructions of illness and health, and the "humanly organized sounds" (Blacking 1973) of healing ceremonies, we discover the cultural logic whereby aesthetic configurations participate in a comprehensive pattern of reality and become therapeutically effective.[11] With the body as a nexus, the gestures of trance conflate movements of the rainforest and movements of humans, the vocalized songs of mediums give rainforest spirits human voices, the bamboo tubes metaphorically overlay insect calls and beating human hearts. The language of humans and the language of forest spirits rustle, for a moment, together.

Appendix A:
Temiar Transliterations

TRANSLITERATIONS FOR CHAPTER 3, BECOMING A HEALER:

DREAM NARRATIVE: AŊAH BUSUU', KELYET, 22-II-82, DN45

1. AB:[1] Na' lah. Mɛntərii' Jɛlmɔl 'i-na' lah 'i-gabag. Kahyɛk. Kahyɛk mɛntərii' 'i-gabag nɔŋ num-tii' 'amɛs yɛh. 'ɛrnɔɔr bəəh yɛh, rɛ'na' na-'ɔɔr, na-pɔ' na-'ɔɔr 'i-gabag ma-mɛntərii'. Na' bəəh yɛh.

Mɛntərii' Jɛlmɔl. Na' cə-cee', Mɛntərii' Jɛlmɔl 'anɔ' Bərintəəh [MMB] 'ɛn-teh. Bərintəəh 'ɛncob gɛ' Tambɯn. Bərintəəh, mɛn Caldaaw, mɛn Tamaay, na' lah 'ɛncob. Na' lah Bərintəəh 'i-gabag na'. Na' yee' halaa' num-tii' 'amɛɛr yeh 'i-pɔ' ma-na-na' mulaa' bərɛnkah.

Ya-ciib yoot. Ya-ciib ma-jɛlmɔl 'a-tɛɛ', jɛlmɔl na-na', na' 'i-tɛ'lɛ' ha-tɔp. Lɔɔ' 'i-tɛ'lɛ' ha-top, na-na'. Na' num-'ɛnlaak.

2. M: 'e-lo' kɛnɯɯh jɛlmɔl ha-ciib?

3. AB: Bərintəəh. 'ə-na' 'i-rii' (hɔj) 'i-deeh na'. Rii' 'a-tɛɛ' na', kɛnɯɯh 'əh. Tataa' Bərintəəh 'a-tɛɛ'.

4. M: Ləpas na'?

5. AB: Na-jal na-ney sɛn'ɔɔy ha-tɔp Bərintəəh.

6. M: ɲob-ley ɲam, ɲob-dɛmdəp?

7. AB: Ya-dɛmdəp. Dɛ'rii' yah na' lah. Tɔ' bə-ləbih. Dɛ'rii' yaar ya-dɛmdəp. Na-səluh ɲam, ya-rɛnrɛc sɔɔj. Yəəl, nɛɛh, kɛrlɯ' na-selɔg na-pɔ'.

8. M: Bəəh hah?

9. AB: Həə', bəəh 'i-na' na-pɔ'. Pɔ' 'i-bəəh 'i-na' [FaAB], pɔ' yee' kuwɛ̧ɛ̧s [AB], ya-yoot ya-pɛ'pɔ'.

[1] AB = Angah Busuu', the narrator; MMB = Minister of Mount Bərintəəh; FaAB = Father of Angah Busuu'; M = Marina Roseman.

10. M: Yoot.

11. BA: Həə', yaar yoot ya-pɔ' layɛg na'. Tɛhnuh gɔb na' "mimpi."
Mimpi yaar yoot. Jadii' ya-pɔ' yah-yoot kah baraŋkalii' na-'ɔɔr na'
'i-na-na' [MMB].
　　"Həə',"
na-roo' [MMB],
　　"Hɔy, 'i-jɛk ma-hą̄' bəəh hah.
　　Ma-bəəh 'i-jɛk, 'i-hǫǫd ma-kəwą̄s ha-doh.
　　'im-bar-bəəh ma kəwą̄s hah.
　　Ma-hą̄h 'im-kɔw yaak yeh.
　　Rɛ'na' yaak 'i-kɔw ma-hah,
　　ma-kəwą̄s ha-doh 'im-bar-bəəh.
　　Rɛ'na'."
[FaAb]: Bolɛh lah, ha-lo'."

Jadii' cɛɛg yee' 'i-pɔ'
na-roo' 'i-rii' 'əh ma-tataa' na'
na-'ɔɔr,
　　"Yee' 'i-hǫǫd na-na',
　　'i-jɛk ma-na-na'
　　'i-hǫǫd ma-hą̄',"
ma-yee' na-tuh, 'i-pɔ' yee' na'.
Na-'ɔɔr lah. Kɛw! Na-gabag.
'i-'ɔɔr yee' [MMB]:
　　"Ham-gabag, 'ɛ-roo', bolɛh."
[AB responds]:
　　"Ha-hǫǫd 'im-gabag?"
[MMB answers]:
　　"Həə'. 'i-hǫǫd. 'ɛ-rooh yee' 'i-hǫǫd."
Na-gabag gənabag doh lah. Gabag kiraa' naar ɲaag na-gabag 'i-
hǫǫh 'i-wad. 'i-wad habis na' hɔj naar langkah nɛ' langkah 'i-wad,
habis lah 'i-lɛk 'a-deh. 'i-maa' ma-deek, 'i-bə-gabag 'ɛ-sərɛgyɔɔg,
'ay'aag 'i-paaw yeh bə-halaa' lah, yi-sɛ'soo' lah ma-baboo' bar-kəd,
ma-papəət bar-tɛŋɔr kuy 'i-sə'soo' bə-jampii':
　　　　　　　　[softly] "jɛg-jɛg-jɛg-jɛg."
Lɔɔy doh, paay sɛ'noo' 'a-tɛɛ' 'i-kɛdkɔɔd hɔj 'i-tataa' doh. 'i- gabag
'a-tɛɛ' mɛn-bungaa' 'a-tɛɛ' paay.

12. M: Na' pərtamaa'?

13. AB: Na-na' pərtamaa' yaŋ mulaa' 'əh.

14. Girl from chorus: Na-na' mulaa' 'aluŋ.

15. AB: Həə', mulaa' 'aluŋ 'ə-na' na-na'.

DREAM NARRATIVE: ADING KERAH, Rəlɔɔy, 10-vi-82, DN5

Na-kɔɔd rəwaay baboo' mənalɛh Rangwɛ̗ɛ̗y, na-kɔɔd rəwaay babəəh jɛlmɔl Galɛɛŋ, nam-səlɔg nam-'ɛn ma-rɛh. Kɛnʉʉh baboo' na' Səleŋɔɔy. Jadii' na-'ɛn ma-rɛh, na-tɛrgəl səhiŋgaa' naar miŋguu', na-tɛrgəl naar miŋguu', na-tɛrmaa' num-rɛh. Na-tɛrmaa' ma-rɛh,

mɔ' nɛ' kolam, gool, deek mɛrgəəh (hɔj ma-bəəh; ma-yee' hɔy, tɔ' na-tə'ɛl lo'-lo').

Ləpas na' na-tɛrmaa' num-rɛh, baruu' na-tuh ma-rəwaay yeh, na-tuh ['i-baboo']:

"mɔ' sɛn'ɔɔy ha-gonaa' ma-hạ̄ạ̄' na'."

Na-tuh:

"Hạ̄ạ̄', kɛnʉʉh 'əh, 'amɛɛ'. 'amɛɛ'· səleŋɔɔy."

Ləpas na', baruu' na-'og ney nɔŋ. Na-'ulang 'ulang, təyab təyab miŋguu'. Ney miŋguu' ney kalii'; ney miŋguu' ney kalii'. Jadii' na-'og nɔŋ na'. Habis na-'og nɔŋ na', bolɛh 'i-gabag pi-mɛs pi-mɛs.

Jadii', na-səmaaɲ wɛl. Na-səmaaɲ kɛnʉʉh na', na-səmaaɲ,

"Ma-cɔɔ' ham-tɛrbə' kɛnʉʉh num-jadii' bə-kɛnʉʉh?"

Masaa' na', tii' paay 'i-səlɔg lɛh 'i-doh [in Rəlɔɔy].

'i-jawab:

"Hɔ̗y, tɔ' 'i-lɛk ma-cɔɔ' 'im-'og kɛnʉʉh,

sɛn'ɔɔy hɔ̗y, kəwạ̄ạ̄s hɔ̗y.

Tɔ' 'i-lɛk."

Na-tuh, na-'oor,

"Ma-lɛh ha-doh bolɛh ha-tɛrbə' kɛnʉʉh 'amɛɛ' səleŋɔɔy."

Hɔj sətəŋah tahon baruu' na-'oor 'im-pɔɔh bar-gɔɔh, bar-cantok. Jadii' hɔj pas mɛn hənelad, mɛn-kɛnʉʉh jɛlmɔl teh, mɛn-macam-macam, bɔ' jadii' 'i-pɔɔh. Na-'oor rii' num-bəəh kɛnʉʉh rii' lɛh yeh pasal kewạ̄ạ̄s hɔ̗y. Sampey 'i-pakey nɔŋ na' sampey doh 'i-pakey.

Na-'og 'ɛm-hənelad, tapii' musim 'i-pɔɔh, boleh 'ɛ-helad hun-tɛ':
mɛn-bungaa', mɛn-lo' lo'. Na-'og ma-lɔɔ' 'ɛm-jəhook, ma-lɔɔ' 'ɛm-
kelʉ' ləgaa', 'ɛm-tɛrwog sɛmpid, ma-lɔɔ' 'ɛm-rɛntak.

DREAM NARRATIVE: UDA PANDAK, KENGKONG, 30-VI-82, DN21

Gɔɔh. Gɔɔh 'ɛ-cantok na'. Na-ba-rəwaay. Laguu' 'ɛ-na' na-mɔɔj
ma-kəlɔɔj 'awɛn. 'i-pɔ' na-tɛrlɔɔs ma-rii'. Layɛg 'i-pɔɔh, 'ɛ-dɔɔl
'awɛn, 'i-maa', 'i-səlɔg, na-həwal baboo' mənalɛh. Na-gɛrsaak,
na-'eed wɔb yee' 'am-gɛrsaak, wɔb rəwaay yeh. Lɛgləjɛg na-pəlɔh.
Na-'eed, pancah [bunyi] ɲaag tɔ' na-lɛylɔy jərʉk, na-'eed
'am-kədəng ma-kawasan doh. Yoot na-'og gənabag wɔb caraa'
gɛnsaak na'.

DREAM NARRATIVE: ALʉJ HITAM, KENGKONG, 30-VI-82, DN27

Nɔŋ bɛɛk. Jɛŋjɛɛg. Kəlomaar, kənoruk jərəək 'əh. Kəlomaar, hup
'ɛ-tuuy.

Baboo' mɛj bəyɛ'. Soog naar dəpaa', səleŋɔɔy 'olah 'əh. 'i-guu' rii'
jɛnjɛɛg, na-kəl. 'i-maa' ma-deek, 'i-bək samɔg 'əh wɔb bek 'əh.
'i-səlɔg lə'aak, 'i-kub. 'i-kub lə'aak. Na-həwal rii'. Baboo'.
Num-kəlɔɔj kəlomaar na-həwal, na-gabag, na-kərook, na-kəl,
na-sabat ma-'ɛɛ'. Kəlomaar na-həwal, na-tɛg ma-hup yeh, "kəlib!"
Cərahaaw 'olah 'əh.

DREAM NARRATIVE: ALʉJ HITAM, KENGKONG, 30-VI-82, DN26

Nɔŋ bɛɛk.
Jəhʉ' rəgəəl.
Cɛp 'un-maa' tabaag,
na-kəl ma-tɛ', mənanuu' 'əh.

Na-kəl ma-tɛ', 'i-tə'ɛl deek.
'i-tə'ɛl deek, 'i-pɔ' kənoruk 'əh.
Na-həwal babəəh, 'i-pɔ' na-həwal na', na-gabag.
Hɔj manah, hɔj 'ənam tahon.
Babəəh litɔw, na-pakey gɔb—
    sɛlwar, baju'.
'i-kɔw dato', kɛnʉʉh 'əh.
Rii' 'ə-na' na-bɛrtuh ma-yee' bɔ' 'ɛ-soo',
'ɛ-kɔɔd cɛnrɔɔs.
Na-helad ma-cɛp.

DREAM NARRATIVE: ABILEM LUM, BAWIK, 7-IX-82, DN2

Nɔŋ Taŋkəb. Jɛlmɔl teeh, nɛɛh, mə-'agaah: "Kəruuh, kəruuh, kəruuh." Sɛgnug. 'un-gɛlgəl jəhʉʉ'. "Kəruuh, kəruuh, kəruuh, kəruuh." Na-na' 'i-cɛgcɔɔg, nɛɛh. Bar-cocok buruŋ. Cɛp təraad 'a-tee'. 'i-cɔɔg-cɔɔg na', ralii' 'i-səlɔg. Bunyii' bunyii' cətəd baboo' mənalɛh. Mɛj ha-nɛɛh 'olah 'əh. Na' 'i-gabag.   Cocok buruŋ. Cɛp, cɛgcɔg cɛp. Cɛp təraad 'a-tɛɛ'. Jadii', 'i-cɔɔg-cɔɔg na' 'a-tɛh, 'i-pɔɔc-pɔɔc, 'i-səlɔg təŋah harii' na'. Lətih, 'i-səlɔg. Bunyii' bunyii' bunyii' na' sədəəb bə-ralii'. Baruu' 'i-pɔ'.

TRANSLITERATION FOR CHAPTER 4, THE DREAM PERFORMED:

DREAM NARRATIVE: PANDAK HIBEL, JɛLGək, 22-VI-82, DN9

Nɔŋ tiw bərɔk doh, təŋkoh Mɛnrak. Samaa' nɔŋ təluuy talʉn wɔb buŋaa' carak 'a-tɛɛ': təluuy ney bulan [bulan tiga'], carak ney bulan.

Bargɔb mɛntərii' tiw na'. Na-tibaa' na' cə-kanɛɛ' bɛɛk, kɛ-gabag bɛɛk. 'i-guu' səlaay kayuu', səlaay baa', na-nɛɛh nɛɛh nɛɛh, na-cəraay (na-bəreycɔɔ', macam 'ɛ-piyara' ma-'ayam), macam baboo' na-mad ma-yee', na-kənan. Na-cəraay na', na-cɛn. Bar-kənan. Baboo' mənalɛh, gid na' [indicates 3 1/2 to 4 ft.].

'e-loo' kuy nam-tuh? Na-gabag hii'.

Appendix B:
Discography

Temiar Dream Music of Malaya, Ethnic Folkways FE4460 (c. 1955); material collected under the direction of H. D. Noone in 1941.

An Anthology of South-East Asian Music: Music of the Senoi of Malacca, Barenreiter-Musicaphon BM 30 L2561 (c. 1977); material collected by Hans Oesch in 1963.

Notes

CHAPTER 1: INTRODUCTION

1. Kirk Endicott (1979) and Howell (1984) note that neighboring aboriginal groups, the Batek De' and Chewong, also express cosmological orientation in daily activities. They urge us to attend not only to traditionally demarcated ritual ceremonies, but to the ritualized activities of everyday life.

2. Several earlier studies of Senoi Semai and Temiar music are primarily descriptive and analytical (Hornbostel 1926; Kolinski 1930; Haden 1939; Blacking 1954–1955). Oesch (1973, 1974a, 1974b) also discusses economic and religious considerations involved in Orang Asli music-making.

3. Hirschman (1987:563), charting the shifting position of the Orang Asli in census classifications from 1881–1980, notes that the aborigines were generally listed under the "Malay" category. "Although some critics believe that the placement of aborigines under the Malay category reflects a political motive," he suggests, "the number of aborigines is too few to affect the relative ethnic demographic balance."

CHAPTER 2: CONCEPTS OF BEING

1. Benjamin (1979) presents a sensitive discussion of the dynamic of bounded soul and unbound spirit in Temiar religion.

2. The term *rəwaay* refers to a "soul" principle among several Orang Asli groups. Blagden lists *ro-wai* as "soul" only among the Semang of Sungai Plus (Skeat and Blagden, 1906, vol. 2:720). Subsequent researchers, however, report cognates among other Aslian speakers. Howell (1984: 127–141) interprets *ruwai* among the Chewong as vital principle, consciousness, and spirit-guide. *Ruai* as "soul" among the Semai is located just behind the center of the forehead and is detachable in dreams (Dentan 1968:82). Jah Hut have seven *ruay* or types of "soul" (Couillard 1980:33). Gérard Diffloth reports cognates in other Mon-Khmer languages, including Khmu' (*rwaay* 'tiger') and Waic (*sivay* 'tiger') (personal communication). See n. 12, below, on etymological links among terms for spirit-mediums and tigers. These terms may be related to the Malay *roh* (< Arabic *ruh, ruah*), the quickening spirit of life. In Moslem belief, *roh* is "a subtle vaporous substance, the principle of vitality, sensation and voluntary movement" that departs the body at death (Wilkinson 1959:978). However, the extent of the Austroasiatic cognates would seem to preclude an Arabic etymology.

3. Benjamin (1967:136) notes that if a child's hair must be shaved for delousing, a tuft of hair is retained (over the forehead for boys and at the crown of the head for girls) for the head soul to reside in.

4. Also: *rəwaay, halaa', pɔ'*, depending on place and speaker.

5. *Rɛywaay* is a morphological derivative of *rəwaay* on the stative-verb/adjective pattern (Benjamin 1976).

6. There is some indication that women's head souls are considered to be more labile than men's: when camping along the river, women do not sleep with their heads towards the water for fear that their roaming head souls might get lost in the water and fail to return to the dreamer. Men sleep with their heads pointed toward the water, without need for such precautions. Both men and women, however, must not sleep with their heads next to the fire out of concern for scorching returning head souls.

7. Among the Argentine Mapuche, the vocalization of *tayil* similarly unbinds and activates the patrilineal soul (Robertson 1976, 1979).

8. By "controlled uttering" I mean properly contexutalized and uttered with intent, not accidentally vocalized.

9. The vital principle of trees and plants among the Chewong is in their sap, *tam*, which also translates as water (Howell 1984:128). The Batek posit a cool dew (*mun* < Malay *embun*) found in the heavens in abundance, on earth in the sap of the Malacca cane, and as the blood of superhuman beings (*hala' 'asal*) and shamans (Kirk Endicott 1979:124–125). Laderman (i.p.) compares the Orang Asli valuation of coolness with aspects of the Malay humoral system.

10. Upper-portion souls of plants are specifically termed *kahyɛk*, while upper-portion souls of mountains are often termed *potərii'* (Malay *puteri* 'princess') and *məntərii'* (Malay *menteri* 'chief,' 'minister') (see Benjamin 1979:13). However, the spiritguides of mountains as well as plants can conduct liquid *kahyɛk* into ceremonial props and the breast of spiritguides. *Kahyɛk* is thus specifically used to refer to the sap of plants and generally used to refer to the spiritual liquid manifesting the upper-portion soul of activiated spiritguides.

11. Benjamin (1967a:153) suggests these terms are Malay borrowings: *kənoruk*, the inflected form of Malay *kurong* 'enclosure', and *sarak* from the Malay word *sarang* 'animal's hole, nest'.

12. The Temiar term for spirit-medium, *halaa'*, also used by the Semai and the Semang, may be related to the Malay term *halak* 'were-tiger'. Malay shamans (in Kelantan, *bomoh belian*) often have the tiger spirit (*hantu belian*) as helpers. *Bomoh belian* are sometimes believed to send their souls out to roam as were-tigers; the souls of deceased *bomoh belian* also take the form of tigers. The tiger form of the *bomoh belian* is called *halak* in Kelantan (Cuisinier 1936:39–41; Endicott 1970:21–22). Cuisinier interprets this as an aboriginal substratum in Malay cultures, or as a borrowing from aborigines. The term may be cognate with the Proto Monic of Dvararati times in Central Thailand, sixth to ninth centuries A.D., **klaa'* 'tiger': *Panthera tigris corbetti* (Diffloth 1984:61).

13. In the information I collected on eighty-eight different individual spiritguides encountered by thirteen mediums, only twelve (14 percent) spiritguides were manifestations of lower-portion souls.

14. *Argusanius argus* (Temiar cɛp kəwɔɔk, cɛp 'ambɯj).

15. *Tor tambroides* (Malay *ikan kelah*).

16. *Oncosperma horrida*.

17. These include the rhinocerus hornbill (*Bucerus rhinocerus*, Temiar tərək), an unidentified game bird (Temiar *hohuy*), and the bay owl (*Phodilius badius*, Temiar taŋkəwɔɔj).

18. *Phodilius badius* (Temiar taŋkəwɔɔj).

19. Reported instances included the Ipoh tree (*Antiaris toxicaria*), whose sap is used for blowpipe dart poison, and the Jelutong tree (*Dyera cosulata*, Temiar bədɔk loŋɯn), whose resin is used as an adhesive.

20. Reported instances include Temiar *bayas* (*Oncosperma horrida*) and Temiar jɛŋjɛɛg (possibly *Ceiba pentandra* or *Arenga pinnata*?).

21. Inhabitants of settlements on the rivers Berok and Nenggiri both traced the origin of odor to the cəhɔɔŋ tree at the source of the Berok River. There is some indication that this belief is more prominent in the Berok river valley. The cəhɔɔŋ tree is sometimes said to contain *badii'*, a dangerous vapor or emanation associated with blood released in the slaughter of animals. This could be the result of the Temiar connection of tree trunks, heart souls, and blood. The concept of *badii'* is also found among the Malays.

22. This short utterance is the most common. A longer version is: "Odor, odor, odor of the cəhɔɔŋ tree, I am walking by."

23. Among the Chewong, a person's smell (*moni*) can be lost while bathing or left behind in one's settlement and must be retrieved and returned to the individual or illness will result (Howell 1984:145).

24. New arrivals are also feared as carriers of various illness beings (*baad, sɛmyaap*) that are picked up as one passes through the jungle and rivers.

25. Not only departing visitors, but even a resident head of a household leaving for a week's journey will sometimes prepare a scrap of cloth imbued with his odor for use in the event that one of his relatives is "eaten" by his odor in his absence.

26. The barking deer (*Muntiacus muntjak*), the silver-leafed monkey (*Presbutis cristata*), the dusky leaf monkey (*Presbytis obscura*), the pig-tailed macaque (*Macaca nemestrina*), the long-tailed macaque (*Macaca fascicularis*).

27. Also *mayaŋ, bayaŋ* (< Malay *bayang* 'shadow').

28. Wilkinson (1959:94) defines the Malay *bayang* as a "Vague outline; shadow. Of a face on a photographic negative; a girl's figure outlined against her dress; the passage of food indicated by the expansion of the throat. . . ." Echols and Shadily (1963) define the Indonesian *bayang* as shadow, reflection, and image. *Wayang* is the Javanese cognate.

29. The medium Abilem Lum of Bawik comments on his patient: "There is something special from me within you. Like liquid sap, there is

a shadow inside the patient guarding her. This is the reason for restrictions [on the patient and other community members] during curative treatment."

30. The neighboring Batek are Orang Asli of the Semang (Negrito) ethnic division speaking a Northern Aslian language. The Batek shadow-soul, *bayang*, is one of two fundamental components of living human beings; the other is the life-soul, *ɲawa*, or "breath of life" that animates the body. The Batek shadow-soul, distinctive for each individual, leaves the body when a person sleeps, its encounters appearing to the sleeper as dreams. Shadow-souls can be seen during dreams and by shamans in trance, where they resemble the person himself (Kirk Endicott 1979:93–96).

31. Ading Kerah addresses his wife as "mother" since he speaks with the voice of his spiritguide, who is like his child. His wife becomes the spiritguide child's "mother."

32. Ading Kerah addresses his wife and her siblings as "Mothers" (see preceding footnote). This address is then metaphorically extended to include all the women who sing choral response and play the bamboo-tube percussion for the singing ceremony.

33. I have bracketed concepts the Temiar say are embedded in the words sung, i.e., extended meanings. The coolness of the body as the song passes through is associated with the cool spiritual liquid *kahyɛk*, which flows from the spiritguide through the medium concurrently with the song.

34. Penghulu Dalam is specifically addressing his and his wife's younger sisters, who become the *waa'* of his child, the spiritguide. By extension, he generally addresses the women participating in the ceremony.

35. The common habitat of the dark-necked tailorbird (*Orthotomus atrogularis*) is undergrowth and thickets in forests and open country (see King and Dickinson 1975:370). This is also where Temiar graves are often located: in the secondary growth and thickets of former swiddens and bordering current swiddens.

36. Perhaps the Temiar, whose notion of the shadow form is less well developed than the shadow-soul of the Batek, have been influenced by some of the Batek concepts about shadows. The Batek shadow-soul goes to live in an afterworld following death, where it retains the distinctive features of the individual from which it came (Kirk Endicott 1979:93). The Temiar generally impute to their more detailed notion of head soul many of the properties that the Batek render as shadow-soul.

37. *Mayaŋ* is the noun form; *'ɛ-mayaŋ*, verb, 'one gives a *mayaŋ*'. When presented during spirit seances, as is often the case, the *mayaŋ* payment may also be referred to as *halad* ('ceremonial prop', also used to refer to ceremonial leaf ornaments and whisks; cf. Malay *alat* 'tool', 'utensil').

38. In her study of the neighboring Chewong, Howell (1984, 1988) similarly finds that "the superhuman beings, far from being extrinsic to

social processes and daily concerns, must be interpreted as members of the society" (1988:2).

39. In an American example of the tension between differentiation and communitarianism, Felker (1983) investigates metaphors of "the team" used to disguise relations of hierarchy in the operating rooms of Western cosmopolitan hospitals.

40. Pərɛnhǫǫd is also referred to by the Temiar terms sərɛnlɔk and sǝlɛntab. Temiar pərɛnhǫǫd is comparable to Semai *punan* (Dentan 1968:55), Chewong *punɛn* (Howell 1984:183), and Malay *kempunan* (Coote 1976).

CHAPTER 3: BECOMING A HEALER

1. See Benjamin (1979, 1981) on the dialectics of Temiar language, religion, and social orientation.

2. The juxtaposed relations between spiritguides and mediums (child-father, teacher-student, female-male, male-male) will be examined further in chapter 4. Spiritguides appear to male mediums predominantly in the guise of females, although male spiritguides also do appear. The ratio of female to male spiritguides is 2:1.

3. The position of dream songs in relation to other Temiar musical genres is discussed in chapter 4.

4. Rather than using the term *soul* which implies a thing existing independently of the physical body, Ellen Basso (1987) suggests the term *interactive self* for emergent entities anthropomorphized to engage with the mind of a human being.

5. I translate ŋɔɔy as "fragrance" in situations where the word is often qualified by Temiar adjectives such as "good" or "sweet" or "bittersweet." This is often the case for flowers, ceremonial leaves, and products burned as incense (e.g., roots, resins, beeswax). Temiars value fragrant odors; they wear fragrant leaves in their hair or tucked at the waist to please one another and suspend them from ceremonial ornaments to entice the spirits. Both fragrant and nonfragrant odors are permeable and capable of crossing categorical boundaries.

6. A piece of *kasay* root, kɛmɲan resin (*Styrax benzoin*; Malay *kemenyan*), or beeswax (Temiar *padaw*, sɯj) is placed in a bed of coals to release its fragrance during incantations and performances.

7. See Dentan 1983 and Domhoff 1985 for further discussion of the circumstances surrounding the colonial and postcolonial transformation of Temiar dream theories. Some psychotherapists involved in the earlier popularization of so-called Senoi dream theories, such as Ann Faraday (personal communication), are readjusting their original statements to fit more recent ethnographic evidence.

8. This sample of fifty does not represent my entire corpus of dream narratives, or even the entire corpus of dream narratives in which familiars began to sing. It includes only those dream narratives that recount events

in daily life that preceded a dream encounter with a familiar who began to sing.

9. Fruit trees and flowerbushes span both these categories: they were placed in the "tended" category when the dream narrative emphasized their planting and cultivation, or situated in the "travel" category when the narrative stressed gathering expeditions or travel through the jungle.

10. On animated nature or "local spirits" (and their incorporation into world religions such as Buddhism, Hinduism, and Islam) see Skeat (1900/ 1967:52–54) and Kirk Endicott (1970:28–46, 96ff) on the Malays, and Shaw (1975:1–10, 77–81, 108–112) on the Malays, Chinese, and Hindus in Malaysia; Tambiah (1970) on Thailand; and Geertz (1960:16–29) on Java.

11. The cultural marking of geographic formations is not restricted to Southeast Asia or Oceania. Allen writes of the narrators, singers, and diviners in Quechua-speaking mountain communities of the Andes:

> We should also recognize another natural resource in the mountain environment, and that is the rugged punctuated character of the landscape itself. For the topography is like an immense piece of undeciphered script, whose meaning people come to know as they live in and with it. The Incas imposed their own complex (and imperialistic) interpretation onto the landscape by drawing the places in their empire into a huge circular system whose hub was Cuzco (Zuidema 1964). More than four hundred years after the Conquest this natural iconography of place continues to provide Andean people with an orientation, with a way of speaking and thinking about themselves and their society. The master speakers are those who know how to hear what the landscape has to tell them [1985:17].

12. *"Ma-lɔɔ'?"* is an abbreviation of the longer phrases *"Malɔɔ' ha-ciib 'a-tɛɛ'?"* "Where have you just been to?" and *"Ma-lɔɔ' ham-ciib?"* "Where are you going?" The comparable standard Malay greeting is: *"Darimana?"* "Where are you coming from?" (or, less frequently, *"Nak gi mana?"* the Indonesian *"Mau ke mana?"* "Where are you going?").

13. MMB = Minister of Mount Bərintəəh; AB = Angah Busuu', the narrator; FaAB = Father of Angah Busuu'; M = Marina Roseman.

14. *ɲaag* 'mouth' = song, song section.

15. Temiar transliteration appears in Appendix A. All Temiar words begin with consonants; thus, initial vowels are preceded by a glottal stop (see Benjamin 1976). In the interests of standardizing capitalization, the glottal stop will not be noted at the beginning of proper names.

16. Seeger, writing on the Suyá of Brazil, defines cosmology as "the way in which the members of a society construct their universe and think of themselves and other beings within it" (1981:21).

17. This phrase is drawn from the repertoire of the annual fruit season genre Tangɔɔy. Ceremonial cult and musical genres will be discussed in chapter 4.

18. *'amɛɛ'* is a term of address for "mother"; *səleŋɔɔy* refers to the graceful, beautiful aspects of a woman: fluid movements, curving body, wavy hair. I translate the Temiar as "Mother Fluid Beauty."

19. The interactive self of Mt. Raŋwɛ̰ɛ̰y is speaking of herself in the third person.

20. Falling level and rising narrowly are spatial metaphors for melodic contour drawn from geographic terms describing the slope of the landscape.

21. Temiar transliteration appears in Appendix A.

22. This is somewhat like the practice surrounding a person's autonym or "true name," which retains a special status despite later superficial name changes.

23. Temiar transliteration in Appendix B.

24. The lower-portion soul is usually termed *hup*, but in the context of mediumship is often termed *jərəək*, *kənoruk*, or *kəlomaar*.

25. An unidentified tree species.

26. Possibly *Arenga pinnata* or *Ceiba pentandra*.

27. Temiar transliteration in Appendix B.

28. Similarly, following Inca and then Spanish Conquests, the mountain spirits of the Andes were reidentified with the new administrators, legal owners, and managers of Andean resources. Previously, these mountain spirits had existed in a relationship of mutual distribution and exchange with the indigenous peoples. Later, they were characterized according to hierarchcal systems of social organization and market principles of ownership (Taussig 1980:182–187).

29. See Roseman 1980 on the metaphorical identification of Orang Asli with upstream and Malays with downstream in history and legend.

30. *Intsia bakeri* (Malay *merbau*).

31. Taking out claws refers to the extraction of portions of the illness agent lodged inside the patient.

32. Temiar transliteration in Appendix A.

33. See Schieffelin 1977 for a comparable process among Kaluli spirit mediums in Papua New Guinea. As in the Temiar case, the Kaluli theory of dreaming and spirit-mediumship is "not merely a symbolic concept," but rather a "living part of [Kaluli] reality and its activity" (Schieffelin 1977:175).

34. *Dato'*, from the Malay 'head of family, elder' < *datu* 'ruler, chief', the old Malay sovereign title borne by the Srivijaya King of the Kota Kapur inscription (A.D. 686) (Wilkinson 1959:260–261). The word is found throughout Austronesian. The term *dato' nenek* (or *datuk nenek*) is used by Malays to refer to ancestors and spirits.

35. *Argusianus argus* (Temiar *cɛp kəwɔɔk*).

36. *Copsychus saularis* (Temiar *cɛp bəraay*).

37. *Phodilius badius* (Temiar *taŋkəwɔɔj*).

38. Temiar *sɛgnug taŋkəb*: 'frog', *sɛgnug* < possibly *sug* 'touch'; *taŋkəb*, an unidentified mountain frog species.

39. *Psilopogon pyrolophus*, Fire-tufted Barbet (Temiar *cɛp təraad*).

40. Temiar transliteration in Appendix A.

41. Dentan (1968:85) similarly defines *halaaq* as a quality of varying degrees among the neighboring Semai.

42. There are, however, traces of "office": Temiars hold that every village should have at least one medium; and a proclaimed medium does find himself under social and moral pressure to perform for others.

43. Amok Jerwan Long succumbed to tuberculosis in 1982. She died before I was able to meet her. She was recorded in 1969 by the Orang Asli Broadcast Unit of Radio-TV Malaysia. Another female medium of renown was recorded in Grik, Perak, in 1958. These materials are archived in the collection of the Orang Asli Broadcast Unit at Radio-TV Malaysia, Kuala Lumpur.

44. The same individual can be both leader and headman.

45. Temiar terms for "discussions" (*bə-caraa'*, *bə-pakad*), are both foreign terms for "discussion, deliberation" from the Malayized Sanskrit and Arabic respectively. See Robarchek 1979b on *be-caraa'* among the Semai.

46. Epidemics of flu or upper respiratory infections can incapacitate a Temiar community. With hunting and gathering at a standstill and hardly any food surplus to draw on, these epidemics can precipitate a major community-wide crisis.

47. For an example of a *jenhook* song phrase, see song transcription, figure 2, at "J" in the *halaa*'s vocal line.

CHAPTER 4: THE DREAM PERFORMED

1. Solo singing devoid of choral response is also called *pəŋjəwɔ'*. Temiars sometimes sing solo while lying on their sleeping mats in the late afternoon or deep in the night. They may be clearing their hearts of longing for a distant lover (see chapter 6), quietly contacting a spiritguide, or fixing in their memories the lines of a song just taught to them by a spiritguide in a dream.

2. *Elateriospermum tapos*.

3. See Benjamin (1968b:9–13) on the institution of Mikong.

4. Keranih Laloh married Ading Kerah's classificatory older sister, that is, the child of one of his parents' siblings.

5. *Elateriospermum tapos*.

6. *Lansium domesticum* (Malay *langsat*).

7. *Nephelium mutabile* (Malay *pulasan*, a *rambutan* species).

8. *Nephelium lappaceum* (Malay *rambutan*).

9. Benjamin (1967a) identifies this as Malay *tabang* or *kesan*. Possibly *Baccaurea bracteata* (Burkhill 1966:280).

10. *Baccaurea griffithii* (Malay *tampoi*).

11. Possibly *Nephelium eriopetalum* (Malay *rambutan asam*).

12. Possibly *Baccaurea brevipes* or *B. wrayi* (Burkhill 1966:280, 284); Malay *buah tajam* (Benjamin 1967: table 3).

13. Malay *habok mas* (Benjamin 1967: table 3).

14. Malay *buah mas*; Temiar *ləyɛg* (Benjamin 1967: table 3).

15. Kemar is four hours' journey past Grik, two hours beyond Ampang Tangor.

16. This is also the last day that fires would have been lit at the head and foot of the grave had the child been buried, followed by a small ceremonial feast and cessation of the first stage of mourning restrictions.

17. Temiarized Malay *dapad* < *dapat* 'get' is used to indicate an encounter with a spiritguide that results in receipt of a way.

18. *Num-bǝlɛɛh* 'to prepare', 'to shape the head-soul like one pats and shapes the earth around a young shoot'.

19. *Num-sapuu'* < Malay *sapu* 'to sweep'.

20. A *paley* is a hut of plaited palm fronds specially constructed inside the house in which a ceremony is to be held. It is only constructed for particular genres such as the Tiger genre. The medium sings from inside the hut with the chorus circling around the outer perimeter. While the Temiar usually use the fronds of the palm *Eugeissona tristis* (Temiar *bɛltɔp*; Malay *bertam*) to construct *paley* huts, Burkhill reports a possible etymology for the term: "The Pagan races make considerable use of species of *Licuala* [a genus of the family Palmae; Temiar *kǝwar*]: the trunks of the larger ones supply uprights for their shelters and the leaves are used for thatch. So it has come about, in the rude art of the Sakai, that a leaf is drawn to suggest a house [Skeat and Blagden, *Pagan Races*, 1, 1906 p. 483]. . . . The [*Licuala*] species are of small size, and do not differ greatly in appearance: so the Malays call them all 'palas'. This name is 'pales' in Semang, and is converted into 'palei' in northern Borneo" (1966:1362).

21. *Licuala* sp. (Malay *palas*).

22. *Nephelium lappaceum* (Temiar *legɔs, susug*).

23. *Kǝnaseh* is the nominalized form of the verb *kaseh* < Malay *kasih* 'to give'. It carries here the implications of the colloquial Malay *kasih sayang*, 'to feel love or affection'.

24. Seasonal changes are also recognized by the arrival of particular bird, insect, and mammal vocalizations.

25. Stories of creation collected by Benjamin make a direct association between the semantic fields of "seasonal fruits" (*bǝrǝk*) and "year" (*pǝnaa', guur, tahut, tawun*) (Benjamin 1967a:60, n. 11). The Temiar often refer to the seasonal fruits with merely the term *tahut* (ibid.); similarly, the Batek De' often refer to seasonal fruits (*kǝbu'*) simply as *tahun* (Kirk Endicott 1979:55).

26. *Sǝpooy* describes a slow dance movement, strolling in place and swaying from the torso. It also refers to a flirtatious downcast sideways glance of the eyes. *Sǝpooy* < Malay *sepuy* 'soft blowing of the breeze' also recalls the image of suspended fruits swaying in the wind described in the song text.

27. *Elasteriospermum tapos*.

28. Despite their cultural and linguistic affinities with the Senoi, the borderline Lanoh exhibit Semang modes of societal integration (the "band" as opposed to the Senoic "tribe") and social units of productive enterprise (the conjugal family, as opposed to the Senoic descent group) [see Benjamin 1985, table 1].

29. Skeat and Blagden report several Semang variants for Rambutan:

tangguɲ (Batek De'), *tanggui*, and *tangoi* (1906, II:690). One of the Temiar words for the seasonal fruits (*kəbəh*) is also cognate with the Batek De' term (*kəbu'*) (Kirk Endicott 1979:55).

30. The combination of seasonal fruits and bees in Abilem's dream may reflect more than their circumstantial appearance together during the fruit season. For while the Temiar collect beeswax for ceremonial purposes from abandoned hives (yet remain uninterested in gathering honey), the Batek De' elaborate honey collection ceremonially with singing sessions marked by special bee songs to attract large numbers of bees to earth and to protect honey collectors (Kirk Endicott 1979:59–61).

31. Benjamin reports a creation myth collected in Humid (along the Perolak River in Kelantan) in which two mountain peaks, the female Mt. Cɛŋkeh and the male Mt. Mərooy (said to lie near Mt. Chingkai, but farther upstream) arose out of the primordial flood waters (1967a:39).

32. On the experiences of the Orang Asli during World War II and the Emergency, see Jones 1968:203–301, and Carey 1976:305–320.

33. On the beginnings of the Ciɲcɛm cult in Perak in the 1930s see Stewart 1948:218f; H. D. Noone 1939, 1955:4; and R. Noone 1972:63–67.

34. Located in Kelantan on the other side of Bihay.

35. This is the only song I recorded that has a triple meter, which may explain why it cannot be sung with the duple-metered bamboo-tube percussion.

36. The rock face with the Rambutan Fruit King at the top, the Tiger King at the bottom, and a beehive hanging from top to bottom in Abilem's dream of Taŋgɔɔy may have its correlate in the stone pillars reaching from the firmament to earth in Batek De' cosmology (Kirk Endicott 1979:42). Endicott notes: "The Aring Batek say that bees nowadays remain in the form of bees even when they are in the sky. They are said to sit in special caves in the stone pillars like 'goods on a shop shelf' " (59).

37. The fruit season is said to be a time when tigers, who are supposed to enjoy eating durian, are especially numerous. Biologists suggest that tigers may be drawn to eat the rodents who consume the fruits.

38. The simultaneous aspects of wife and child will be discussed further below.

39. These include *jəyɛs*, *rambey*, *pərah*, *bətaar*, and *pɛrgɛs*.

40. *Macaca fasicularas* (long-tailed macaque, Temiar *raŋkuu'*, *sənaluh*).

41. The Malay medium, originally from Pahang, was reportedly named Hassan Chu. He lived in a Malay settlement, Kampung Sungkai, then located downstream from Blau's current site.

42. The younger sister of Penghulu Kechik of Sintang.

43. From the Malay martial arts movements (*silat*) sometimes performed to musical accompaniment.

44. In his name for this Malay spirit, Penghulu Dalam uses the Arabic term *jin* for "spirit." Jin bohmin is probably the Malay Earth Spirit, *jin bumi*.

45. *Instia bakeri*.

46. On the *naga* in Indic symbolism, see Bosch 1960.

47. The Hakka Chinese community of Pulai is located near the lowland Temiar communities around Kuala Betis (See Carstens 1980). Interaction between this community and upstream Temiars dates back to before the Emergency (1948–1960). Even earlier interactions between Hakka-speakers (as well as other Chinese groups) and Temiars have occurred (see Schebesta 1928). Abilem Lum reports that before the Japanese War, the Temiar used to hold trance-dancing ceremonies together with the Chinese in Pulai. *'Ahuuh,* a Chinese caretaker of an altar in Pulai called The Altar of the Mother (*Tukuŋ Mɛɛ'* < *tokong* 'Chinese temple', 'joss-house'; *mɛɛ'*, Temiar 'mother'), told Abilem that the altar was dedicated to a Temiar woman who had married a Chinese man. She is considered to be the matriarchal ancestor of the Chinese of Pulai, and a picture of her inserted inside a bottle is kept in the altar.

48. The classificatory brother of one of Ading Kerah's parents.

49. During Malay-style ceremonies, I observed Penghulu Hitam insert kernels of popped rice in his waistband at both sides and in back, and then crunch together and tear off the tip of his leaf whisk. He then inserted the tips of the leaves behind his left ear.

50. The *bəranɔ'* is a single-headed drum with a larger head and flatter frame than the traditional single-headed *batak* drum. The shape of the *bəranɔ'* is said to have been copied from the Malays.

51. This is the position of the assistant, Sədin, mentioned above.

52. In most other ceremonial genres, the medium makes comments to and questions the general audience, who are free to answer him. Projecting the role of verbal respondent onto the *mindok* segregates the two specialists from the audience-at-large in a manner congruent with the Malay tendency toward fragmentary specialization in performance roles (see below, "Male Mediums and Female Chorus").

53. Admirable attempts to correlate social structure, subsistence technologies, and musical and dance forms have been made by Alan Lomax (1968, 1976). For a comparison and contrast of our approaches to this topic, see Roseman 1984, Feld 1984, and the Comments section following the two articles.

54. Women commonly gain renown as midwives; knowledge is gained primarily through experience assisting other midwives. The task is fraught with ritual danger and proscriptions. In difficult births, a medium will assist, calling on his spiritguides to intercede with the obstructing illness beings.

55. Although Friedl (1975) devalues the importance of small-game distribution, Temiars do not differentially value small game and large game. It is all good to eat. Karen Endicott's work with the neighboring Batek De' Semang (1979) supports the Temiar case.

56. Karen Endicott argues similarly that in evaluating women's productive roles we must look to the exceptions. She notes the distribution of tubers and vegetables (the products of women's gathering) to neighboring households among the Batek De' (Semang), aboriginal neighbors of the

Temiar. She suggests that there is a single sharing network among the Batek, and that the products of men's and women's endeavors have equivalent value in a manner consistent with generalized reciprocity (Karen Endicott 1979:63–64).

57. The root morpheme *bəəh* is used to generate the kinship reference term, *bəəh*, and address term *'ambəəh*, for "father." It also generates the gender term for "male," "man" (*babəəh*, singular; *bɛhbəəh* plural). Similarly, the root morpheme *boo'* generates the kinship reference term *boo'* and address term *'amboo'* for "mother," as well as the gender term for "female," "woman" (*baboo'*, singular; *bɛ'boo'*, plural). Furthermore, there is a pair of quite distinct words which do encode parenthood: *doo'* and *ɲɔɔ'*. With the terms *bəəh* and *boo'*, then, it would seem that we are not really dealing with "fatherness" or "motherness" in the kinship or parental mode; rather, the core of the issue is encoded maleness and femaleness.

58. In a study of forty-one songs recorded with dream source stories by male mediums, twenty-one spiritguides were female, ten spiritguides were male, and six were unspecified. (The forty-one songs were received from a total of thirty-seven spiritguides; the same spiritguide sometimes gives more than one song.) This is a two to one ratio of female to male spiritguides received by male mediums. We are reminded of the probable etymology for the Temiar term *gonig* 'spiritguide' < Malay *gundik* 'consort'.

59. Temiar transliteration in Appendix A.

60. Geoffrey Benjamin's informants from the Perolak River Valley identified *Tohaat* as *Yaa' sɔy 'is*, 'Grandmother Sunset,' a deity dwelling in the Temiar "Land of the Dead"—a 'flower garden' (*kəbun boŋaa'*) located toward the sunset, where head, heart, and eye-souls were said to go after death (Benjamin 1967a:143–144). My informants from the Bərɔk river valley (including members originally from Jalong, Simpak, Perak) remained ambivalent on the sex of *Tohaat*, and strongly denied the existence of a "flower garden" afterworld. This is a good example of the extreme variability (by region, river valley, and even settlement) in Temiar beliefs—a testament to the segmentary nature of Temiar cosmological structure and ceremonial practice, as well as a testament to the reification of individual revelation in local Temiar cosmological details. Yet, my Temiar informants in Blau on the Bərɔk River denied that "each river valley has its own truth about the cosmos." They could accept, indeed espoused regional variability in food restrictions, ceremonial practice, spiritguide preferences, and so forth, but not regarding an afterworld: about this "flower garden," they said, Benjamin's informants from Humid were either wrong, or were fabricating for the anthropologist.

61. The payment for services rendered is termed *mayaŋ*. See chapter 2, "Shadow."

62. See Ellen Basso (1987) and DaMatta (1984) for further examples of symbolic inversion in musical performance.

63. This dynamic is reminiscent of Shivaite-Buddhist tendencies operative in the Southeast Asian region. For example, the Javanese concept of

"power" involves concentrating opposites—"not their merging, but their dynamic simultaneous incorporation within a single entity" (Anderson 1972:14). This simultaneous juxtaposition of male and female elements is found in the *hari-hara ardhanari* sculptural image: the left portion of the statue is anatomically female, the right, male (ibid.; Holt 1967:81; O'Flaherty 1980:296, 317). Each side retains its respective gender characteristics, combining to express the vitality of the ruler: "He is at once masculine and feminine, containing both conflicting elements within himself and holding them in a tense, electric balance" (Anderson 1972:14). On the sacred marriage (hierogamy) of god and goddess; god and human; object of devotion and devotee in Hinduism expressed variously as heterogeny, androgyny or transvestitism, see O'Flaherty 1973, 1980; and Goswami 1982. Sexual union and marriage often serve as root metaphors for the dynamics of reciprocal exchange in social organization (Lévi-Strauss 1964:46) and cosmological symbolism (see, for example, Taussig 1980:163–164 on the Andes).

CHAPTER 5: SETTING THE COSMOS IN MOTION

1. *Antiaris toxicaria.*

2. *Na-tərɛlhəwal* '[the medium] causes [the spiritguide] to emerge'.

3. *Genhaa'* animals include Malayan pangolin (*Manis javanica*, Temiar *wɛjwooj*); siamang (*Hylobates syndactylus*, Temiar *'amaaŋ*); monitor lizard (*Varanus nebulosus*, Temiar *tərakɔl*); Argus pheasant (*Argusianus argus*, Temiar *cɛp kəwɔɔk*); toad sp. (*Bufo melanostictus*, Temiar *sɛgnug mənuu'*). See Benjamin 1967a, table 5, for an extended list of *genhaa'* animals. Different animals may be considered *genhaa'* in different settlements or river valleys.

4. The disease-causing potential inherent in *genhaa'* animal species renders them too dangerous to be consumed by young children or parents with young children.

5. *Varanus nebulosus* (Temiar *tərakɔl*).

6. Angah Pandak uses the word *pəmalii'* [< Malay *pemali* 'taboo in effect at all times' (as distinguished from temporary taboos such as birth or menstrual taboos)] to help define the Temiar term. The Ma' Betisek, an Austronesian-speaking Orang Asli group of the "Aboriginal Malay" division, use the term *kemali'* to describe a complex of beliefs involving anthropomorphic ideas about plants and animals who, when offended by certain actions, cause illness, injury, or misfortunes connected with natural contingencies such as drought, thunderstorms, and whirlwinds (Wazir-Jahan 1981).

7. Temiar *mayaŋ*, see chapter 2, "Shadow."

8. Temiar *misik* < possibly Malay *bisik* 'speaking in a whisper'. Benjamin suggests an alternative etymology from the Malay *bising* 'noise' 'incessant chatter' (personal communication, 1985).

9. *Misik* species include a number of birds, such as the crested jay (*Platylophus galericulatus*, Temiar *cəralah*); Malaysian rail-babbler (*Eupetes*

macrocerus, Temiar *hooŋ*); chestnut-backed scimitar-babbler (*Pomatorhinus montanus,* Temiar *huldɔk*); greater racket-tailed drongo (*Dicrurus paradiseus,* Temiar *kəmɛlwak*); ferrigunous babbler (*Trichastoma bicolor,* Temiar *payɛh*); white-winged black jay (*Platysmurus leucopterus,* Temiar *səmɛrluŋ*); white-hooded babbler (*Gampsorhynchus rufulus,* Temiar *sorah*); a wagtail sp. (possibly *Motacilla cinerea* or *Dendronanthus indicus,* Temiar *tayɛt*); paradise fly-catcher (*Terpsiphone paradisi,* Temiar *wɛdwaad*). Several cicada species (e.g., Temiar *ya' sikɛt, ya' 'ɛnrɛl*), caterpillars (Temiar *taluug, talaay*), and butterflies (Temiar *tawag*) are also *misik.* Benjamin (1967a: table 1) also lists several *misik* mammals: siamang (*Hylobates syndactylus,* Temiar *'amaaŋ*); slow loris (*Nycticebus coucang,* Temiar *tampɛl*); and white-handed gibbon (*Hylobates lar,* Temiar *tawɔh*).

10. Possibly a Temiar version of the Malay *sawan.*

11. *Lestudo pseudemus,* Serrated large land tortoise (Temiar *kənɔg*).

12. Other family members commented on the saliva produced during Bubung's attacks.

13. Diffloth (1981) discusses speech taboos and linguistic improvisation among the Semai.

14. *Sus scrofa.*

15. Case studies of *rɛywaay* are examined in detail in chapter 6.

16. Laderman's research on dietary rules among rural Malays (1979, 1981) and Dentan's among the Semai (1965) suggest that playing with cultural rules, shifting and adjusting according to the demands of expediency or personal experience, may be a universal tendency operating along a continuum, with some cultures allowing greater latitude for personal adjustment than others.

17. Derrida notes the association between "chance" and "the unforeseeable." Chance, the unforeseen "alterity of the other—that which does not reduce itself to the economy of our horizon," is opposed to anticipation, which "sees the *objectum* coming ahead, faces the object" (1984:5–6).

CHAPTER 6: REMEMBERING TO FORGET

1. Temiar terms for "desire" include the verbs *pət* ('i-pət *ma-* . . . 'I miss, long for . . .'), *cɛn* 'want', *hɔ̧ɔd* 'desire', and *hɔg* 'desire sexual intercourse'. Of these, the last is most explicitly and immediately sexual. The second and third may be used to express both material desires and human passions. These two, *cɛn* and *hɔ̧ɔd,* are the verbs reportedly used by spiritguides when expressing their intentions toward humans.

2. As noted in chapter 4, a study of forty-one songs recorded with dream source stories by male *halaa'* showed twenty-one female spiritguides, ten male spiritguides, and six of unspecified gender. (The forty-one songs were received from a total of thirty-seven spiritguides; the same spiritguide sometimes gives more than one song.) This is a two to one ratio of female to male spiritguides received by male spirit-mediums.

3. Recall the etymology of *gonig* 'spiritguide' < Malay *gundik* 'consort'. When the *halaa'*/spiritguide relationship is unisexual (male-male), the seductive nature of the relationship is subordinated to the generational dimension (father-child or older brother-younger brother).

4. *Hɛwhəyaaw* is an expressive found in poetic speech and song texts. Everyday words for longing and associated sadness include the verbs *pət* ('*i-pət ma-* . . . 'I miss, long for . . .') and *rəyaak* 'to long [for]', 'to pine [for]'.

5. *Bərɛnlii'* is conceivably related to *ralii'* (*be-ralii'* 'unconscious', 'otherawareness').

6. *Megalaima franklini* (Temiar *cɛp təwaal*).

7. *Elateriospermum tapos* (Temiar *sɔc*).

8. Solo instruments include *pɛnsɔɔl* (noseflute), *si'ɔɔy* (mouthblown flute), *kərəb* (tube zither), *gɛŋgɔɔɲ* (metal mouthharp), and *raŋgɔɲ* or *raŋgɔc* (mouthharp made from the midrib of the palm, *Eugeissona tristis*). For additional discussion of instrumental genres, see chapter 4.

9. *Nephelium lappaceum* (Temiar *ləgɔs, susug*).

10. For a remarkably similar linkage of natural sounds, instrumental repertoire and symbolic meanings among the T'boli of Mindanao, Philippines, see Mora 1987. The T'boli link themes of longing, cosmology, mythology, and music in a complex that metaphorically associates interlocking percussion parts encoding male/female polarity and complementarity, musical composition emerging from cross-sexual relations between human dreamer and spiritguide, the cross-sexual relations of the deities themselves, and a cultural interpretation of the antiphonal duet of the crimson-breasted barbet (*Megalaima haemacephala*). One is tempted to begin speaking about themes of a Southeast Asian culture area.

CHAPTER 7: SONGS OF A SPIRITED WORLD

1. Scholars of oral history debate the relative value of genealogy and legend in reconstructing a positivist historical timeline. Ethnohistorical approaches examine indigenous historical narratives for more than their timeline; they are also studied for their phenomenological value as records of the experience of time, event, and person. See Reid and Marr (1979) and Rosaldo (1986) for notable examples.

2. Iris Young builds upon Adorno's concept of the negative dialectic (Adorno 1973), which opposes differences without totalizing them in a Hegelian manner. Derrida and the poststructuralists also recognize difference as a defining property of essentially interrelated categories (Derrida 1976; Kristeva 1977).

3. The Temiar system of revelation contrasts, for example, with that of the Yir Yoront, Australian aborigines described by Lauriston Sharp (1952). Flora, fauna, and items of material culture were originally dreamed into being by the Dreamtime ancestors; new items threaten the wisdom of the Dreamtime ancestors, disrupting both the cosmology and the social structure it legitimates. Sharp discusses the limited success of improvisations

devised to encompass new items such as the steel axe into the original system.

4. Hood Salleh, working among the Jah Hut, documents a marked increase in healing ceremonies held in villages where roads have been built. He hypothesizes that the stress of social change produces illness, which the Jah Hut treat ceremonially. Alternatively, as nontraditional influences intensify, Jah Hut respond and attempt to counterbalance them with an intensification of traditional ceremonial activity (Hood Salleh and Hasan Mat Nor 1982).

5. Carol Laderman, writing on the Malay incorporation of the Galenic humoral medical system as it reached Malaysia through Islamic medicine, suggests that its adoption was eased by traditional hot-cold oppositions still seen in Orang Asli medical systems (Laderman 1991).

6. See Daniel (1984) for a Peircean semiotic analysis of signs of Tamil body and person. Daniel notes that in Hindu India, iconicity is valued over arbitrary symbolization (1984:40); the Temiar data indicates a similar preference for iconicity. The intimation of indexicality within iconic bodily signs is in keeping with that aspect of the sign that Daniel terms polychromy or multimodality: one sign may contain many modes of signification (39).

7. See Robarchek (1979a), Howell (1986), and Dentan (1968, 1978) for similar qualities in Semai and Chewong socialization processes.

8. Renaat Devisch uses this analogy in his investigation of Yaka healing rites in Zaire (1977, 1984). He combines post-Saussurian semiotics with a processual orientation to examine the semantic configurations that correlate body, society, and cosmos. See Bibeau (i.p.) for a penetrating review essay on Devisch and European semiology.

9. Ortner (1984) projected such a combination in her history of anthropological theory since the 1960s. Csordas (1990) draws together Merleau-Ponty's phenomenological studies of perception and Bourdieu's poststructural theory of practice to articulate a paradigm of embodiment. He shows how the mind-body distinction between "subjective facts of psychocultural reality" and "objective facts of biology" can be collapsed: "When both poles of the duality are recast in experiential terms, the dictum of psychological anthropology that all reality is psychological (Bock 1988) no longer carries a mentalistic connotation, but defines culture as embodied from the start" (Csordas 1990:37).

10. "Culture," Boas wrote, "may be defined as the totality of the mental and physical reactions and activities that characterize the behavior of the individuals composing a social group collectively and individually in relation to their natural environment, to other groups, to members of the group itself and of each individual to himself. It also includes the products of these activities and their role in the life of the groups." Yet, he emphasized, "The mere enumeration of these various aspects of life, however, does not constitute culture. It is more, for its elements are not independent, they have a structure" (Boas 1911/1938:149). Structural-functionalists

continued to examine the interrelation of cultural elements, investigating the interrelationship among parts (Malinowski 1922/1984), and of parts to the whole, showing how particular actions or institutions contributed to social solidarity (Radcliffe-Brown 1952/1965). Building upon the work of linguists such as de Saussure (1915/1966) and carrying the insights of Durkheim and Mauss in a different direction, structuralists in the tradition of Lévi-Strauss (1962/1966) developed another approach, suspending the search for cause and effect and focusing rather upon the structural relations among cultural terms as they are constituted through relations of difference and transformed in codes of color, gender, space, time *ad infinitum*.

Interpretive anthropologists turn from the functionalist emphasis on the instrumental end of social integration and add yet another dimension. An interpretive account grounds encoded meanings in social life, showing how central values or a cultural sensibility are differentially expressed and experienced in various domains—not, however, in the totalizing cultural configurations of Benedict (1934/1959), but rather with an eye (and ear) toward subtle twists and turns that allow not only for iconicity or associations based on resemblance, but also for symbolic inversions and inconsistencies.

11. See David Schneider (1976:219) for his discussion of the "culturalogic", and Guss (1988) for a brilliant demonstration of this dynamic in his study of Yekuana basketry and house-building.

Glossary

badii'   A dangerous vapor or emanation associated with blood released in the slaughter of animals.

gənabag   Singing; singing and trance-dancing ceremonies. Nominalized form of the verb *gabag*, 'sing'.

gonig   Spiritguide.

halaa'   Spirit-medium, referring alternatively to the person, the ability, or the spiritguide.

hənum   Breath. Associated with heart soul.

hup   Heart soul, lower-portion component of self. Seat of internal experience, thought, memory, emotion.

kahyɛk   A cool spiritual liquid, a form that the upper-portion soul of a spiritguide takes when it flows through a medium.

kampung   A Malay term for village or settlement.

mɛ'maa'   To return (home); used to refer to the return of the medium from trance, and the return of the visiting spiritguide to its original source.

nɔŋ   Path; can be used to refer to a footpath or river route, a song or melody, an opinion in a discussion.

ŋɔɔy   Odor; a component of self.

palɛy   A small circular hut constructed from plaited palm fronds. A *palɛy* is constructed inside a Temiar house for ceremonies involving the Tiger Spirit.

pɛhnɔɔh   Singing and trance-dancing ceremonies.

pərenhɔ̧ɔ̧d   A state of unfulfilled desire resulting from an unanswered request or broken promise that leaves the unfulfilled person vulnerable to illness or other misfortune.

pərenlʉb   The action whereby a medium conducts the cool spiritual liquid from his spiritguide into the head and heart soul of a recipient.

rəwaay   Head soul, upper-portion component of self. Vital animating force. Associated with voice and expression.

rɛywaay   Soul loss.

wɔɔg   Shadow-form or shadow-soul; a component of the self.

Bibliography

Abu-Lughod, Lila
    1986   *Veiled Sentiments: Honor and Poetry in a Bedouin Society.* Berkeley, Los Angeles, London: University of California Press.

Adams, Richard Newbold
    1975   *Energy and Structure: A Theory of Social Power.* Austin: University of Texas Press.

Adorno, Theodor W.
    1973   *Negative Dialectics.* New York: Continuum Publishing Company.

Allen, Catherine J.
    1985   Time, Place, and Narrative in an Andean Community. Unpublished paper presented in the "Symposium on Performance and Aesthetics in Andean South America and Southeast Asia," Cornell University.

Anderson, Benedict R. O'Gorman
    1972   The Idea of Power in Javanese Culture. In *Culture and Politics in Indonesia,* ed. Claire Holt, assisted by B. R. O'G. Anderson and James Siegel. Ithaca: Cornell University Press.

Armstrong, Robert Plant
    1971   *The Affecting Presence: An Essay in Humanistic Anthropology.* Urbana: University of Illinois Press.
    1981   *The Powers of Presence: Consciousness, Myth, and the Affecting Presence.* Philadelphia: University of Pennsylvania Press.

Babcock, Barbara
    1978   *The Reversible World: Symbolic Inversion in Art and Society.* Ithaca: Cornell University Press.

Bahr, D. M., and J. R. Haefer
    1978   Song in Piman Curing. *Ethnomusicology* 22(1):89–122.

Bakhtin, Mikhail M.
    1981   *The Dialogic Imagination: Four Essays by M. M. Bakhtin,* ed. Michael Holquist, trans. Caryl Emerson and M. Holquist. Austin: University of Texas Press.
  1984/1965 *Rabelais and His World,* trans. Helene Iswolsky. Bloomington: Indiana University Press.

Barthes, Roland
    1989   *The Rustle of Language,* trans. Richard Howard. Berkeley, Los Angeles, London: University of California Press.

Basso, Ellen
    1987   The Implications of a Progressive Theory of Dreaming. In
            Dreaming: The Anthropology and Psychology of the Imaginal, ed.
            Barbara Tedlock. Albuquerque: University of New Mexico
            Press.
    1984   Responses to Feld and Roseman. *Ethnomusicology* 28(3):461–
            463.
Basso, Keith H.
    1984   "Stalking with Stories": Names, Places, and Moral Narratives
            among the Western Apache. In *Text, Play, and Story: The Con-
            struction and Reconstruction of Self and Society*, ed. Edward M.
            Bruner, pp. 19–55. Prospect Heights, Ill.: Waveland Press.
Bauman, Richard
    1977   *Verbal Art as Performance*. Rowley, Mass.: Newbury House.
Bauman, Richard, and Joel Sherzer, eds.
    1974   *Explorations in the Ethnography of Speaking*. New York: Cam-
            bridge University Press.
Becker, Judith
    1979   Time and Tune in Java. In *The Imagination of Reality: Essays in
            Southeast Asian Coherence Systems*, ed. A. L. Becker and Aram
            Yengoyan, pp. 197–210. Norwood: Ablex.
Becker, Judith and Alton
    1981   A Musical Icon: Power and Meaning in Javanese Gamelan Mu-
            sic. In *The Sign in Music and Literature*, ed. Wendy Steiner, pp.
            203–215. Austin: University of Texas Press.
Béhague, Gerard, ed.
    1984   *Performance Practice: Ethnomusicological Perspectives*. Westport:
            Greenwood Press.
Bellwood, Peter
    1985   *Prehistory of the Indo-Malaysian Archipelago*. New York: Aca-
            demic Press.
Benedict, Ruth
    1959/1934 *Patterns of Culture*. Boston: Houghton Mifflin.
Benjamin, Geoffrey
    1966   Temiar Social Groupings. *Federation Museums Journal* 11 n.s.:1–
            25.
    1967a   Temiar Religion. Ph.D. dissertation, University of Cambridge.
    1967b   Temiar Kinship. *Federation Museums Journal* 12 n.s.:1–25.
    1968a   Temiar Personal Names. *Bijdragen Tot de Taal-, Land- en Vol-
            kenkunde* 124:99–134.
    1968b   Headmanship and Leadership in Temiar Society. *Federation
            Museums Journal* 13 n.s.:1–43.
    1976   An Outline of Temiar Grammar. In *Austroasiatic Studies*, pt. 1.
            Ed. P. Jenner et al., pp. 129–187. Honolulu: University Press of
            Hawaii.
    1979   Indigenous Religious Systems of the Malay Peninsula. In *The*

Imagination of Reality: Essays in Southeast Asian Coherence Systems, ed. A. L. Becker and Aram Yengoyan, pp. 9–27. Norwood, N.J.: Ablex.

1981   The Anthropology of Grammar: Self and Other in Temiar. Unpublished manuscript.

1986   Between Isthmus and Islands: Notes on Malayan Palaeo-Sociology. Working Paper No. 71, Sociology Department, National University of Singapore.

Benvéniste, Emile

1971   *Problems in General Linguistics.* Coral Gables, Fla.: University of Miami Press.

Berger, Peter

1967   *The Sacred Canopy: Elements of a Sociological Theory of Religion.* New York: Doubleday and Company.

Berger, Peter L., and Thomas Luckmann

1966   *The Social Construction of Reality: A Treatise in the Sociology of Knowledge.* New York: Anchor.

Bibeau, Gilles

In press   European Semiotics, Praxiology and Medico-Psychiatric Anthropology: Dead-ends or New Avenues? An Essay-Review on Devisch's Interpretation of Yaka Medical Culture. *Culture, Medicine and Psychiatry.*

Blacking, John

1954–1955 Musical Instruments. *Federation Museums Journal* 1/2 n.s.:35–52.

1973   *How Musical Is Man?* Seattle: University of Washington Press.

1985   The Context of Venda Possession Music: Reflection on the Effectiveness of Symbols. *Yearbook for Traditional Music* 17:64–87.

Blumer, Herbert

1969   *Symbolic Interactionism: Perspective and Method.* Englewood Cliffs, N.J.: Prentice-Hall.

Boas, Franz

1938/1911 *The Mind of Primitive Man,* rev. ed. New York: Free Press.

Bock, Phillip

1988   *Rethinking Psychological Anthropology.* San Francisco: Freeman.

Bourdieu, Pierre

1977   *Outline for a Theory of Practice,* trans. Richard Nice. Cambridge: Cambridge University Press.

Bosch, Frederik David Kan

1960   *The Golden Germ: An Introduction to Indian Symbolism.* 's-Gravenhage: Mouton.

Burkhill, I. H.

1966/1935 *A Dictionary of the Economic Products of the Malay Peninsula.* Kuala Lumpur: Ministry of Agriculture and Co-operatives.

Carey, Iskandar
1961   *Tenglek Kui Serok: A Study of the Temiar Language, with an Eth-nographical Summary.* Kuala Lumpur: Dewan Bahasa dan Pus-taka.
1976   *Orang Asli.* Kuala Lumpur: Oxford University Press.
Carstens, Sharon
1980   Images of Community in a Chinese Malaysian Settlement. Ph.D. dissertation, Cornell University.
Collier, Jane F., and Michelle Z. Rosaldo
1981   Politics and Gender in Simple Societies. In *Sexual Meanings: The Cultural Construction of Gender and Sexuality*, ed. Sherry B. Ort-ner and H. Whitehead, pp. 275–329. Cambridge: Cambridge University Press.
Coote, E.
1976   *Malay-English, English-Malay Dictionary.* Kuala Lumpur: Mac-millan.
Corbin, Henry
1966   The Visionary Dream in Islamic Spirituality. In *The Dream and Human Societies*, ed. G. E. von Grunebaum and Roger Caillois. Berkeley and Los Angles: University of California Press.
1972   *Mundus Imaginalis*, or the Imaginary and the Imaginal. *An An-nual of Archetypal Psychology and Jungian Thought* (Spring):1–19.
Couillard, Marie André
1980   *Tradition in Tension: Carvings in a Jah Hut community.* Penang: Universiti Sains Malaysia.
Coville, Elizabeth
1984   Others, Origins, and the Transmission of Toraja Knowledge. Unpublished paper presented at the 36th Annual Meeting of the Association for Asian Studies, Washington, D.C.
Csordas, Thomas J.
1983   The Rhetoric of Transformation in Ritual Healing. *Culture, Medicine and Psychiatry* 7:333–375.
1990   Embodiment as a Paradigm for Anthropology. *Ethos* 18(1):5–47.
Cuisinier, Jeanne
1936   *Danses magiques de Kelantan.* Paris: Institut D'Ethnologie.
Dallmayr, Fred R., and Thomas A. McCarthy, eds.
1977   *Understanding and Social Inquiry.* Notre Dame: University of Notre Dame Press.
DaMatta, Roberto
1984   On Carnaval, Informality,and Magic: A Point of View from Brazil. In *Text, Play, and Story*, ed. E. Bruner. Prospect Heights, Ill.: Waveland Press.
Daniel, E. Valentine
1984   *Fluid Signs: Being a Person the Tamil Way.* Berkeley, Los Angeles, London: University of California Press.

Dentan, Robert Knox

1965   Some Senoi-Semai Dietary Restrictions: A Study of Food Be-
        havior in a Malayan Hill Tribe. Ph.D. dissertation, Department
        of Anthropology, Yale University.

1968   *The Semai: A Nonviolent People of Malaya*. New York: Holt, Rine-
        hart & Winston.

1978   Notes on Childhood in a Non-Violent Context: The Semai
        Case. In *Learning Non-Aggression*, ed. A. Montagu. London:
        Oxford University Press.

1983   *A Dream of Senoi*. (Council on International Studies, Special
        Studies No. 150.) Buffalo: State University of New York at
        Buffalo.

Department of Statistics, Malaysia

1983   *1980 Population and Housing Census of Malaysia: General Report of
        the Population Census*. Khoo Teik Huat, Chief Statistician and
        Commissioner of Census, Malaysia. Kuala Lumpur: Depart-
        ment of Statistics.

Derrida, Jacques

1976   *Of Grammatology*. Baltimore: Johns Hopkins University Press.

1984   My Chances/Mes Chances: A Rendevous with Some Epicurean
        Stereophonies, trans. Irene Harvey and Avital Ronell. In *Tak-
        ing Chances: Derrida, Psychoanalysis, and Literature*. Baltimore:
        Johns Hopkins University Press.

Devisch, Renaat

1977   Processes for the Articulation of Meaning and Ritual Healing
        among the Northern Yaka (Zaire). *Anthropos* 72(5/6):683–708.

1984   *Se recréer femme: Manipulation sémantique d'une situation d'infé-
        condité chez les Yaka du Zaïre*. Berlin: Reimer.

Diffloth, Gérard

1976   Expressives in Semai. In *Austroasiatic Studies*, pt. 1, ed. Phillip
        N. Jenner et al., pp. 249–264. Honolulu: University Press of
        Hawaii.

1981   To Taboo Everything at All Times. *Proceedings of the Berkeley
        Linguistic Society*: 157–165.

1984   *The Dvarati Old Mon Language and Nyah Kur. Monic Language
        Studies*, vol. 1. Bangkok: Chulalongkorn University Printing
        House.

Dinesen, Isak

1972/1937 *Out of Africa*. New York: Vintage Books.

Domhoff, G. William

1985   *The Mystique of Dreams*. Berkeley, Los Angeles, London: Uni-
        versity of California Press.

Douglas, Mary

1966   *Purity and Danger*. New York: Praeger.

1970   *Natural Symbols*. New York: Vintage.

Durkheim, Emile
  1947/1915 *The Elementary Forms of the Religious Life: A Study in Religious Sociology*, trans. Joseph Ward Swain. Glencoe: Free Press.
Durkheim, Emile, and Marcel Mauss
  1963/1903 *Primitive Classification*, trans. Rodney Needham. Chicago: University of Chicago Press.
Echols, John, and Hassan Shadily
  1963   *An Indonesian-English Dictionary*, 2d. ed. Ithaca: Cornell University Press.
Endicott, Karen
  1979   Batek Negrito Sex Roles. M.A. thesis, Department of Prehistory and Anthropology, Australian National University, Canberra.
Endicott, Kirk
  1970   *An Analysis of Malay Magic*. Oxford: Clarendon Press.
  1979   *Batek Negrito Religion: The World-View and Rituals of a Hunting and Gathering People of Peninsular Malaysia*. Oxford: Clarendon Press.
  1983   The Effects of Slave Raiding on the Aborigines of the Malay Peninsula. In *Slavery, Bondage, and Dependency in Southeast Asia*, ed. A. Reid and J. Brewster, pp. 216–245. Brisbane: University of Queensland Press.
Errington, Shelly
  1983   Embodied *Sumange'* in Luwu. *Journal of Asian Studies.* 42(3):545–570.
Fabrega, Horacio, Jr.
  1972   Medical Anthropology. In *Biennial Review of Anthropology, 1971*, ed. B. Siefel, pp. 167–229. Stanford: Stanford University Press.
  1974   *Disease and Social Behavior*. Cambridge, Mass.: MIT Press.
  1975   The Need for an Ethnomedical Science. *Science* 189:969–75.
Faraday, Ann
  1972   *Dream Power*. New York: Coward, McCann & Geoghegan.
Feld, Steven
  1981   'Flow Like a Waterfall': The Metaphors of Kaluli Musical Theory. *Yearbook for Traditional Music* 13:22–47.
  1982   *Sound and Sentiment: Birds, Weepings, Poetics and Song in Kaluli Expression*. Philadelphia: University of Pennsylvania Press.
  1984   Sound Structure as Social Structure. *Ethnomusicology* 28(3):383–409.
  1988   Aesthetics as Iconicity of Style, or 'Lift-up-over-sounding': Getting into the Kaluli Groove. *Yearbook for Traditional Music* 20:74–113.
Felker, Marcia
  1983   Ideology and Order in the Operating Room. In *The Anthropology of Medicine: From Culture to Method*, ed. L. Romanucci-Ross et al., pp. 346–365. South Hadley, Mass.: Bergin and Garvey.

Firth, Raymond
   1966   Bilateral Descent Groups: An Operational Viewpoint. *Royal Anthropological Institute Occasional Papers* 16:22–37.
Fried, Morton H.
   1967   *The Evolution of Political Society: An Essay in Political Authority.* New York: Random House.
Friedl, Ernestine
   1975   *Women and Men: An Anthropologist's View.* New York: Holt, Rinehart and Winston.
Friedson, E.
   1970   *Profession of Medicine: A Study of the Sociology of Applied Knowledge.* New York: Harper and Row.
Garfield, Patricia
   1974   *Creative Dreaming.* New York: Ballantine Books.
Geertz, Clifford
   1960   *The Religion of Java.* University of Chicago Press.
   1966   *Person, Time and Conduct in Bali: An Essay in Cultural Analysis.* Cultural Report No. 14, Southeast Asia Studies. New Haven: Yale University Press.
   1973   *The Interpretation of Cultures.* New York: Basic Books.
   1983   *Local Knowledge: Further Essays in Interpretive Anthropology.* New York: Basic Books.
Godelier, Maurice
   1986   *The Mental and the Material,* trans. Martin Thom. London: Verso.
Goffman, Erving
   1967   *Interaction Ritual: Essays in Face-to-Face Behavior.* Chicago: Aldine.
Goldman, Irving
   1979   *The Cubeo: Indians of the Northwest Amazon,* 2d ed. Urbana: University of Illinois Press.
   1974   *Frame Analysis.* New York: Harper and Row.
Good, Byron
   1977   The Heart of What's the Matter: The Semantics of Illness in Iran. *Culture, Medicine and Psychiatry* 1:25–58.
Goswami, Shrivatsa
   1982   Radha: The Play and Perfection of *Rasa.* In *The Divine Consort: Radha and the Goddesses of India,* ed. John Stratton Hawley and D. M. Wulff. Berkeley: Berkeley Religious Studies Series.
Guss, David
   1988   *To Weave and Sing: Art, Symbol, and Narrative in the South American Rainforest.* Berkeley, Los Angeles, London: University of California Press.
Haden, R. Allen
   1939   Dance Music of the Temiar. *Asia* 39:114–15.

Hillman, James
  1982   Anima Mundi: The Return of Soul to the World. *Spring*. Dallas: Spring Publications.
Hirschman, Charles
  1987   The Meaning and Measurement of Ethnicity in Malaysia: An Analysis of Census Classifications. *Journal of Asian Studies* 46(3):555–582.
Hocart, A. M.
  1937   Kinship Systems. *Anthropos* 32:245–251.(Reprinted in *The Life-giving Myth*. London: Methuen and Co., 1952.)
Holt, Claire
  1967   *Art in Indonesia: Continuities and Change*. Ithaca: Cornell University Press.
Hood H. Mohamad Salleh and Hasan Mat Nor
  1982   Roads are for Development? Some Aspects of Jah Het Social Change. Paper presented at UNESCO Regional Workshop on "Sociocultural Change in Communities Resulting from Economic Development and Technological Progress," Bangi, Selangor, Malaysia, October 4–6, 1982.
Hornbostel, Erich M. von
  1926   Die Musik der Semai auf Malakka. *Anthropos* 21:227.
Howell, Signe
  1984   *Society and Cosmos: Chewong of Peninsular Malaysia*. Singapore: Oxford University Press.
  1986   To Be Angry Is Not To Be Human, but To Be Fearful Is. Paper presented to the Conference on Peace, Action, and the Concept of Self. Edinburgh.
  1988   Total Prestations as the Life-giving Acts among the Chewong. Paper presented at the American Anthropological Association, Annual Meetings, Phoenix, Ariz.
Huntington, Richard, and Peter Metcalf
  1979   *Celebrations of Death: The Anthropology of Mortuary Ritual*. Cambridge: Cambridge University Press.
Hymes, Dell
  1964   Introduction: Toward Ethnographies of Communication. *The Ethnography of Communication. American Anthropologist* 66(6:2):1–34.
  1971   Sociolinguistics and the Ethnography of Speaking. In *Social Anthropology and Language*, ed. Edwin Ardener, pp. 47–93. London: Tavistock Publications.
Johnson, Frank
  1985   The "Western Concept of Self." In *Culture and Self: Asian and Western Perspectives*, ed. Anthony J. Marsella, G. De Vos, and F. L. K. Hsu. New York: Tavistock.
Jones, Alun
  1968   The Orang Asli: An Outline of Their Progress in Modern Malaya. *Journal of Southeast Asian History* 9(2):268–292.

Kapferer, Bruce
  1979*a* Introduction: Ritual Process and the Transformation of Context. *Social Analysis* 1:3–19.
  1979*b* Entertaining Demons: Comedy, Interaction and Meaning in a Sinhalese Healing Ritual. *Social Analysis* 1:108–52.
  1983 *A Celebration of Demons: Exorcism and the Aesthetics of Healing in Sri Lanka.* Bloomington: Indiana University Press.

Keil, Charles
  1987 Participatory Discrepancies and the Power of Music. *Cultural Anthropology* 2(3):275–283.

Kessler, Clive
  1977 Conflict and Sovereignty in Kelantanese Malay Spirit Mediumship. In *Case Studies in Spirit Possession*, ed. Vincent Crapanzano and V. Garrison. New York: Wiley-Interscience.

King, Ben F., and E. C. Dickinson
  1975 *A Field Guide to the Birds of South-East Asia.* London: Collins.

Kleinman, Arthur
  1980 *Patients and Healers in the Context of Culture: An Exploration of the Borderland between Anthropology, Medicine, and Psychiatry.* Berkeley, Los Angeles, London: University of California Press.
  1989 *The Illness Narratives: Suffering, Healing and the Human Condition.* New York: Basic Books.

Kolinski, Mieczyslaw
  1930 Die Musik der Primitivstämme auf Malaka und ihre Beziehung zur samoanischen Musik. *Anthropos* 25:585–649.

Koskoff, Ellen, ed.
  1989 *Women and Music in Cross-Cultural Perspective.* Urbana: University of Illinois Press.

Kristeva, Julia
  1977 *Polylogue.* Paris: Editions du Seuil.

Laderman, Carol
  1979 *Wives and Midwives: Childbirth and Nutrition in Rural Malaysia.* Berkeley, Los Angeles, London: University of California Press.
  1981 Symbolic and Empirical Reality: A New Approach to the Analysis of Food Avoidances. *American Ethnologist* 8(3):468–493.
  1988 Discussant: Comments on the Panel "Cultural Dimensions of Healing in Southeast Asia." 40th Annual Meetings of the Association for Asian Studies, San Francisco, 1988.
  1991 *Taming the Wind of Desire: Psychology, Medicine and Aesthetics in Malay Shamanism.* Berkeley, Los Angeles, Oxford: University of California Press.

Lévi-Strauss, Claude
  1964 Reciprocity, The Essence of Social Life. In *The Family: Its Structure and Functions*, ed. Rose L. Coser. New York: St. Martin's Press.
  1966/1962 *The Savage Mind.* Chicago: University of Chicago Press.

1969/1964 *The Raw and the Cooked* (*Mythologiques*, vol. 1), trans. J. and D. Weightman. New York: Harper and Row.

Lock, Margaret
    1988   Introduction. In *Biomedicine Examined*, ed. M. Lock and D. R. Gordon. Dordrecht: Kluwer Academic Publishers.

Lomax, Alan
    1968   *Folk Song Style and Culture*. Washington: American Association for the Advancement of Science.
    1976   *Cantometrics: An Approach to the Anthropology of Music*. Berkeley: University of California, Extension Media Center.

Malinowski, Bronislaw
    1984/1922 *Argonauts of the Western Pacific*. Prospect Heights, Ill.: Waveland Press.
    1965/1935 *Coral Gardens and Their Magic*, vol. 2: *The Language of Magic and Gardening*. Bloomington: Indiana University Press.

Mannheim, Bruce, and Dennis Tedlock, eds.
  In press *The Dialogic Emergence of Culture*. Philadelphia: University of Pennsylvania.

Mauss, Marcel
    1967/1925 *The Gift: Forms and Functions of Exchange in Archaic Societies*, trans. Ian Cunnison. New York: W. W. Norton.
    1950/1934 Les techniques du corps. In M. Mauss, *Sociologie et anthropologie*. Paris: Presses Univ. de France.
    1950/1938 Une categorie de l'espirit humain: la notion de personne, celle de "moi". In *Sociologie et anthropolgie*. Paris: Presses Univ. de France.
    1979/1935 Body Techniques. In *Sociology and Psychology, Essays*, trans. Ben Brewster. London: Routledge & Kegan Paul.

McLeod, Norma, and Marcia Herndon, eds.
    1980   *The Ethnography of Musical Performance*. Norwood: Norwood Editions.

Mead, Margaret
    1977   *Letters from the Field 1925–1979*. New York: Harper and Row.

Medway, Lord
    1978   *The Wild Mammals of Malaya (Peninsular Malaysia) and Singapore*, 2d ed. Kuala Lumpur: Oxford University Press.

Merriam, Alan P.
    1964   *The Anthropology of Music*. Evanston: Northwestern University Press.
    1977   Anthropology and the Arts. In *Horizons of Anthropology*, 2d ed., ed. Sol Tax and L. G. Freeman, pp. 332–343. Chicago: Aldine.

Mora, Manolete
    1987   The Sounding Pantheon of Nature: T'boli Instrumental Music in the Making of an Ancestral Symbol. *Acta Musicologica* 59(2):187–212.

Needham, Rodney
   1963   Introduction. In *Primitive Classification*. Emile Durkheim and
           M. Mauss, pp. vii–xlviii. Chicago: University of Chicago
           Press.
Neher, Andrew
   1961   Auditory Driving Observed with Scalp Electrodes in Normal
           Subjects. *Electroencephalography and Clinical Neurophysiology*
           13:449–451
   1962   A Physiological Explanation of Unusual Behavior in Ceremo-
           nies Involving Drums. *Human Biology* 34(2):151–160.
Nettl, Bruno
   1983   *The Study of Ethnomusicology: Twenty-Nine Issues and Concepts.*
           Urbana: University of Illinois Press.
Noone, H. D.
   1939   Chinchem: A Study of the Role of Dream Experience in
           Culture-Contact Amongst the Temiar Senoi of Malaya. *Man*
           39(April):55.
   1955   Introduction and Notes. Accompanying *Temiar Dream Songs
           from Malaya*. New York: Ethnic Folkways Library FE4460 (33 1/3
           rpm recording).
Noone, Richard D.
   1972   *In Search of the Dream People.* New York: William Morrow.
Oesch, Hans
   1973   Musikalische Kontinuität bei Naturvölkern. Dargestellt an der
           Musik der Senoi auf Malakka. *Studien zur Tradition in der Musik.
           Kurt von Fischer aum 60. Geburstag*, ed. H. H. Eggebrecht and M.
           Lötolf, pp. 227–246. München.
   1974a   Musikalische Gattungen bei Naturvölkern. Untersuchungen
           am vokalen und instrumentalen Repertoire des Schamanen
           Terhin und seiner Senoi-Leute von Stammer der Temiar am
           oberen Nenggiri auf Malakka. *Festschrift für Arno Volk*, ed. Carl
           Kahlhaus and Hans Oesch, pp. 7–30. Köln: Musiverlage Hans
           Gerig.
   1974b   Oekonomie und Musik. Zur Bedeutung der Produktionsver-
           hältnisse für die Herausbildung einer Musikkultur, dargestellt
           am Beispiel der Inlandstämme auf Malakka und der Balier.
           *Convivium Musicorum: Festschrift Wolfgang Boetticher zum sechzig-
           sten Geburstag am 19. August 1974*, ed. H. Höschen and D. P.
           Moser, pp. 246–253. Berlin: Verlag Merseburger.
O'Flaherty, Wendy Doniger
   1973   *Asceticism and Eroticism in the Mythology of Siva.* Oxford: Oxford
           University Press. (Issued as an Oxford University Press paper-
           back, 1981, under the title *Siva: The Erotic Ascetic*.)
   1980   *Women, Androgynes, and Other Mythical Beasts.* Chicago: Uni-
           versity of Chicago Press.

Ohnuki-Tierney, Emiko
    1981   *Illness and Healing among the Sakhalin Ainu: A Symbolic Interpretation.* Cambridge: Cambridge University Press.
Ortner, Sherry B.
    1984   Theory in Anthropology since the Sixties. *Comparative Studies in Society and History* 26: 126–66.
Parker, Richard
    1987   Acquired Immunodeficiency Syndrome in Urban Brazil. *Medical Anthropology Quarterly* 1 n.s.(2):155–175.
Phillips, Herb
    1965   *Thai Peasant Personality.* Berkeley, Los Angeles, London: University of California Press.
Radcliffe-Brown, A. R.
    1965/1952 *Structure and Function in Primitive Society.* New York: Free Press.
Reid, Anthony, and David Marr, eds.
    1979   *Perceptions of the Past in Southeast Asia.* Singapore: Heinemann Educational Books.
Robarchek, Clayton A.
    1979a   Conflict, Emotion, and Abreaction: Resolution of Conflict among the Semai Senoi. *Ethos* 7(2):104–123.
    1979b   Learning to Fear: A Case Study of Emotional Conditioning. *American Ethnologist* 6(4):555–567.
Robertson, Carol E.
    1976   *Tayil* as Category and Communication among the Argentine Mapuche: A Methodological Suggestion. *Yearbook of the International Folk Music Council* 8:35–52.
    1979   "Pulling the Ancestors": Performance Practice and Praxis in Mapuche Ordering." *Ethnomusicology* 23(3):395–416.
Rosaldo, Michelle Z.
    1980   *Knowledge and Passion: Ilongot Notions of Self and Social Life.* Cambridge: Cambridge University Press.
Rosaldo, Renato
    1986   Red Hornbill Earrings: Ilongot Ideas of Self, Beauty, and Health. *Cultural Anthropology* 1(3):310–316.
Roseman, Marina
    1980   Malay and Orang Asli Interactions: Views from Legendary History: Unpublished paper, Department of Anthropology, Cornell University.
    1984   The Social Structuring of Sound: The Temiar of Peninsular Malaysia. *Ethnomusicology* 28(3):411–445.
    1988   The Pragmatics of Aesthetics: The Performance of Healing among Senoi Temiar. *Social Science and Medicine* 27(7):811–818.
Rouget, Gilbert
    1977a   Instruments de musique et musique de la possession. *Musique en Jeu* 28(September):68–91.
    1977b   Music and Possession Trance. In *The Anthropology of the Body,*

ed. J. Blacking, pp. 233–239. ASA Monograph No. 15. London: Academic Press.

1980   *Music and Trance.* Chicago: University of Chicago Press.

Sahlins, Marshall

1965   On the Sociology of Primitive Exchange. In *The Relevance of Models for Social Anthropology,* ed. M. Banton, pp. 139–236. London: Tavistock Publications.

1968   *Tribesmen.* Englewood Cliffs, N.J.: Prentice-Hall.

Sapir, J. David

1977   The Anatomy of Metaphor. In *The Social Uses of Metaphor: Essays on the Anthropology of Rhetoric,* ed. J. D. Sapir and J. C. Crocker, pp. 3–32. Philadelphia: University of Pennsylvania Press.

Sapir, J. David, and J. C. Crocker, eds.

1977   *The Social Uses of Metaphor: Essays on the Anthropology of Rhetoric.* Philadelphia: University of Pennsylvania Press.

Saussure, Ferdinand de

1966/1915 *Course in General Linguistics,* trans. Wade Baskin. New York: McGraw-Hill.

Schebesta, Paul

1928   *Among the Forest Dwarfs of Malaya,* trans. Arthur Chambers. London: Hutchinson.

Schechner, Richard

1983   *Performative Circumstances: From the Avant garde to Ramlila.* Calcutta: Seagull.

Scheper-Hughes, Nancy, and Margaret M. Lock

1987   The Mindful Body: A Prolegomenon to Future Work in Medical Anthropology. *Medical Anthropology Quarterly* 1 n.s.(1):6–41.

Schieffelin, Edward L.

1976   *The Sorrow of the Lonely and the Burning of the Dancers.* New York: St. Martin's Press.

1977   The Unseen Influence: Trance Mediums as Historical Innovators. *Journal de la Société des Oceanistes* 33(56–57):169–178.

1979   Mediators as Metaphors: Moving a Man to Tears in Papua New Guinea. In *The Imagination of Reality: Essays in Southeast Asian Coherence Systems,* ed. A. L. Becker and Aram Yengoyan, pp. 127–144. Norwood: Ablex.

1985   Performance and the Cultural Construction of Reality. *American Ethnologist* 12(4):707–724.

Schlegel, Alice

1977   *Sexual Stratification: A Cross-Cultural View.* New York: Columbia University Press.

Schneider, David

1976   "Notes toward a Theory of Culture." In *Meaning in Anthropology,* ed. Keith H. Basso and Henry A. Selby. Albuquerque: University of New Mexico Press.

Schutz, Alfred
  1967   *Collected Papers I: The Problem of Social Reality*, ed. M. Natanson.
          The Hague: Nijhoff.
Seeger, Anthony
  1979   What Can We Learn When They Sing? Vocal Genres of the
          Suya Indians of Central Brazil. *Ethnomusicology* 23 (3):373–394.
  1981   *Nature and Society in Central Brazil: The Suya Indians of Mato
          Grosso*. Cambridge: Harvard University Press.
  1988   *Why Suya Sing: A Musical Anthropology of an Amazonian People*.
          Cambridge: Cambridge University Press.
Sharp, Lauriston
  1952   Steel Axes for Stone-age Australians. *Human Organization*
          11:17–52.
Shaw, William
  1975   *Aspects of Malaysian Magic*. Kuala Lumpur: Muzium Negara.
Simons, Ronald C.
  1985   The Resolution of the Latah Paradox. In *The Culture-Bound
          Syndromes: Folk Illnesses of Psychiatric and Anthropological Interest*,
          pp. 43–62. Dordrecht: D. Reidel.
Skeat, Walter W.
  1967/1900 *Malay Magic*. New York: Dover.
Skeat, Walter W., and Charles O. Blagden
  1966/1906 *Pagan Races of the Malay Peninsula*, vols. 1 & 2. London: Frank
          Cass & Co.
Solheim, Wilhelm G., II
  1980   Searching for the Origins of the Orang Asli. Federation Muse-
          ums Journal. n. s. 25: 61–75.
Stewart, Kilton R.
  1948   Magico-Religious Beliefs and Practices in Primitive Society—A
          Sociological Interpretation of Their Therapeutic Aspects. Ph.D.
          dissertation, London School of Economics.
  1951   Dream Theory in Malaya. *Complex* 6:21–33. (Reprinted in *Al-
          tered State of Consciousness*, ed. C. Tart. New York: John Wiley,
          1969)
Tambiah, Stanley J.
  1970   *Buddhism and the Spirit Cults in North-East Thailand*. Cambridge:
          Cambridge University Press.
  1977   The Cosmological and Performative Significance of a Thai Cult
          of Healing through Meditation. *Culture, Medicine and Psychiatry*
          1:97–132.
Taussig, Michael T.
  1980   *The Devil and Commodity Fetishism in South America*. Chapel Hill:
          University of North Carolina Press.
Tedlock, Barbara, ed.
  1987   *Dreaming: The Anthropology and Psychology of the Imaginal*. Al-
          buquerque: University of New Mexico Press.
Tedlock, Dennis
  1983   *The Spoken Word and the Work of Interpretation*. Philadelphia:
          University of Pennsylvania.

Turner, Victor
   1967   A Ndembu Doctor in Practice. In his *The Forest of Symbols*. Ithaca: Cornell University Press.
   1968   *The Drums of Affliction: A Study of Religious Processes among the Ndembu of Zambia*. Oxford: Clarendon Press.
   1975   Symbolic Studies. In *Annual Review of Anthropology*, vol. 4, ed. B. J. Siegel, A. R. Beals, and S. A. Tyler, pp. 145–161. Palo Alto: Annual Reviews.
Watkins, Mary
   1986   *Invisible Guests: The Development of Imaginal Dialogues*. Hillsdale, N.J.: Analytic Press.
Wazir-Jahan Karim
   1981   *Ma' Betisek Concepts of Living Things*. London: Athlone Press.
Weber, Max
   1964/1922   *The Theory of Social and Economic Organization*, ed. Talcott Parsons, trans. A. M. Henderson and T. Parsons. New York: Free Press.
   1977/1905   "Objectivity" in Social Science and Social Policy. In *Understanding and Social Inquiry*, ed. Fred R. Dallmayr and T. A. McCarthy, pp. 24–37. Notre Dame: University of Notre Dame Press.
Wilkinson, R. J.
   1959   A *Malay-English Dictionary* (Romanized). 2 pts. London: MacMillan & Co.
Wilson, Edward O.
   1989   Threats to Biodiversity. *Scientific American* 261(3): 108–116.
Wilson, Edward O., and F. M. Peter, eds.
   1988   *Biodiversity*. National Academy Press.
Winstedt, R. O.
   1927   The Great Flood, 1926. *Journal of the Malay Branch of the Royal Asiatic Society* 5:295–309.
Wolters, Oliver W.
   1979   Khmer "Hinduism" in the Seventh Century. In *Early South East Asia: Essays in Archaeology, History, and Historical Geography*, ed. R. B. Smith and W. Watson, pp. 427-442. Oxford: Oxford University Press.
   1982   *History, Culture, and Region in Southeast Asian Perspectives*. Singapore: Institute of Southeast Asian Studies.
Wurm, S. A., and S. Hattori, eds.
   1983   *Language Atlas of the Pacific Area*, pt. 2. Map 37: Peninsular Malaysia. G. Benjamin, comp. Pacific Linguistics, Series C, no. 66. Canberra: Australian Academy of the Humanities and the Japan Academy.
Yap, P. M.
   1952   The *Latah* Reaction: Its Pathodynamics and Nosological Position. *Journal of Mental Science* 98:515–564.

Young, Iris
   1986   The Ideal of Community and the Politics of Difference. *Social
            Theory and Practice* 12(1):1–26.
Zemp, Hugo
   1979   Aspects of 'Are'are Musical Theory. *Ethnomusicology* 23(1):5–
            48.

Index

Abdomen: and illness, 38–40
Abilem Lum (Taa' Ariŋ), 70, 92–99, 109 Fig. 2
Aboriginal Malay, 17–18, 19
Ading Kerah, 41, 88
Adoption, 124
Aesthetics, 183–184; dance and movement, 11, 153, 161–165; and emotion, 151–173; fluid beauty, 64–65, 196 n. 18; music, 16, 151, 157–159, 169–173; pragmatic effects, 11; pulsation, 151, 169–173; sound, 11; sway, 161–165
Aggression, 180
Agriculture: crops, 2; cycle, and musical events, 9, 84; and dream songs, 54, 55–56, 58; and hunting, 4; metaphors in healing, 25, 53; metaphors in music, 26, 52–53; ownership, 55; slash-and-burn, 1, 76, 92
Along Indan, 114 Table 2, 141–142
Altitude: Temiar settlements, 2
Aluj Hitam (Taa' Rəgəəl), 67, 69, 130–131, 145
Aŋah Busuu', 60–62
Anger. See Emotion: anger; Illness, causation: emotion of anger
Anthropology: interpretive, theory, 11–12; Temiar understandings of, 20
Argusanius argus. See Great Argus pheasant
Aslian: language, Temiar classified in, 2; Orang Asli language groups, 3 Fig. 1 (map), 17–18
Austroasiatic: language, Temiar classified in, 2; Orang Asli language groups, 3 Fig. 1 (map), 17–18
Austronesian: language, 17–18; peoples, in Malaysia, 19

Baad, 29
Babcock, B., 127
Bakhtin, M., 127

Batek, 17, 41, 42, 93, 95, 191 n. 1, 192 n. 9, 194 n. 30, 194 n. 36
Bateson, Gregory, 8
Bə-caraa'. See Speech: discussions
Becker, A. L. and J., 171
Bees, 94, 97; beeswax, 55
Being: concepts of, 16, 21; and shadow, 40–45
Benjamin, Geoffrey, 177–178
Besisi. See Mah Meri
Biomedicine, 13. See also Medicine, Western cosmopolitan
Birds: bay owl, 70, 197 n. 37; dark-necked tailorbird, 43, 194 n. 35; fire-tufted barbet, 71, 197 n. 39; golden-throated barbet, 169–173, 170 Fig. 5; great Argus pheasant, 35, 70, 197 n. 35; magpie robin, 70, 197 n. 36; in myth, 70; omens, 43, 70; owls, 35; sounds as cues, 24, 70; sounds in music, 85, 151, 169–173; species identified, 193 n. 14, 193 n. 17, 193 n. 18, 203 n. 9
Birth, 108 Pl. 9, 201 n. 54. See also Midwives
Blacking, John, 172
Blood (lɔɔt): badii', 193 n. 21; heart, 30; illness causation, 36, 138
Blowpipe. See Hunting, equipment
Body, 179–181; aesthetics, 71; odor, 37. See also Dance; Movement
Breath (hənum): association with heart, 30; and illness treatment, 45
British: interactions with Temiar, 68. See also Colonialism
Burke, Kenneth, 107

Carey, Iskandar, 88
Chewong, 17, 18, 137, 140, 191 n. 1, 192 n. 9, 193 n. 23
Childbearing, 138, 139 Table 3
Children: food restrictions, 138; head souls, 27, 29, 148; learning about

Designer : U.C. Press Staff
Compositor : A-R Editions, Inc.
Text : 10/13 Palatino
Display : Palatino